Also by David Blake Knox

The Curious History of Irish Dogs (2017)

Ireland and the Eurovision: The Winners, the Losers and the Turkey (2015)

Hitler's Irish Slaves (2012, 2017)

for: Anna
from: Mariana. ♡

FACE DOWN

The Disappearance of Thomas Niedermayer

David Blake Knox

NEW ISLAND

FACE DOWN: THE DISAPPEARANCE OF THOMAS NIEDERMAYER
Second edition published in 2023 by New Island Books
Glenshesk House
10 Richview Office Park
Clonskeagh
Dublin D14 V8C4
Republic of Ireland
www.newisland.ie

First edition published under the title *The Killing of Thomas Niedermayer* in 2019

Print ISBN: 978-1-84840-847-0
Epub ISBN: 978-1-84840-735-0

British Library Cataloguing in Publication Data. A CIP catalogue record for this book is available from the British Library.

Edited by Kerri Ward
Index by Jane Rogers
Typeset by JVR Creative India
Cover design by Spinnaker
Cover photos courtesy of Blueprint Pictures (top) and *Belfast News Letter* (bottom)
Printed by L&C, Poland, lcprinting.eu

New Island Books is a member of Publishing Ireland.

Set in Calluna in 11.5 pt on 17 pt
10 9 8 7 6 5 4 3 2 1

For Georgie Bennett and Edie Blake Knox

Contents

Abbreviations

BBC	The British Broadcasting Corporation
CID	The Criminal Investigation Department of the RUC
CPGB	The Communist Party of Great Britain
DFA	The Department of Foreign Affairs (Ireland)
EEC	The European Economic Community
ETA	Euskadi Ta Askatasuna: an armed Basque separatist organisation
EU	The European Union
FARC	Fuerzas Armadas Revolucionarias de Colombia: a guerrilla organisation in Colombia
FBI	The Federal Bureau of Investigation (USA)
FLQ	Front de libération du Québec: a paramilitary separatist group in Québec
GOC	General Officer Commanding the British army (Northern Ireland)

INLA	The Irish National Liberation Army: a republican paramilitary group
IRA	The Irish Republican Army: a republican paramilitary group, also known as the Provisional IRA
NICRA	The Northern Ireland Civil Rights Association
NIO	The Northern Ireland Office
ODCs	'Ordinary Decent Criminals' who were not part of any paramilitary group
PSNI	The Police Service of Northern Ireland
PTSD	Post-traumatic Stress Disorder
RPG	Rocket Propelled Grenades
RTÉ	Raidió Teilifís Éireann: Ireland's national broadcaster
RUC	The Royal Ulster Constabulary
SB	The RUC Special Branch
SDLP	The Social Democratic and Labour Party
UDA	The Ulster Defence Association: a loyalist paramilitary organisation
UDR	The Ulster Defence Regiment: a locally recruited part of the British army
UNESCO	The United Nations Educational, Scientific and Cultural Organisation
UVF	The Ulster Volunteer Force: a loyalist paramilitary organisation

Introduction

There is an inherent and understandable tension between the desire, on one hand, to move on from the political turbulence that convulsed Northern Ireland across four decades and the need, on the other hand, to confront and understand the causes of the personal and communal traumas experienced by both of its major communities.

I can relate to both compulsions. During much of the 1980s, I worked as a television producer for Ireland's national broadcaster, Raidió Teilifís Éireann (RTÉ), covering the 'Troubles' – a term which understates the years of violence that ended, scarred or ruined many thousands of lives. It was often a grim assignment. Between 1966 and 2006, close to 3,700 people died in the Troubles. Almost every day of the year marks the death of someone killed in this conflict, and it has been estimated that almost 50,000 individuals were also maimed or injured. In total, it has been reckoned that around 500,000 people have been directly affected by acts of political violence. Given that the population of Northern Ireland is less than 2 million, these are remarkable (and shocking) statistics.

There is a phenomenon known in Northern Ireland (and elsewhere) as 'whataboutery'. This usually occurs when a particular atrocity perpetrated by members of one community in the conflict is mentioned and the immediate response is to ask 'what about' some equal (or worse) atrocity committed by the 'other' side – and there is always an 'other' side in Northern Ireland. It seems inevitable that, when one community assigns particular meanings to events in the past, it will antagonise the community that interprets the same historical events in a radically different way. In this context, language can become weaponised and even the choice of individual words may be seized upon as evidence of some underlying bias.

I do not accept George Santayana's famous claim that 'those who cannot remember the past are condemned to repeat it'. That maxim strikes me as demonstrably untrue: both major communities in Northern Ireland regularly invoke 'memories' of events that occurred hundreds of years ago. That does not serve to inoculate them against the iniquities of the past. Indeed, such memories are sometimes called upon to justify their current prejudices and recurring acts of violence. There are, in any case, very few (if any) occasions when historical events can simply be said to have 'repeated' themselves.

In that context, I am inclined to sympathise with the views of the American writer David Rieff, who has argued that it is sometimes better to choose to forget traumatic and divisive incidents in any country's past. Rieff has identified Ireland as a country that is particularly slow to let go of its historic grievances. He believes that Irish history provides an 'illuminating case study of the uses and misuses of the past in the construction, reconstruction, amendment and transformation of the collective memory'.

That is certainly true of Northern Ireland where the recitation of historical wrongs can often be self-serving and lead to toxic political effects. As Edna Longley has observed, the past 'as a continuum' often looms larger in Northern Ireland than the past 'as mortality'. For David Rieff, remembering historic events is not so much a moral imperative as a moral option. I agree with him that there may be some occasions when it is better to let the dead bury the dead, but I also believe there are occasions when that temptation should be resisted. Indeed, there is sometimes a compelling need to interrogate the past and question its accepted narratives.

In 2013, I was contacted by my former colleague Ann Marie Hourihane. I knew Ann Marie as an author and journalist. She referred me to *A Knock on the Door,* a recent radio documentary on RTÉ, and subsequently sent me an article she had written about it. The documentary and her article both related to the kidnapping of a businessman called Thomas Niedermayer. That name stirred a distant memory: I could dimly recall something about a German businessman who had been kidnapped and murdered by the IRA in the early 1970s.

When I listened to the documentary on the RTÉ Player, more memories were revived. It was presented by Joe Duffy, one of Ireland's leading broadcasters and someone who has shone a much-needed light on neglected aspects of Ireland's social and political history. The radio documentary was produced by Ciaran Cassidy and it revealed some of the terrible collateral damage that Thomas Niedermayer's abduction and death inflicted on his family.

It was, in many respects, a very dark story, but it was greatly to the credit of Duffy and Cassidy that their programme was made. Ann Marie proposed that we should try to make a film documentary about this case and, over the following months, we explored the background to the story. (I should add that any faults or errors contained in this book are entirely my responsibility.) Ann Marie forwarded to me some very valuable documentation that she had obtained in the German Foreign Office's Political Archive. The film she had proposed was never made, but the story of the Niedermayers had snagged in my mind and I was drawn back to it in subsequent years. Eventually, I was able to make a feature documentary film about this case with Gerry Gregg – my friend and former colleague – and Kelda Crawford-McCann from Strident Media in Belfast. This became – thanks to Colm O'Callaghan, its first commissioning editor – a co-production between RTÉ, ARTE (the French-German channel), BBC Northern Ireland and Fís Éireann/Screen Ireland.

In the course of making that film, I learned a good deal more about Thomas Niedermayer, as well as the impact his abduction had, not just on his wife and children, but also on his granddaughters, Tanya Williams-Powell and Rachel Williams-Powell. Speaking with them, it was clear that the events that took place in Ireland many years before have continued to impact on their lives. It must have been difficult at times for them to re-visit painful memories but they brought a crucial perspective both to this book and to our film. They also brought a sense of hope for the future in their determination that the devastating legacy of their grandfather's abduction and killing would not be passed on to the next generation.

In a sense, this is the story of two men: Thomas Niedermayer and Brian Keenan. They came from somewhat similar social backgrounds and they both trained to be electronic engineers. They also shared some personal characteristics: they were both intelligent, energetic and single-minded in the pursuit of their respective goals. The two men knew each other and once worked for the same company, but they were not friends and their paths in life were very different. One of them became actively involved in the political violence that enveloped Northern Ireland during the years of the Troubles, while the other became his innocent victim.

But this is also a story about women. One of those women is Ingeborg Niedermayer. Like her husband, she managed to survive the horrors of the Second World

War, but both were deeply affected by the traumatic experiences they had undergone. Ingeborg would suffer further anguish when Thomas was abducted, and then throughout the long years of uncertainty that followed his disappearance. Her two daughters, Renate and Gabriele, also underwent great suffering, and all three women were later to end their lives in desperate circumstances.

In that context, it seems deeply unjust that the only one of those who were centrally involved in this story and who died of natural causes was Brian Keenan – the IRA leader who organised the abduction of Thomas Niedermayer and who ordered the subsequent concealment of his body.

This book is primarily about the victims of political violence. Some of those victims suffered physically – others, psychologically or emotionally. Neither Catholics nor Protestants, unionists nor nationalists, are without blame for the violence in Northern Ireland. But that does not mean that everyone is equally accountable for each violent incident. In the case of Thomas Niedermayer, the guilt lies overwhelmingly – indeed, exclusively – in one direction. An innocent man was abducted solely in order that his kidnappers could use his life as a bargaining chip to advance a political cause with which he had no connection. Their brutal incompetence led to his death and their cynical denial of responsibility for his disappearance added to the terrible distress experienced by his family.

Those who abducted and killed Thomas Niedermayer might have considered themselves to be soldiers in an underground army, but, even when judged by military criteria, their actions were criminal, cowardly and callous. In the catalogue of heartache, misery and loss caused by the Troubles, the story of the Niedermayers is particularly poignant. The killing of Thomas Niedermayer may have been pointless, but it was not without meaning. In this book, I have tried to untangle the complex web of circumstances that combined to ensnare and destroy Niedermayer and his immediate family.

The traumatic legacy of what occurred in 1973 has been felt – and continues to be felt – in different countries and continents and across successive generations. Ballads are sung, parades are staged, murals are painted and monuments are erected to honour some of those who terrorised innocent civilians during the Troubles. There are few ballads, parades, murals or monuments to remind us of those who suffered grievously as a result of that terror. I hope this book contributes – in however small a way – to some redress of that shameful neglect.

1.

The Body in the Glen

It took them four weeks to find his corpse.

A small group of workmen from the 'West Belfast Environmental Action Group' spent a month clearing thousands of tons of stinking rubbish that had been dumped illegally in Colin Glen, an area of public parkland. Apart from the dreadful stench of rotting material, the site was infested with rats and other vermin.

The workmen's objective was apparently to restore the Glen to its former natural beauty. In reality, they were all undercover RUC officers and they kept Walther PPK automatic handguns hidden under their waterproof jackets.

Colin Glen is located close to what was an IRA stronghold in Andersonstown and the policemen's lives would have been in grave danger if their true identities had been discovered. The RUC officers were searching for the body of someone they believed had been murdered by the IRA. They were on the verge of abandoning their mission when one of them discovered some muddy grey trousers. The RUC had been led to Colin Glen by a well-placed source inside the IRA. Now, they realised that the information that he had provided was accurate.

There were human leg bones inside the trousers. Some slippers were found nearby. A few minutes later, they dug up a skull. The hands of the body they excavated had been tied behind the victim's back. He had been gagged and his feet had been bound together by a pair of women's tights. His body had been buried in a shallow grave, face down. In the chilling words of one of his killers, that was so he could 'dig himself deeper'.

2.

The Victim

The body had a name, a history and a life: Thomas Niedermayer was a German businessman. He and his family had been living in Northern Ireland since 1961, but he was born in 1928 in Bamberg, a small Bavarian town on the River Regnitz in Upper Franconia in south-western Germany. A large part of this medieval town is now a UNESCO World Heritage Site, but Bamberg also has a darker side to its more recent history.

The town was the location of an important conference convened by Adolf Hitler in 1926. He had become concerned that the Nazi Party was about to split into two regional factions. One of these consisted of *Gauleiters* (District Leaders) from northern Germany, who were generally regarded as more urban, more radical and more sympathetic to socialist ideas. The others were *Gauleiters* who came from more conservative rural areas in southern Germany and who were less interested in abstract theory than in nationalist and racist ideology.

Hitler wanted the issue to be resolved as clearly as possible and the fact that he chose to hold this conference in a small southern town like Bamberg indicated where his own preferences lay. The Bamberg Conference proved decisive in determining the future development of the Nazi Party and in establishing the dominance of its conservative faction. However, in some respects, the final act of the conference in Bamberg did not take place until eight years later. That was during the 'Night of the Long Knives' when scores of members of the Nazis' radical faction were murdered by the SS on Hitler's orders.

Thomas Niedermayer was born two years after the Bamberg Conference and he was 4 years old in 1933 when Hitler and the Nazi Party took control of the German state. Like other fascistic or extreme populist parties, the Nazis claimed to represent a movement of youth – and 'fresh blood' – that was somehow destined to supplant the older generations and correct their grievous mistakes. In that context, Hitler believed that the indoctrination of children – and male children, in particular – with Nazi ideology was essential for the future of his 'thousand-year Reich'. He wanted to produce boys that were 'as tough as leather and solid as steel'. The Hitler-Jugend (Hitler Youth) programme was designed to create future generations of such loyal and dedicated Nazis. It was established in 1925 and by 1930 had enrolled almost 25,000 members. When Hitler came to power in 1933, all other youth organisations in Germany were compelled to disband and become part of the Hitler-Jugend. By the end of 1933, its membership had reached almost 2 million.

As the 1930s progressed and Nazi control of Germany tightened, it became increasingly difficult for children to avoid membership of the Nazis' youth movement. By the end of the decade, there were almost 8 million members of the Hitler-Jugend. When Thomas Niedermayer was 7 years old, the Reichstag had passed the *Gesetz über die Hitler-Jugend*: a law which made it mandatory for all male German children who were aged 14, free of physical or mental disabilities and of proven 'Aryan' descent to become members of the Nazi Youth organisation. Thomas turned 14 in 1942.

In some respects, Thomas Niedermayer was fortunate in his date of birth. In the closing years of the Second World War, large numbers of boys in the Hitler-Jugend were drafted and trained to fight as infantry troops in support of the regular army. *Wehrertüchtigungslager* (Defence Strengthening Camps) were set up throughout Germany and boys were taught how to use modern weaponry. In the final stages of the war, the Nazis even recruited an entire SS Panzer Tank Division from the Hitler-Jugend. These child-soldiers proved ready to die for their Führer and the 12th Panzer Division suffered 60 per cent casualties following the Allied landings in Normandy in June 1944.

In 1942, however, members of the Nazi youth movement had not yet been assigned to military service. Instead, they were sent to work in war-related industries. So many men had been drafted into the Wehrmacht (the German Army) that there was a chronic shortage of labour in Germany. This shortfall had been met, in part, by the introduction of German women into occupations previously reserved for men, and the use of vast numbers of slave labourers from countries invaded and occupied by Nazi Germany. However, even that was not enough to feed the ravenous appetite of the German war machine, and young boys who were members of the Hitler-Jugend were also recruited. Some, like Thomas, were specifically assigned to work for the Luftwaffe (the German air force). He concluded his formal education in school at the age of 14 and was sent to be trained as an aircraft mechanic in Friedrichshafen where the Zeppelin and Dornier plane factories were based. From there, he was taken to work in a Luftwaffe plant in Karlsruhe on the French-German border.

This assignment may have helped to ensure that Thomas Niedermayer survived the war, but it does not mean that he escaped unscathed. In the 1930s, the Nazis had established Karlsruhe as an important training base for Luftwaffe pilots and so it was an obvious location for aircraft factories. During the early years of the war, Karlsruhe had managed to escape relatively undamaged in comparison with some other German towns and cities. Air raids did take place, but they were infrequent and spread over a period of time. This allowed Karlsruhe's inhabitants to prepare effective forms of defence such as the construction of underground civilian shelters and the digging of large water pits to assist firefighting. Reproductions of Karlsruhe's aircraft factories were built in nearby forests, and these were bombed repeatedly by the RAF before advances in radar technology revealed them to be fakes.

By 1942, however, the Allies had identified the factories where Thomas worked as being of strategic importance to the Luftwaffe, and RAF Bomber Command had listed Karlsruhe as one of the top 25 German cities that they wanted to destroy. The Allies' stated objective was not only to attack the city's aircraft factories, but also 'to break the morale of the civilian population'. In the middle of 1943 – soon after Thomas Niedermayer had arrived in Karlsruhe – Allied bombing raids on the city began to increase in number, in efficiency and in ferocity. In the early morning of 27 September 1944, the RAF launched a major raid on the city. A formation of 248 bombers dropped over 200,000 incendiary devices as well as hundreds of tons of high explosives. A tsunami of fire swept through Karlsruhe's eastern districts. However, the cold, wet weather and the determined efforts of the city's fire fighters managed to limit the damage. Ironically, this meant that Air Marshal Arthur Harris, of RAF Bomber Command, ordered further massive assaults on Karlsruhe in order to ensure its complete destruction. On 4 December 1944, the city was attacked by 513 RAF planes, which carpet-bombed the city – dropping huge numbers of heavy aerial mines, explosive bombs and incendiary devices. There were more massive air raids later that month – one involving almost 1,000 planes – and large tracts of the city centre were completely obliterated. In the closing years of the war, everyone in Karlsruhe lived under constant threat of sudden death. By the beginning of 1945, hundreds of the city's inhabitants had been killed in the bombings as well as hundreds of slave workers. Less than 4,000 family homes – out of 17,000 – were left standing.

By all accounts, the final months of the Second World War generated widespread fear and panic among the city's inhabitants. According to witnesses, the cacophony of roaring aircraft engines, howling sirens, exploding bombs and defensive gunfire was incessant and terrifying. Much of Karlsruhe's population spent the final weeks of the war hiding in dark and dank underground shelters. They could hear French tanks and infantry troops advancing closer to their city. It seemed that nowhere was safe: even carts in the fields and individuals walking home were strafed by low-flying Allied planes.

In the last weeks of the war, German military engineers blew up a number of bridges to prevent Allied troops crossing the Rhine and the road entrances to Karlsruhe were also barricaded. But, on the morning of 4 April 1945, after a heavy artillery bombardment, French forces began to enter the city. It seems that the only armed resistance that the French encountered in Karlsruhe came from some small units of the Hitler-Jugend. These were subdued within a matter of hours and the French had taken complete control of the town by eleven o'clock of that spring morning.

All males in the city who were between the ages of 16 and 45 were required to report to the French military authorities to be examined and questioned. Around 300 adult men were sent to an internment camp in nearby Offenburg, but 700 or so were held as prisoners in Karlsruhe. These prisoners included many former members of the Nazis' youth movement, one of whom was Thomas Niedermayer. The Allies' plan was to re-educate these young people and try to counteract their years of indoctrination by the Nazis. This usually involved compelling them to watch graphic footage of the atrocities that had taken place in camps such as Belsen and Treblinka.

As part of this re-education, in Bavaria, former members of the Hitler-Jugend were taken to visit the concentration camp at Dachau, where many thousands had died as a result of starvation, neglect, brutality and illness – as well as in hideous medical experiments when prisoners were frozen alive and subjected to violent decompression. Soon after the war ended, part of the camp at Dachau was used to house ethnic German refugees from Eastern Europe. Many of these came from what had formerly been known as East Prussia: one of them was a young woman who would play a key role in Thomas's life. Her name was Ingeborg Tranowski.

Thomas Niedermayer remained in an American internment camp for around six months. By the time he emerged he was still only 16 years old and had spent some of his formative years in a war zone. Judith Lewis Herman, a Professor of Psychiatry at Harvard Medical School, described to me that environment as 'a zone of prolonged and repeated trauma where one is under a death threat pretty much all of the time and escape is pretty much impossible'. Some of the boys from the Hitler-Jugend who had lived through the collapse of Nazi Germany regarded their ability to survive as a source of pride in itself. They had, after all, been members of an organisation whose motto was taken from Friedrich Nietzsche: '*Was mich nicht umbringt, macht mich stärker*' ('What doesn't kill me makes me stronger'). Indeed, the determination of German men and women to escape from the collective trauma of the Second World War was evident in Konrad Adenauer's inaugural speech as Chancellor of the new Federal Republic of Germany in the first session of the Bundestag (the German parliament). He urged his fellow countrymen to 'put the past behind us' and move forward with a renewed sense of purpose. For understandable reasons, Thomas Niedermayer and many young Germans like him did not wish to dwell on the horrors they had recently witnessed. It seems that one of the ways they repressed the traumatic experiences of their youth was to embrace the material opportunities that were available in Germany in the post-war years.

In the aftermath of the war, some of the young survivors applied themselves to advancing their careers with an impressive level of commitment. And many of those young Germans found that an unprecedented range of personal opportunities had opened up for them. These opportunities arose, in part, because of the post-war boom in the German economy and also because of the Western Allies' commitment to establish the West German state as a bulwark against the expansion of Soviet Russia. But it was chiefly due to the colossal number of young German men who had been killed in the world war. Close to 3 million had died and that left innumerable vacancies in the professions, in commerce and in industry that needed to be filled. Thomas Niedermayer was one of those who benefited from these opportunities.

After his release, and like many of his contemporaries, Niedermayer did not return to school. Instead, he went back to Bamberg where he trained as a toolmaker. By 1947, when he was just 18, Niedermayer had already become a foreman in a local factory. At the time of his abduction, there may have been an impression in Ireland that Niedermayer was some sort of fat-cat capitalist who came from a privileged social background. He was described in some Irish newspapers as a 'German industrialist' and even as a 'tycoon'. In reality, Thomas came from a modest working-class family – his father was a car mechanic – and he was conscripted into an adult occupation when he was still a child. While in Northern Ireland, he worked as the general manager of a factory that was moderately sized by German standards and he did not own shares or exert boardroom authority in that or any other company.

In 1953, Niedermayer moved back to Karlsruhe to work as an assistant to the Company Director in an electronics plant. This was his first step on the managerial ladder. By then, he had already met and married Ingeborg Tranowski, the young refugee from East Prussia who had been housed at Dachau. Thomas and Ingeborg both had direct experience of the horrific effects of violence while they were still very young, but it seems highly unlikely that either of them could ever have imagined that the small-scale nature of the Troubles in Northern Ireland would prove as lethal as the global conflict they had both survived.

3.
An Army of Rapists

Ingeborg Tranowski became one of the *Heimatvertriebene* – the 12–16 million 'displaced' Germans who fled or were expelled from the territories that had been annexed by Poland, Lithuania and the Soviet Union in the aftermath of the Second World War. This was the largest forced migration in European history, and it had far-reaching consequences for the whole of German society as well as for the individuals involved. Ingeborg grew up at the opposite end of Germany to Thomas Niedermayer, and it seems doubtful that they would ever have met – let alone married – if it were not for the catastrophic effects of what Josef Goebbels, the Nazi Minister for Propaganda, had enthusiastically described as 'total war'.

Ingeborg was born in 1927 – the year before Thomas. Like her husband, she had spent some of her formative years caught up in the brutality and trauma of a world war. She was one of nine children and grew up in a small village called Hohenweise in the far north of what was then known as East Prussia. By the end of the First World War, the Western Allies were determined that Prussia would never again be strong enough to pose a military threat to the rest of Europe. As a result, most of the major territorial losses that were imposed on Germany by the Treaty of Versailles involved the dismemberment of what had once been the Prussian state. Some parts of Prussia were ceded to Belgium; other parts to Lithuania, to Denmark, to Czechoslovakia and to Poland.

This loss of German territory became a major source of grievance during the years of the Weimar Republic and a focus for Hitler's condemnation of the 'November Criminals' who had signed the Versailles Treaty. Under that Treaty, the principal Prussian port of Danzig was designated an open or 'free' city to be administered by the League of Nations, while the eastern region of Prussia became an isolated enclave that could only reach the rest of Germany by ship or by the railway line that led through the 'Polish Corridor' to the remainder of the German state.

In 1939, East Prussia was mainly an agricultural region that held around two-and-a-half million inhabitants, most of whom were ethnic Germans. Ingeborg Tranowski was one of them but, as her name (which is of Polish origin) suggests, different ethnicities had co-existed and mingled for centuries in this part of Europe. In 1938, the Nazis had tried to erase that diverse history by 'Germanising' thousands of individual surnames and renaming hundreds of villages and towns. When Hitler came to power, there were also around 10,000 Jews living in East Prussia; when the war ended, there were none.

The British and French governments had agreed to Germany's occupation of the Sudetenland in what was then Czechoslovakia in 1938. They accepted Hitler's assurance that this would be 'the last of Germany's territorial claims in Europe'. However, shortly after that agreement had been signed in Munich, the Nazis stepped up their demands for the inclusion of Danzig and the Polish Corridor in the new German Reich. Nazi newspapers whipped up nationalist sentiment, claiming that ethnic Germans needed immediate protection from brutal Polish repression. Hitler proposed building a new motorway through the Polish Corridor which would be under German control. This would have reconnected East Prussia to the rest of Germany while, at the same time, denying Poland direct access to the sea and its vital trade routes.

For understandable reasons, the Polish government declined to give way to the German demands. The Nazis' response was to stage a 'false flag' attack on a German radio station in Gleiwitz, a small Prussian town that was close to the border with Poland. On 31 August 1939, a group of SS men dressed in Polish army uniforms acted as agents provocateurs. They seized the radio station in Gleiwitz and proceeded to broadcast political messages that purported to come from Polish nationalists. The day after the alleged 'incursion' had taken place, Hitler sent German troops into Poland and it was this act that finally triggered the world war.

East Prussia escaped with relatively little damage in the opening years of hostilities. There were few urban centres and the region was not a major centre of armaments production and was, therefore, not an obvious target for Allied air raids. However, almost all of the young men in East Prussia were soon drafted into the Wehrmacht. Their roles in agriculture and industry were taken by slave workers from countries occupied by Nazi Germany and by thousands of young German women like Ingeborg Tranowski. In 1939 it had become mandatory for all German girls aged between 14 and 18 to join the Bund Deutscher Mädel (League of German Maidens) – the girls' section of the Hitler-Jugend – and Ingeborg was 14 years old in 1941. The Bund's original purpose was to prepare German girls for their future role as mothers of the Third Reich. However, as the war progressed, its members were called upon to function as a type of reserve labour force. Indeed, it was the recruitment of young German women – as well as foreign slave workers – that enabled the Nazis to sustain and prolong the war despite a series of crushing military defeats.

At the age of 16, Ingeborg began her training as a nurse but this was interrupted the following year due to serious illness in her family. She would not resume working as a nurse for many years. When she did, she was living in Northern Ireland and had returned to nursing as a means of distraction in the wake of her husband's disappearance.

The relative peace that East Prussia had enjoyed was shattered in the summer of 1944. In August of that year, Königsberg, the medieval city where Immanuel Kant was born, was almost obliterated by successive RAF bombing raids. By that time, the Red Army was driving the Wehrmacht out of Eastern Europe and the roads into East Prussia had already become crowded with ethnic German refugees fleeing before the Soviet advance.

There was still time for the German authorities to arrange an orderly mass evacuation of civilians before the Red Army arrived, but the local Gauleiter, Erich Koch, was an ardent Nazi who regarded such a measure as an admission of defeat. The civilian population of East Prussia would pay a high price for Koch's refusal to countenance their departure. It was, however, a price that Koch did not have to pay himself; he managed to arrange his own escape from East Prussia and died of natural causes almost forty years later.

The refugees from eastern Europe who arrived in East Prussia in 1944 brought with them stories of the dreadful savagery of the Soviet invaders, and Joseph Goebbels' Ministry of Public Enlightenment (sic) and Propaganda was keen to amplify the fears that such stories generated. The Nazi press and newsreels accused Soviet soldiers of heinous war crimes which included the mass murder of

German children and the rape of German women 'from 8 to 84'. Goebbels even arranged for observers from neutral Switzerland to visit one of the villages – close to Ingeborg's home – where multiple rapes and murders by Soviet troops had taken place for them to witness the carnage. 'For once', as Antony Beevor observed, Goebbels's horror propaganda 'turned out to be no exaggeration'. There is no doubt that terrible atrocities were committed by the Red Army. What is also clear is the terror that reports of these atrocities induced in the population of East Prussia.

By then, the entire population of Germany had been systematically misled for years by their leaders about the real state of the war. When, on 13 January 1945, Soviet forces launched their first major offensive into the Reich, the speed at which the Eastern front collapsed was entirely unexpected and deeply shocking to the German citizens of East Prussia. January 1945 was also one of the coldest winters ever recorded in north-eastern Europe. The earth was frozen solid and night temperatures fell 25 degrees below zero. This meant that the ground could not easily be dug up to create defensive positions for the German troops. It also meant that rivers were frozen and did not form serious obstacles for any assault force. In other words, conditions were ideal for a Soviet invasion of East Prussia. Within a week, Soviet forces had severed most road and railway links, leaving the region cut off from the rest of Germany.

In that bitter weather, tens of thousands of Prussian civilians packed their possessions onto sledges and horse-drawn carts and fled in confusion from the rapid advance of the Red Army. No one seemed to know for certain where the Russian troops were, or from which direction they would come. Huge caravans of half-starved and panic-stricken people who were desperate to leave East Prussia clogged the roads. Many had left with little more than the clothes they were wearing. Parents searched in despair for lost children and semi-feral hordes of children wandered through forests and abandoned farmsteads looking for their families.

One German officer described this grim exodus: these were, he wrote, 'columns of misery: the children, the women, the sick and the old, the wounded and the ever more wounded, and all with their helpless, pleading eyes'. Another German soldier saw one young woman on her own, riding a horse as far and as quickly away from the Red Army as its hooves could carry her. The young woman's ancestors, he imagined, had probably arrived in East Prussia many generations ago. Now, he believed, he was watching 'six hundred years of history' disappear before his eyes.

In the first four months of 1945, many thousands of refugees died while trying to flee the Soviet army. They starved, froze to death, drowned at sea, succumbed to epidemics, exhaustion and injuries, or were killed by the Russians. But some Prussians died by their own hands. Nazi propaganda had glorified *Selbstmord* – 'self-murder' – as preferable to defeat, and, between January and May of 1945, large numbers of German civilians took their own lives. The first of these mass suicides took place in East Prussia, but, eventually, they spread like an epidemic through other regions of Germany on a scale that was unprecedented in European history. German men tended to hang or shoot themselves, while one of the most common methods used by German women to kill themselves – and often their children as well – was suicide by drowning.

It could, of course, be argued that the Third Reich was a regime that carried from the start the seeds of its self-destruction. The German armies that invaded the Soviet Union in 1941 had waged war with exceptional ruthlessness and indiscriminate brutality. Now, it seemed the time of retribution was at hand. Soviet forces advanced into East Prussia in immense columns – according to Stalin, 'quantity has its own quality' - and many of the Russian troops believed that there was no such thing as an innocent German. Natalya Gesse was a Russian journalist who observed the Soviet soldiers in action during their invasion of East Prussia. She described them as 'an army of rapists'.

The future Nobel Prize-winner Aleksandr Solzhenitsyn served as a Soviet artillery officer during the invasion of East Prussia. He wrote later that it was commonplace for any German women that Russian soldiers encountered 'to be raped and then shot'. (Solzhenitsyn was arrested and imprisoned in a gulag for criticising such actions in a letter sent from the front.)

At least 2 million women are thought to have been sexually assaulted by Soviet soldiers during the Red Army's invasion of Germany, and a substantial minority, if not an actual majority, appear to have suffered multiple rapes. One tank commander even boasted that, when the Red Army finally left Germany, it had left 'two million of our children' in its wake. However, given the immense misery that Nazi Germany had inflicted on the world, there was little sympathy for the suffering of these women. The use of rape as a weapon to terrorise women and subdue a civilian population seems to have been regarded with a high degree of tolerance – and sometimes active encouragement – by the commanders of the Red Army.

Much of the German population of East Prussia – which by 1945 was largely composed of women, children and old men – managed somehow to escape the Red Army. Ingeborg was one of those who fled in terror before its advance. In normal circumstances, it would have taken a matter of hours to travel by train from Königsberg in East Prussia to Berlin. But by January of 1945 many railway tracks had been destroyed by Allied bombs, and the trains that were still running attracted huge crowds that were desperate to board them. It took Ingeborg almost six months to make her way through the mayhem and chaos of this mass exodus and find safety in a zone of Germany that was occupied by Allied forces.

There was a chronic lack of accommodation in north-western Germany for refugees from the east.

Allied bombing raids had concentrated for years on its urban and industrial centres, and that had resulted in the complete destruction of great swathes of housing in those towns and cities. In the aftermath of the war, there were millions of ethnic German refugees that needed to be housed, and that created a huge logistical problem for the Western Allies.

Their solution was to send these immigrants to rural areas, where there were smaller populations, less war damage and more available housing. Bavaria was one of the principal locations where immigrants were sent, and by 1950 almost a quarter of its total population consisted of ethnic Germans from Poland, Czechoslovakia and East Prussia. The Germans who arrived in Bavaria in 1945, as Ingeborg did, were not welcomed by many of Bavaria's local inhabitants. The immigrants were often mocked for their regional accents and customs – some could not even speak German.

That reaction was, perhaps, understandable. According to Jürgen Müller-Hohagen of the Dachau Institute, 'the awareness of the horrors (the immigrants) had experienced was very, very low.' One writer noted that the farmers in Bavaria had 'never been stuck in air-raid shelters when the bombs rained down and the lives of their loved ones were extinguished', and had 'never trekked, shivering and hungry, along foreign country roads'. For such people, he believed, it was as if the dreadful ordeals of the East Prussians had never happened, or, at least, 'had nothing to do with them'.

It is not surprising then that Ingeborg, according to her sister-in-law Marianne Niedermayer, never wished to speak about or recall her flight from East Prussia. According to Jürgen Müller-Hohagen, 'what had been done' to and seen by refugees like Ingeborg 'was so terrible that they could not talk about it. There had been wounds inflicted that were so deep they could not heal for the rest of their lives.'

The German immigrants were held in detention camps for many months after their arrival in Bavaria: indeed, the last of these camps did not close until 1966. The largest of the detention centres was in Dachau – the first concentration camp opened by the Nazis in 1933, where more than 55,000 prisoners had died. There is an inescapable irony in these ethnic Germans being held in buildings that had previously been used as concentration centres for those ethnic and racial groups that the Nazis believed to be sub-human.

Many of the German immigrants from Eastern Europe had believed that the exile from their former homes was only temporary, and that they would soon be able to return to them. However, it soon became obvious that these refugees would not be allowed to return to East Prussia. Indeed, any Germans who remained there were forcibly expelled in the years that followed the end of the Second World War. At the Potsdam Conference in July 1945, British, American and Russian leaders had agreed to remove millions of ethnic Germans from Eastern

Europe. Winston Churchill had proposed that 'a clean sweep [should] be made' of all Germans in the east. He believed that such expulsion was necessary to ensure that there would be no future 'mixture of populations to cause endless trouble'. As Antony Beevor has observed, this involved 'the abrupt and total destruction of a whole region with its own marked character and culture'. Today, this policy might be described as one of 'ethnic cleansing'.

Apart from Ingeborg, there was only one surviving member of her family: her sister, Renate, after whom she would name one of her own daughters. To lose seven of her brothers and sisters in so short a time was nothing short of a catastrophe and such a blow might overwhelm the emotional stability of any individual. But, when they were released from the Dachau camp, Ingeborg and Renate began to build a new life for themselves in the nearby town of Bamberg. Not long after they arrived there, Ingeborg met a good-looking, energetic and ambitious young man called Thomas Niedermayer. Like him, she had survived the cataclysm of the war. And, like him, that did not mean she had emerged undamaged by the experience. Indeed, the trauma of what had happened in East Prussia in 1945 appears to have cast a dark shadow over the rest of Ingeborg's life.

It seems likely that she suffered from post-traumatic stress disorder (PTSD): a psychological condition that can occur when individuals are exposed to shocking and deeply disturbing events. This can result in recurring feelings of depression and anxiety, and any person with PTSD is regarded as being at a significant risk of killing themselves. The war may have brought them together, but, like many Germans who had survived its horrors, Thomas and Ingeborg followed Konrad Adenauer's advice and focused firmly on the future and not the past.

The couple were married in Thomas's hometown of Bamberg in 1952. Their union may have seemed to exemplify the ways in which the recent immigrants to Bavaria could become fully integrated with the local population. The Niedermayers' future looked bright when, a few years after their marriage, Thomas joined the large and successful Grundig electronics factory in Nuremberg as a works manager. They could not know it, but he was setting out on a path that would eventually lead both him and his wife to their premature deaths in Ireland.

If the story of the Niedermayers is inextricably linked to a world war, then the family is also bound to another bitter conflict – and to the history of the Troubles in Northern Ireland during their most savage years. As civil unrest and political violence grew more intense during that period, changes in the strategy followed by the IRA would have a direct and calamitous impact on all of Thomas Niedermayer's family.

At times, it can seem that a noose was slowly being tightened around the lives of these innocent Germans; one that would eventually bring all of them to their deaths. What happened to the Niedermayers was, of course, a dreadful personal tragedy, but it also represents an indictment of the politics of terror. And, in order to understand some of the reasons why they died, it is necessary to examine something of the social and political context in which their deaths took place.

4.
Fear and Loathing

In the early 1920s, the island of Ireland was partitioned into two separate jurisdictions that still exist today: one of these comprises twenty-six Irish counties to the south while the other comprises just six counties in the north. There were a number of factors that contributed to Ireland's partition and one of them was religious affiliation. Most Catholics in the northern province of Ulster were nationalist in their political sympathies and wished to become part of the new, independent Irish state that was being created in the south. Most northern Protestants were unionists who wished to remain part of the United Kingdom and they were in an overall majority in much of Ulster.

Partition was conceived as the answer to what the British liked to call 'the Irish Question'. However, many Irish nationalists viewed the new border as nothing but an imperial imposition. Éamon de Valera was the founder and first leader of Fianna Fáil, the party that dominated southern

Irish politics for more than forty years. He believed that the division of Ireland was 'entirely artificial' and had been 'fostered by British money and British influence'. Nationalists like de Valera assumed the way to end the partition of Ireland was to convince the British of that necessity. It was thought that, once the northern unionists realised that they could no longer count on Britain's support, they would acquiesce peacefully to the reunification of the country. That was, perhaps, a naive assumption.

In reality, partition was not a solution that was imposed arbitrarily by a colonial power on Ireland. Instead, it was an outcome that had been dictated by the existence of acute political, economic and religious divisions and by the possibility of a full-scale civil war engulfing the entire island. That possibility was averted: instead, two separate and relatively contained types of civil war did take place. One of those was fought in the south of the island, in what had become Saorstát Éireann, or the Irish Free State. That conflict was between those who accepted the provisions of the Anglo-Irish Treaty signed in 1921 – which included the partition of Ireland – and those who rejected its terms. By the time the bloodshed ended in 1923, more Irish combatants had been killed in this civil war than in the whole of the preceding War of Independence.

The other conflict that was fought in the early 1920s was in Northern Ireland. Fewer people may have died than in the south, but it had a more explicitly sectarian dimension. Sectarianism in Ulster has never been fuelled simply by questions of religious affiliation. Instead, religion has been closely linked to issues of ethnic, cultural and political identity. This has been a recipe for intermittent conflict between Protestants and Catholics and this conflict erupted in the early 1920s in vicious communal violence. When the tumult of those years finally subsided, the two governments of the new Irish states viewed each other with some loathing and a good deal of mutual suspicion and distrust.

While nationalists were dominant in the Dublin-based Irish parliament, the northern legislature was dominated by unionists. The northern parliament would eventually meet at Stormont, an imposing structure in the classical Greek style built just outside Belfast's city boundaries. Ironically, some of the leaders of Ulster's unionists were opposed to any devolution of power from the imperial parliament at Westminster. They suspected that the British might use a local parliament as the staging post to an all-Ireland state. There were some solid grounds for their suspicions: the Government of Ireland Act of 1920 that created Northern Ireland had explicitly stated Britain's desire for 'the eventual establishment of a Parliament for the whole of Ireland'.

In Northern Ireland, the unionist population spanned a number of different religious denominations and social backgrounds. These came together in several pan-Protestant organisations, such as the Orange Order. The ostensible purpose of that institution was to

promote the religious principles of the Reformation of
the sixteenth century. In practice, the Order helped to
unify members of unionism's diverse social classes and
multiple Reformed churches – and there were more than
fifty different Protestant denominations listed in the 1961
census of Northern Ireland taken in the year that Thomas
and Ingeborg Niedermayer arrived there.

The anti-Treaty (or republican) forces in the south
of the island had denied the moral and legal authority of
the Irish Free State. They lost the subsequent civil war,
and the vast majority of republicans were reconciled
with the new regime in the course of the 1930s. However,
a rump of militant republicans continued to deny the
legitimacy of both the parliaments in Dublin and Belfast.
They remained committed to an armed campaign by the
IRA. Indeed, according to its 'Green Book' – the so-called
'Bible' of the IRA – Sinn Féin, the political party that
represented the IRA's views, remained the only 'legal and
lawful government of the Irish Republic'. As such, the
Green Book claimed that only Sinn Féin had 'the moral
right to pass laws for, and to claim jurisdiction over, the
whole island of Ireland'.

North of the Irish border, the constitutional status of
Northern Ireland remained the major political issue. There
were periods in the following decades when this issue was
to the forefront of political debate and controversy and
other times when its importance seemed less critical, but
it was always present to a greater or lesser extent. This

meant that, in effect, all elections in Northern Ireland were understood as *de facto* referendums on the state's continued existence. That tended to produce a sense of political stasis in both the unionist and nationalist parties elected to the Northern Irish parliament.

This was dramatically reflected in the large number of constituencies in which candidates for Stormont were returned unopposed. On average, almost half of all seats in the Northern Irish parliament – those constituencies with a clear majority of either Catholics or Protestants – were seldom, if ever, contested in general elections. This meant that, in the first fifty years of the state's existence, few MPs at Stormont ever lost their seats as a result of electoral defeat; whether unionist or nationalist, they were usually only replaced when they had retired or died. Indeed, in February 1969 when the fundamentalist Protestant minister, the Rev. Ian Paisley, contested the Bannside constituency of the unionist Prime Minister, Terence O'Neill, this was the first time in over twenty years that O'Neill had faced another candidate: he had been returned unopposed in every election since 1946. By conventional standards, this would indicate that the form of democracy that had prevailed in Northern Ireland for half a century was constrained and exceptional.

Northern Ireland was once described by the Unionist Party leader David Trimble as 'a cold house for Catholics', and there were good reasons for nationalists to believe that they were treated as second-class citizens. There were several constituencies in the west and south of the northern state where there were more Catholics than Protestants and these had been gerrymandered to ensure unionist control of local government. In 1968, there were just eleven urban district and county councils out of seventy-three that were controlled by nationalists: roughly half the number that might have been expected. Since councils could allocate houses, those controlled by unionists were prone to discriminatory practices that favoured Protestants.

That background may help to explain why Northern Ireland has sometimes been portrayed as a fascistic 'Orange state' in which the most fundamental of civil rights – such as the right to vote – were consistently denied to some of its citizens on the basis of their religion. Indeed, it is sometimes assumed that Catholics were totally disenfranchised. Northern Ireland has been compared to the apartheid regime in South Africa and to the southern states of the USA during the imposition of the racist Jim Crow laws. Such comparisons only serve to understate and trivialise the scourge of genuine racism. Discrimination certainly existed in Northern Ireland, but there needs to be some sense of proportion in assessing its extent and impact. It was not enforced as a systematic government policy and no one was ever denied the right to vote in local council elections, Stormont elections or Westminster parliamentary elections because of their religion. There was never any mandatory segregation of public schools, public places or public transport, similar to the system that existed for years in the southern states of the USA. In fact, such discrimination was specifically prohibited in the legislation that established the northern state.

In the early years, there were some half-hearted attempts made to follow this legal obligation. In 1921, the first Stormont cabinet announced that the new government 'intended to enroll members of all creeds in their staff'. Unfortunately, northern governments honoured that ambition more in the breach than the observance. It may have been illegal to practise religious discrimination, but that did not prevent it soon becoming established on a widespread and, at times, blatant scale. In particular, those public appointments that were the gift of state authorities were often dispensed with what Patrick Bishop and Eamonn Mallie have accurately described as 'ruthless partiality'.

There were some obvious similarities between the two Irish states born in the 1920s. Indeed, they mirrored each other in several ways and it seems impossible to consider the northern state without some reference to the southern one. Both states, for example, tended to hold similar conservative positions on certain social issues and there was little scope for women to play leading roles in the political life of either state. In 1935, James Craig, the northern Prime Minister, reacted when the Free State vaunted its Catholic ethos: 'They still boast of Southern Ireland being a Catholic State. All I boast of is that we are a Protestant

Parliament and a Protestant State.' At the time that Craig spoke, Catholics constituted more than one-third of the northern state's population. The following year, Éamon de Valera, the leader of the Fianna Fáil government in Dublin, declared in public that Ireland was 'a Catholic nation' – although nearly one quarter of those living on the island were Protestants. It seems that the religious minorities in both parts of Ireland were excluded, when convenient, from the calculations of both men.

There were, however, some crucial differences between the two Irish states. Protestants living south of the Irish border may have felt marginalised and unsympathetic to the religious and cultural ambitions of the government in Dublin. As Marianne Elliott has observed, many of them 'felt isolated in a country whose ethos was now so demonstrably Catholic and whose national narrative bore so little resemblance to their own'. By 1926, the Protestant population in the territory of Saorstát Éireann was almost 30 per cent less than it had been in 1911. The situation was very different for northern Catholics. Southern Protestants constituted a very small minority in the southern state but, at the time of partition, Catholics made up around 35 per cent of the total population of Northern Ireland and their numbers and proportion grew in the decades that followed. Indeed, they now constitute the majority religion in Northern Ireland.

Protestant and Catholic communities in Northern Ireland have tended to live separate but parallel lives and each has maintained their own networks of social and commercial organisation. They have typically attended different schools, read different newspapers, played different sports and voted for different political parties. However, the two communities have also lived beside each other for centuries and have often shared the same – usually conservative – attitudes towards a range of social issues. It would have been considered quite unusual for Ulster's Protestants and Catholics not to have any friends, or neighbours, or co-workers – or relatives – from the other community. Even during the worst years of the Troubles, the distinctions between the two communities were not always clear-cut.

This peculiar combination of closeness and distance between the two communities gained further resonance during the years of the Troubles. As Henry McDonald has observed, in the villages and small towns across rural Ulster, 'killers and victims have had to live side by side in relatively close proximity'. Both of the major communities in Northern Ireland had developed an acute and intuitive understanding of the complex nuances that served to define their differences. These 'dog whistles' often went unheard by outsiders like Thomas Niedermayer, but, on occasion, they could be used deliberately to provoke or antagonise the 'other side'. As the Nobel Laureate Seamus Heaney wrote about his fellow northerners: 'Smoke signals are loud-mouthed compared to us.'

By and large, the leaders of the unionist party that governed Northern Ireland for almost half a century did not operate as professional politicians. The regime that they controlled was one of part-time ministers and a parliament that often met for no more than two afternoons a week while in session (and often less). This was, in the words of Henry Patterson, an 'amateurish political culture' in which major policy decisions were frequently not made by ministers or parliament but by senior civil servants. It could even be argued that the amateurish nature of Northern Ireland's government was beneficial to its citizens in that it helped to prevent the creation of a more aggressively sectarian state. Whatever those benefits may have been, they were not enough to redress the deep sense of grievance felt by many northern Catholics.

5.
The Miracle-Worker

To many nationalists, Ulster unionism may have seemed like a monolithic political bloc that was utterly resistant to change. However, unionism contained its own internal conflicts and these were influenced by a wide range of regional, social and denominational factors. Given that the Unionist Council included some members of the landed gentry – as well as many small farmers – and members of the commercial bourgeoisie, along with those of the industrial working class – the wonder is that their alliance held together for so long. In the early 1970s, under the intense pressure of the Troubles, Ulster unionism fragmented into its constituent elements of social groups and classes.

In fact, significant divisions had already begun to open up within the Unionist Party by the end of the Second World War. A small group of relatively progressive MPs had emerged who favoured reducing the influence of the Orange Order and wished to make unionism more acceptable to the minority Catholic population. One of these was Morris May, who was elected in 1949 and soon became a member of the unionist cabinet: in the early 1950s he urged his party to loosen its links with the Orange Order. May also blocked an attempt by some unionist MPs to limit the numbers of children entitled to state benefits. Although it was claimed that this proposal was designed to save the exchequer money, it would clearly have disadvantaged Catholic families which tended to be larger than Protestant ones. Brian Maginess was another senior minister in the Stormont cabinet. In 1959, he proposed that Catholics should be encouraged to join the Unionist Party. Maginess also recommended that unionists should treat their political opponents 'not as enemies but as fellow members of the community' and criticised those who made abusive references to the religious beliefs of others. His views were subsequently endorsed by Clarence Graham, the chairman of the influential Standing Committee of the Ulster Unionist Council.

By the mid-1950s, Maginess, Graham and May were not the only unionist politicians who seemed a good deal more professional and capable than their predecessors. Some of these MPs were not only involved in efforts to reform and modernise the Unionist Party, they also led the campaign to regenerate the Northern Irish economy. There was an obvious and critical need for such regeneration. Unlike the rest of Ireland, the north-eastern corner of the island had become industrialised in the course of the nineteenth century. However, in the twentieth century, its traditional industries of ship-building, heavy engineering and rope manufacture had experienced an unremitting and terminal decline. By focusing energies on economic regeneration, it seemed that the liberal faction within unionism could avoid splitting their party, while at the same time improving the living conditions of both Catholics and Protestants in Northern Ireland. This was the context in which Stormont governments began to seek foreign investment through offering a range of financial incentives.

Brian Faulkner was one of the younger unionist MPs who was associated with this process at that time. He would later become the sixth and last Prime Minister of Northern Ireland but, in the late 1950s, his principal focus was on the Northern Irish economy. Faulkner was first elected to the Stormont parliament in 1949, but before then he had spent almost ten years working in the family business which was then one of the world's largest shirt manufacturers. Although he did not become Minister for Commerce until 1963, Faulkner was involved throughout the preceding decade in formulating a new and effective economic strategy and had identified his major concern as the 'industrial issues confronting the Government'. He believed that Germany was of particular importance to Northern Ireland, and he made frequent visits there in his attempts to attract foreign investment.

In the early 1960s, the Northern Ireland Labour Party (NILP) had made significant electoral gains in areas where working-class Protestants lived. Faulkner and others believed that their new economic strategy offered concrete political benefits to the Unionist Party, since it could erode the appeal of socialist groups. Even intelligent and capable unionist MPs like Faulkner did not grasp that the real threat to their party's control of the northern state would not come from within their own Protestant community. There had been some clear indications that a growing number of northern Catholics were prepared to play a more active role in the internal affairs of Northern Ireland. Faulkner and other unionists did not grasp that opportunity and failed to realise that the prolonged and systematic exclusion of Catholics from political power in the northern state was already building to an unprecedented and overwhelming crisis.

But, in the early 1960s, that gathering political storm still lay ahead and unionist MPs like Faulkner could feel confident about their party's future. The investment of international companies such as ICI, DuPont and Goodyear had generated new and reasonably well-paid jobs throughout Northern Ireland and this growing economic prosperity promised to improve the lives of both Catholics and Protestants. There was evidence that such prosperity had already halted the electoral advance of the NILP and other socialist parties in Belfast and other Northern Irish towns. At the beginning of 1960, the Stormont government was ready to announce another major economic coup. This one involved a man who appeared to embody the *Wirtschaftswunder* (economic miracle) that had transformed West Germany in the aftermath of the Second World War. His name was Max Grundig and he was to prove instrumental in bringing Thomas and Ingeborg Niedermayer and their young family to Northern Ireland.

Grundig was born twenty years before Thomas but he came from a somewhat similar background. Like Niedermayer, he was born in the Franconian region of Bavaria to a family of modest means. His father died when he was 12 and, like Niedermayer, Grundig left school at 14. He began his working life as a trade apprentice to a plumber. However, Grundig had developed a consuming interest in modern technology and, by the age of 22, he had already set up a small shop in Nuremberg selling and repairing radios. The rapid growth of this enterprise was greatly aided by the advent of the Nazi regime.

In 1933, radio sets were still relatively new and expensive devices and the Nazi leadership had grasped their potential as a medium of propaganda. Indeed, Joseph Goebbels, the Minister for Propaganda, believed that the National Socialists could never have come to power in Germany without their skilful exploitation of the medium. One of Goebbels' political goals was to ensure that radio sets were affordable and widely available throughout the new Reich.

Soon after the Nazis came to power, Goebbels commissioned a new type of radio. The result was the

Volksempfänger, the so-called 'people's radio'. It was a simple two-band set with limited reception. That limitation appealed to the Nazis because it meant that they did not have to worry about German listeners tuning in to foreign stations. *Volksempfänger* sets were heavily subsidised by the Nazi regime: they cost just 76 Reichsmarks – about half the price of the nearest equivalent – making them the cheapest radio sets in the world. They were also the most successful and popular of the Nazis' range of 'people's products', such as the Volkswagen, and they came to assume an iconic role in the political imagery of Nazi Germany. As the outbreak of war grew closer, the production of these sets intensified until, by the autumn of 1939, over 7 million *Volksempfänger* had been sold.

By 1938, Max Grundig's company was generating more than one million Reichsmarks in annual turnover. By the time he turned 30, Grundig had become a very wealthy man. Despite his wealth, Grundig followed a restrained lifestyle. His passion was his work and it seemed that everything else was of secondary importance to him. His original business had involved two partners, but he bought them both out. He had the reputation of someone who made all decisions on his own and who was absorbed in the smallest details of his business. During the Second World War, Grundig managed to continue to run his business as before. In fact, his electronics output became so important to Germany's war economy in the manufacture of V1 and V2 rockets that he was ruled exempt from any military service.

Towards the end of the war, the German economy was in a state approaching total collapse. Industrial output in 1947 was one-third of its 1939 level; basic food supplies were severely limited; a system of barter had replaced many cash exchanges; and a very high percentage of German men of working age had been killed in the war. However, within twenty years, the German economy had staged an extraordinary recovery and was envied by most of the rest of the world. Max Grundig played a central role in that recovery.

His company was now called 'Grundig AG' and its owner quickly identified the scale of the market that was emerging in consumer electronics. Within a few years, the brand name of Grundig had come to signify products that were solid and reliable and conformed to the highest standards of technical specification. By the time Thomas Niedermayer joined the company, Grundig was on its way to becoming a market leader in home entertainment products across Western Europe.

After a war that had reduced much of their country to a state of rubble, there was an obvious need for some escape mechanisms. Television sets and radios brought entertainment into ordinary people's homes and allowed them to forget the devastation around them. They could glimpse the possibilities of other happier worlds and believe they had a brighter future. Max Grundig was able to meet that critical need. By the end of the 1950s, his company employed tens of thousands of workers in its German plants and was one of the biggest manufacturers in Europe. Max Grundig usually relied on his own instincts when it came to making important business decisions and now his instincts told him the time was right to locate the first of his operations outside of Germany.

Grundig had become aware of the incentives that were available to foreign investors in Northern Ireland. In 1945, the Stormont government had introduced an Industries Development Act that provided assistance for job creation through a series of substantial financial grants. These inducements included the building of advance factories, valuable fuel subsidies and the provision of housing for new workforces. Most of the investment that these incentives attracted came from outside Northern Ireland. Initially this originated in Great Britain, but European and American companies soon saw the commercial opportunities and also began to invest in significant numbers.

The impact of such external investment should not be exaggerated, but by 1960 one in every six manufacturing jobs in Northern Ireland was provided by foreign firms that had received financial assistance from the Stormont government. This allowed the contraction of traditional industries to be offset by the growth of alternative ones and resulted in the creation of tens of thousands of new jobs, particularly in the east of the country. These foreign firms had little interest in following any recruitment policy that favoured one section of Northern Ireland's population over another and their complete indifference to the religious affiliation of their employees was soon reflected in the composition of their workforces.

In the years since he joined the Grundig company, Thomas Niedermayer had risen rapidly within its management structure. In 1955, at the age of just 27, he had entered Grundig's top echelon when he was appointed as a department head at the company's headquarters in Nuremberg where Max Grundig had built two large tower blocks to house his workforce. Niedermayer was regarded by his colleagues as ambitious, hard-working and highly capable. He was also someone who had a shop floor understanding of the electronics industry. He was, in short, a man after Max Grundig's own heart, so it was no great surprise that he was chosen to be the first General Manager of the new overseas operation. The first location ear-marked for a Grundig factory outside Germany may have seemed a more unlikely choice. It was a village a few miles to the south-west of Belfast called Dunmurry.

Soon after they arrived in Ireland, Thomas and Ingeborg recorded an 'audio letter' for their relatives back in Germany. This tape recording was never sent to them and remained unheard for over sixty years. However, it provides a unique and revealing insight into the Niedermayers' early impressions of their new home.

It soon becomes clear from the tape that the family are greatly enjoying life in Northern Ireland. Thomas acknowledges that, at first, they found it difficult to understand the local dialect: 'people talked and talked and we just nodded without understanding anything'. However, he reports that things had greatly improved since then, and now 'Inge speaks more English than I had anticipated.' They had visited local beauty spots, such as the Giant's Causeway, and he looked forward to showing visitors from Germany the Irish countryside so that 'you will see for yourself how beautiful Ireland is'. Thomas admits that initially he thought that it seemed to rain a good deal, but he notes that 'people (here) do not pay much attention to that, and now we are doing the same'.

Thomas includes on the tape a recording of 'an Irish folk song'. The song in question is 'There's One Fair County in Ireland', also known as 'The Boys of the County Armagh', and the singer is Bridie Gallagher. The lyrics lavish extravagant praise on the northern county of Armagh, 'the orchard of Erin's green land', and the record was a huge hit in Ireland in the late 1950s and early 1960s. Listening to the song, I wondered if its insistent tempo reminded Thomas of the *Schlager* or 'oompah' music popular in his native Bavaria. The singer's yearning for her 'Irish home' may also have echoed some of the '*Heimat*', or 'homeland', themes that feature in the sentimental ballads that Thomas would have heard growing up in Franconia.

On the same tape, Ingeborg tells her German relatives that the people in Northern Ireland are very friendly, and their neighbours are 'always ready to help'. She appears surprised that each family 'has a house like the newer homes in Germany'. They also have both front and back gardens, the front gardens have a lawn 'with roses and beautiful flowers', and the back gardens are 'for the children to play in'. She notes that 'it's a well-known fact that there are many children in Ireland', so there is always a lot of noise in the street when they come out of school. She praises the 'wonderful black tea' that is available locally but asks if some camomile tea can be sent to her from Germany since it was unobtainable in Ireland.

Given subsequent events, some parts of the tape recording have taken on a further resonance. In one sequence, Thomas looks forward to exploring more of Ireland – including the 'South and West coast' – but explains that he is not in any rush because 'we have quite a few more years to do so'. In fact, Thomas and Ingeborg were able to visit many parts of Ireland during those early years. Writing to his brother in 1969, Thomas mentioned that he and his family were about to spend two weeks of their holidays in County Wexford, followed by another week spent in Bundoran in County Donegal.

In another part of this audio letter, Ingeborg talks about family visits to the seaside: she had never lived so close to the sea before and she was captivated by the experience. 'Sometimes,' she writes, 'when I walk on the beach it is as beautiful as a fairy tale.' But she also expresses a degree of apprehension: 'when you go into the water, it is ice-cold to your feet and you have soon to come out'. A few days previously, she adds, Thomas had driven the family to a nearby beach: 'the others got undressed and went into the water, but I only took my shoes off and walked along [the shore].' When she went back for her shoes, they were gone: 'the tide had come in and carried them away'. Twenty or so years later, an Irish tide would also carry Ingeborg away.

For most of its existence, Dunmurry – where the new Grundig factory was located – had a predominantly Protestant population. In the nineteenth century, the village was one of the many linen centres with small factories and mills that were scattered throughout rural Ulster. By the 1920s, the character of the village had begun to change and its green field sites were used to re-house some of Belfast's most deprived city-dwellers. This trend accelerated in the aftermath of the Second World War. The war years had been a time of considerable social, economic and cultural change in Northern Ireland. Local businesses had boomed and unemployment had fallen. Cinemas and pubs were allowed to open on the Sabbath and the hundreds of thousands of US servicemen, stationed in Northern Ireland during the war, had also helped to expand local horizons.

The Northern Ireland Housing Trust was established in 1945 and soon became widely accepted as a 'religion-blind' agency that did not discriminate between Protestants and Catholics. This dismayed those unionists who wanted housing to be distributed in favour of Protestants. However, an analysis of the Trust's operations shows that its allocation of housing accurately reflected the denominational proportions of Northern Ireland. Basil Brooke, the third Prime Minister of Northern Ireland, had the reputation of being prejudiced and deeply sectarian in his personal beliefs. However, he threw his political weight behind the Housing Trust's central policy – its rejection of religious discrimination – and that helped ensure that its legitimacy was accepted by both major communities in Northern Ireland.

In the 1950s, the Trust purchased land in and around Dunmurry and began to build new housing units. One-third of these units was reserved for residents of run-down areas of Belfast, including a large number of families from the Lower Falls area of West Belfast. This changed the religious demographics of Dunmurry and established new housing estates whose inhabitants were now almost all Catholic. The Grundig factory was the first occupant of the new industrial estate at Derriaghy Park. The plan was that its new labour force would be recruited from nearby housing estates, such as Andersonstown –which meant that the majority of the workforce was likely to be Catholic.

One of those who came to work in the new plant was a young man called Brian Keenan. He had previous experience of working in the electronics sector and was intelligent and articulate with a very forceful personality. Keenan may not be well known to the general public in Ireland – or elsewhere, for that matter – but he would play a pivotal role in shaping the IRA that emerged in Northern Ireland during the early 1970s, and in formulating the strategy that it would follow throughout that decade.

Soon after he joined Grundig, Keenan was chosen to be one of the shop stewards who represented its workers. In that capacity, he had frequent meetings with Niedermayer. They came from similar social backgrounds, though Keenan's family had arguably a somewhat higher social status. Despite some similarities – or, perhaps, because of them – it seems that their encounters could often become heated and acrimonious. According to Thomas's former secretary, there was no love lost between these two men and that personal antagonism may be one of the reasons why Brian Keenan would come to play a central role in the death of Thomas Niedermayer.

6.

The Apprentice

Brian Keenan's family came from the New Lodge Road in Belfast's inner city. The New Lodge area had been developed as Belfast became industrialised during the course of the nineteenth century. Many of its residents had escaped rural poverty and had come to work in nearby mills and factories. For many years, the population of New Lodge was 'mixed', meaning that it was home to both Protestants and Catholics.

During the Second World War, Belfast produced large quantities of ships, aircraft and munitions to support the Allied war effort. In addition to this, a great deal of food grown in Northern Ireland passed through the city on its way to Britain. All of this made Belfast an obvious target for the Luftwaffe and the Stormont government had been well advised of the imminent likelihood of German bombing raids.

In comparison with other large cities in the UK, Belfast remained poorly defended. This was largely due to the negligence of the Stormont government. Hardly any air-raid shelters had been prepared. There were no available searchlights. There were no night fighters. Of the twenty-two anti-aircraft guns in the city, only seven were deemed fit for purpose. The extreme vulnerability of the city to German attack was identified by some unionist MPs and several ministers resigned from the Stormont cabinet in protest at what one termed the 'slack, dilatory and apathetic' conduct of the government.

As a result of such neglect, the city offered the Luftwaffe an easy and inviting target. In April and May 1941, scores of German bombers conducted a series of devastating air raids. Hundreds of civilians died as a result of these raids and more than half of Belfast's houses were destroyed by high explosives or incendiary bombs. In proportionate terms, these were the most damaging raids inflicted by the Luftwaffe on any city in the UK.

New Lodge was in one of the areas that was badly damaged by the Luftwaffe. Whole streets were flattened and many of their residents were killed. Given Keenan's subsequent role in the IRA, there is a certain irony at work here as the IRA had been seeking an alliance with Nazi Germany for several years – in fact, the relationship between the IRA and the Nazis ran rather deeper than a merely tactical arrangement. The previous August, the IRA's main propaganda sheet, the *War News*, had described Jews as 'unscrupulous wretches' and promised its readers that, once it gained power, the IRA would 'rid the country of such vermin'. The *War News* – whose title referred to the IRA's campaign against the British presence in Ireland, not to the global conflict – also assured its readers that, if troops from Nazi Germany ever invaded Irish territory, they would come 'as friends and liberators'.

The Luftwaffe's bombs did not discriminate between the Protestant and Catholic citizens of Belfast and both communities suffered commensurate casualties. The threat of further air attacks led more than 200,000 of Belfast's citizens – almost half its total population – to move out of the city in 1941 and seek refuge in rural Ulster. Brian Keenan's family was one of those that left Belfast. They moved to the small village of Swatragh in County Derry where he was born in 1942. Swatragh was in the Mid-Ulster electoral constituency, which was at that time fairly evenly balanced between Catholics and Protestants. This meant that it was one of the constituencies that was regularly contested in parliamentary elections. Over the years, the winners of these contests had see-sawed between unionist and nationalist MPs and, on a few occasions, republican candidates from Sinn Féin – the 'political wing' of the IRA – were also returned.

Protestants and Catholics both lived in Swatragh and in the surrounding countryside. Although it still has only a few hundred inhabitants, the village boasts three churches: Roman Catholic, Church of Ireland and Presbyterian – the three major Christian denominations in Northern Ireland. While the village is very small, it did not escape its share of sectarian violence in the most recent Troubles. One case illustrates the kind of domestic intimacy that has often been a feature of such violence in rural Ulster.

In 1981, a part-time policeman called John Proctor was shot dead by the IRA. Proctor was 25 years old when he was killed. He had just left the Mid-Ulster Hospital where he had been visiting his wife, June, and their newborn son. June walked her husband to the door of the maternity ward and told him to 'watch himself'. Then, she went to a window to wave goodbye. As she waited there, she heard the sound of gunshots. 'I knew it was Johnnie, and I knew he was dead,' she said later, 'because I heard the number of shots they put in him. It wasn't just one shot – they riddled him.' Proctor had been shot thirteen times at point-blank range with a semi-automatic assault rifle. As she stood by the window, June watched as her husband's body was carried into the hospital. She recognised him by his clothes: he had been murdered just a few hours after the birth of his son.

Earlier that day, Proctor had helped to carry the coffin of another young man: a close friend of his called Alan Clarke who had been killed two days previously by the same unit of the IRA. On the afternoon that Proctor died, RUC officers were able to tell his widow the name of the IRA gunman whom they believed had killed him. His name was Seamus Kearney and he was a local man who lived in Swatragh.

For most of the next thirty-two years, June Proctor saw Kearney almost every day: 'He lived less than a mile away, and would drive past my place of work,' she said. 'He would just look at me. He knew who I was, and he knew that I knew who he was.' However, there was not sufficient evidence for Kearney to be charged and he was not tried for the murder of Proctor until 2013. By then, new forensic technology was able to connect his DNA with the scene of the killing.

Kearney declined to give evidence or speak at his trial and Sinn Féin denounced his conviction as 'vindictive'. He was sentenced to twenty years, but, under the terms of the Good Friday Agreement of 1998, the maximum term he could serve was two years and he was soon released. Proctor's widow still believed that 'justice had been done for Johnnie' – after more than three decades. (Subsequently, it was reported that Kearney asked the police to prosecute June for a 'hate crime' because of the comments she had made.) Proctor's son, also called John, spoke of his personal loss in 'never getting to meet my father', but he also expressed his family's relief that Kearney had been publicly identified as his father's killer. 'Justice is justice for any innocent family,' he said, 'whether they are Protestant or Catholic.'

In the 1940s, Keenan's family was not known for its republican politics. According to Jeanette Keenan, one of his daughters, Keenan's father was a civil servant and accountant; that accorded the family 'a perceived higher status' in relation to other Catholics. Keenan's father also served in the RAF in England during the Second World War. He was a warrant officer and was commended for bravery when he waded through aviation fuel that had spilled onto the runway to help rescue an air crew whose plane had crashed on take-off. There may be another irony here: when Brian Keenan was later sentenced for serious terrorist offences, he would spend some years in Full Sutton. This was one of four high-security prisons in England where IRA prisoners were sent. It had been built in northern Yorkshire, beside the old aerodrome at Pocklington where Keenan's father had once served with distinction.

After the war, Keenan's father moved back to Northern Ireland and his family returned from Swatragh to the New Lodge area of Belfast. Like Niedermayer, Brian Keenan left school in his early teens and, according to his daughter, this resulted in him 'educating himself'. Like Niedermayer, Keenan was intelligent and capable. And, like Niedermayer, he began training to become an electronics engineer. Engineering was an occupation in Northern Ireland that had traditionally been associated with Protestants. Apprenticeships were often passed on within families and it could prove difficult for Catholics to gain access to the trade. According to some accounts, Keenan experienced sectarian prejudice when he began to train as an apprentice in the largely Protestant town of Larne in north Antrim. That may help to explain why he decided in 1958, while still only 16 years old, to move to Corby, an industrial town in Northamptonshire in the north of England.

At that time, Corby was undergoing a period of rapid commercial expansion and the town attracted many immigrants from both Ireland and Scotland. Keenan moved in with his brother who was already living in Corby and continued his apprenticeship as an electronics engineer. While Keenan was living in England, he came to the attention of the police on more than one occasion. He was arrested after a vicious fight with his own brother which continued even after they had both been taken to the police station. In another incident, he was arrested for vandalism and the damage he had caused to a cigarette dispensing machine. These offences were relatively minor and may have faded in his memory, but it meant that Keenan had been fingerprinted by the English police and his prints were kept on file. More than fifteen years later, they would be used to help ensure his conviction for serious terrorist crimes.

Keenan later claimed that his education in radical politics began in England. He became involved with the Electrical Trades Union, which at that time was dominated by members of the British Communist Party (CPGB). In the following years, Keenan was often labelled a convinced Marxist and even as a 'Stalinist' who subscribed to a strict doctrine of 'democratic centralism'. Although Keenan sometimes described himself as a 'communist', there seems to be little evidence that he was familiar with Marxist theory and his alleged 'Stalinism' might only refer to his single-minded and autocratic character. Indeed, it is hard for me to believe that Keenan's political opinions conformed to any theoretical system, whether Marxist or otherwise.

In an interview he gave towards the end of his life, Keenan named three books that had inspired his beliefs. It is worth examining each of these works briefly and considering what they might contribute to an understanding of Keenan's character and the perspective he brought to his role in the IRA.

Keenan identified *The War of the Flea* as one of these seminal texts. In this short study, Robert Taber provides an informative but largely uncritical summary of Mao Zedong's theories on how asymmetric guerrilla wars could be won through creating a 'climate of collapse', in which it becomes impossible to maintain the existing regime. The central metaphor suggests that even a large and powerful animal, such as a dog, can be worn down by the persistent attacks of a much smaller but elusive creature, such as a flea. (Perhaps the metaphor is not entirely convincing: dogs, after all, are seldom killed by fleas.)

Taber's book suggests that the incoming tide of revolution in the developing world is an irresistible force and he seems confident in his prediction that western governments will prove unable to contain or defeat its armed insurgencies. Ironically, this projection has similarities with the 'domino' theory advanced at that time by some conservative ideologues in the USA. According to their understanding, the loss of one country to Communism would lead inexorably to a succession of comparable defeats and, ultimately, to the loss of American global hegemony. Such predictions have proven to be flawed. With a few exceptions, such as the Viet Cong's campaign in South Vietnam, Mao's theories of guerrilla warfare have failed in those countries where elected governments have had the means to prevent insurgents from establishing substantial base (or 'liberated') areas.

Taber was an American journalist who had covered the aftermath of the collapse of Fulgencio Batista's corrupt regime in Cuba and his wholehearted enthusiasm for Castro's government may now seem rather naive. Back in the USA, Taber had founded the 'Fair Play for Cuba Committee', which was characterised in US Senate hearings as the 'publicity agent' for Castro's regime. The Committee later achieved notoriety when one of its members, Lee Harvey Oswald, was charged with the assassination of President John F. Kennedy. In Cuba, a relatively small group of armed and determined revolutionaries had managed to seize control of the state and ruthlessly suppressed all political opposition. It is not hard to imagine why this political scenario might appeal to Keenan's forceful and unyielding character. One of his former associates in the IRA told me that Keenan often referred to Taber's book in conversation and would recommend it to others as an essential guide to future strategy in the IRA's armed campaign. In particular, he was attracted to the idea of producing a 'climate of collapse' in Northern Ireland that would be similar to the one that Castro had created in Cuba.

Keenan also cited *Small is Beautiful: A Study of Economics as if People Mattered* as one of the books that had most influenced him. In this appropriately slim volume, E. F. Schumacher argued in favour of what he termed a 'Buddhist approach to economics' and urged a return to the traditional values that he believed could still be found in the small villages of India and Burma. In addition to being interested in Buddhism, Schumacher was also a recent convert to Catholicism at the time he wrote *Small Is Beautiful,* and his book reveals a strong underlying religious impulse. This is evident in his open dislike of the agnostic materialism of contemporary capitalism and his rejection of what he considered to be the vacuous morality of modern society. Schumacher acknowledged that his thinking had been influenced by the teaching of various papal encyclicals on socio-economic issues, such as Leo XIII's *Rerum novarum* and Pius XI's *Quadragesimo anno* in which both popes advocated a return to small-scale and family-run businesses.

It might seem rather odd for a committed Marxist, as Keenan is alleged to have been, to identify so strongly with the work of someone like Schumacher who wrote from an explicitly anti-materialist position and who deplored what he considered to be the Marxist reduction of human life and values to the determinants of economic forces and class struggles. Perhaps Keenan's familiarity with both Schumacher's work and Marxist theory was only superficial, and Schumacher's appeal to him was driven by the economist's abhorrence of multinational capitalism – even if that abhorrence was rooted in religious precepts.

Keenan also cited one work of fiction as central to the evolution of his political opinions: Robert Tressell's *The Ragged Trousered Philanthropists*. This novel is widely regarded as a classic text of socialist literature. Across more than 600 pages, Tressell excoriates the capitalist system as it existed in Edwardian England. The work is passionate, intense and persuasive, but it is also highly repetitive and its depiction of conflict between different social classes is often extremely crude and reductive.

There is much less characterisation than caricature in this novel and this is evident even in Tressell's schematic use of surnames such as 'Slyme' and 'Sweater' to signify both class roles and personality traits. (The two are often treated by Tressell as identical.) In the black-and-white world he describes, there is no such thing as an employer who is not brazenly dishonest, or a Christian who is not a transparent hypocrite. But what is, for me, most striking about this book is not its absence of social nuance, but the impatience, anger and contempt that its socialist hero feels for his fellow workers.

They are the unwitting 'philanthropists' of the book's title: dopes and dupes who do not realise that their endless drudgery only serves to enrich their masters. The novel's central character, the aptly named Frank, admits to feeling 'hatred and fury against the majority of his fellow workmen'. He regards them as 'the real oppressors' of their own class and likens them to 'so many cattle' that have not only endured impoverished circumstances but have 'opposed and ridiculed any attempts to alter [them]'. Such people, he believes, have chosen to embrace their 'poverty and degradation' and are content that the children they have 'brought into existence' will experience the same degree of hardship.

For me, this novel not only expresses a view of politics that is relentlessly dogmatic, but it also displays an extreme degree of intolerance for anyone who might hold differing opinions. That may even have been part of the novel's appeal for Brian Keenan. He was described by one of his former colleagues as someone who was possessed with 'demonic energy' and who was also not prepared 'to tolerate any form of dissent'. That attitude seems to have extended to his immediate family. According to one of his daughters, his views were never challenged in his home by any of his children. In that context, the hierarchical structure and the sense of discipline and control – as well as the military elitism and machismo – of the IRA seems likely to have appealed to him.

7.
The Shape of Things to Come

Keenan had married and started a family while he was still in England, but he returned to Northern Ireland in 1963 when he was in his early twenties. His previous experience seems to have helped him find work in the new Grundig factory in Dunmurry. The following year, he was arrested by the RUC after riots broke out in nationalist areas of Belfast. These disturbances, which took place over four nights in September and October 1964, marked the most serious civil unrest in Northern Ireland for over thirty years.

A British general election was called in 1964 and one of the candidates contesting the constituency of West Belfast stood as an 'Irish Republican' since Sinn Féin, along with the IRA, were then both proscribed organisations in Northern Ireland. At that time, the Protestant fundamentalist minister, the Rev. Ian Paisley, was regarded by most political commentators as a marginal figure and a relic of a previous era in Northern Irish history. However, Paisley objected vociferously and in public to the display of an Irish tricolour flag in the campaign headquarters of the republican candidate and demanded that it be removed by the RUC. The flying of this flag was technically illegal in Northern Ireland, if its display were likely to lead to a breach of the peace. In practice, the RUC usually ignored this law when the flag was flown in Catholic and nationalist areas.

On this occasion, however, Paisley announced that, if the flag were not physically removed by the RUC, his supporters would do so themselves. In the context of the Westminster general election, the unionist government did not wish to seem tolerant of republicans flouting the law and the RUC was instructed to remove the flag. RUC officers did so, but over the next two days the situation worsened after another tricolour was displayed in the front window of the republican office. A large crowd had gathered overnight and was clearly hostile to any RUC intervention. The flag was again removed, but this time the police used an armoured tender to storm the republican headquarters. This reaction was seen by many not only as excessive but also as counter-productive since it helped to escalate the immediate crisis.

Over the following nights, hundreds of republican sympathisers gathered in the area and full-scale rioting was soon underway. The police were pelted with stones, bottles and petrol bombs. A small number of IRA gunmen also opened fire on the police and one RUC officer was wounded by gunshot. Others were hospitalised and many protesters were arrested. One of those was Brian Keenan. He was later convicted of committing a breach of the peace and sentenced to three months in prison or a fine. After a short time in jail, Keenan paid his fine of £85, and was released to resume working in the Grundig plant.

The Divis Street riots are sometimes viewed as a harbinger of what was to come. They played a significant role in the emergence of two men whose political futures would become inextricably linked over the subsequent decades. Gerry Adams and Ian Paisley would both become leading – though bitterly opposing – figures in the Troubles, until, eventually, the two political parties that they led would form a most unlikely coalition. These two men would also share remarkably long periods as leaders of their respective political parties: Adams was President of Sinn Féin for thirty-five years while Paisley led the Democratic Unionists for thirty-seven.

The Divis Street riots also proved to be the first real test for the man who had recently become the new Prime Minister of Northern Ireland. In 1963, Terence O'Neill might have seemed an ideal choice to lead his fellow unionists through a period of long overdue political change. He was, by then, a seasoned politician who had served in both junior and senior ministerial posts since his election to Stormont in 1946. Although he was a member of the Orange Order, O'Neill pledged himself to end religious discrimination and to build better relations with the southern Irish state. He was also associated with progressive economic policies and aimed to attract new industries to Northern Ireland, while forging fresh and constructive relations with Ulster's trade unions.

It seemed that O'Neill had come to power at an opportune time. The year before he became Prime Minister, the IRA had formally abandoned 'Operation Harvest', more commonly known as its 'border campaign'. This armed offensive against the northern state was launched in 1956 and focused on the counties that bordered the Irish Republic. The IRA's goal was to 'liberate' successive areas of the state where there was a Catholic and nationalist majority and render them beyond the control of the northern authorities. Six RUC officers had been killed in this campaign and so had eight IRA men – four of whom were blown up by their own bombs.

The campaign had proved wholly unsuccessful – except, perhaps, south of the border where the IRA men killed in the campaign were given huge public funerals and Sinn Féin was able to win several seats in Dáil Éireann (the Irish parliament). These deaths also gave rise to a number of popular, if somewhat lachrymose, ballads in which the dead IRA members were lamented as 'martyrs for old Ireland'. However, in military terms, 'Operation Harvest' was considered a disaster even by some members of the IRA. A major factor in its failure was the lack of support the campaign had received from Northern Ireland's Catholics. According to the IRA communiqué that announced the end of its campaign, this was because their minds had been 'deliberately distracted' from what republicans identified as 'the supreme issue' facing Ireland: the 'unity and freedom' of the country.

Unionists, on the other hand, tended to believe that a principal factor in the IRA's defeat was the use of internment. This had also been introduced by the Fianna Fáil government on the southern side of the Irish border and had led to the imprisonment of hundreds of suspected IRA members without trial. Brian Faulkner was the unionist Minister for Home Affairs who introduced internment in Northern Ireland, and its apparent success in the 1950s may have tempted him to adopt the same strategy some years later. However, he did so in very different circumstances and with catastrophic results.

In the year that Terence O'Neill became Prime Minister, Brian Faulkner had stated that he 'doubted that there was any other country which has shown such universal political stability as Northern Ireland'. Against that background, O'Neill had claimed that his mission was to reform the state and conciliate its different traditions. Instead, he would witness the revival of sectarian conflict and political violence on a scale not seen in Ireland for almost half a century.

8.

The Storm Breaks

Thanks, in part, to foreign investment from companies like Grundig, Northern Ireland experienced relative economic prosperity in the post-war years. Along with rising living standards came rising expectations. This was particularly true for Ulster's Catholics. They had benefited not only from the growing prosperity but also from the reforms and investment in education introduced by the Westminster parliament and followed (somewhat reluctantly) by the Stormont government. By 1961, the expenditure per capita on education in Northern Ireland was almost four times that spent south of the Irish border. It was customary among many working-class Protestants to leave school at an early age in order to enter apprenticeships in trades where there was already a family history. But working-class Catholics often did not have that option and they proved more prepared to avail of the new opportunities for third-level education. This tendency was evident in the dramatic increase in the proportion of Catholic students attending Queen's

University in Belfast and other third-level institutions. It also became evident in the growing number of Catholics to be found in professional and managerial occupations.

By the late 1960s, it appeared that many young Catholics were no longer prepared to settle for any kind of second-class citizenship in Northern Ireland and 1967 marked a critical juncture for them. In that year, the Northern Ireland Civil Rights Association (NICRA) was formed. It was intended to appeal across the sectarian divide and attract liberal and fair-minded Protestants. Later in 1967, the Derry Housing Action Committee was established. Both organisations began to stage marches, rallies and other forms of public protest that focused on the reform of a system of local government where the voting franchise was still restricted to property owners and rate-payers.

The Labour government at Westminster was led by Harold Wilson, who liked to boast that he had more Irish constituents in Liverpool than most elected politicians in Ireland could claim. That might help to explain some of the sympathy that Wilson felt for the cause of Irish nationalism and the hope that he expressed for the political reunification of Ireland. There were other reasons for his antipathy to the Ulster unionists: he believed that their support for the Conservatives at Westminster made it more difficult for Labour to gain an overall majority in parliament and, in 1964, he had even proposed that Northern Ireland's MPs should be excluded from the British House of Commons.

It was not surprising that the Stormont cabinet soon came under pressure from Wilson to introduce some basic democratic reforms. These would have brought Northern Ireland into line with the rest of the UK and some unionist MPs recognised that such change had become unavoidable. However, the Unionist Party was also under pressure from within the Ulster Protestant community to resist making any concessions to Irish nationalism. This was of particular concern to unionists in the western counties who feared losing control of local government in some areas where nationalists were in the majority. In retrospect, the alarm that this caused seems disproportionate, since losing a few councils would not have affected the constitutional status of Northern Ireland as part of the UK state. However, in the eyes of some Protestants, the loss of even a few councils would have involved a symbolic defeat for unionism and nowhere was that felt more acutely than in relation to the 'Maiden City' of Derry (otherwise known as Londonderry).

In the course of the nineteenth century, unionists had become a minority in Derry and the city corporation was controlled by nationalists. In the early 1920s it was one of a number of nationalist councils that rejected the authority of the Stormont government and voted to give their allegiance to Dáil Éireann in Dublin. The unionist government responded by abolishing proportional representation in local elections, which had tended to reflect the actual demographic balance in Northern

Ireland, and by redrawing local electoral boundaries. As a result, they were able to regain control of Londonderry Corporation through the gerrymandering of its electoral wards so that the Catholic majority in the city was only able to win a minority of corporation seats.

When the political storm finally broke in 1968, it seems almost inevitable that Derry would be its epicentre. In October 1968, the local Housing Action Committee invited NICRA to join them in a protest march in Derry. Loyalists quickly announced that they would stage a counter-demonstration. Both marches were banned by William Craig, the unionist Minister for Home Affairs, but the Housing Action Committee decided to go ahead and about 400 people showed up for the demonstration. The RUC blocked the route the marchers intended to take. The marchers refused to disperse and some began to throw missiles at the RUC. By any standards, the police over-reacted and baton-charged the demonstration.

Among those injured in the baton charge were several Westminster MPs, including Gerry Fitt, the irrepressible Republican Labour MP for West Belfast, who roundly condemned the 'stormtrooper tactics' of the RUC. Many years later, he showed me the blood-stained shirt he had worn on that day, which had been framed and kept for posterity. Gay O'Brien, a news cameraman from RTÉ was also present and the footage of police violence he shot that day was screened around the world. The date of 5 October 1968 is usually regarded as the start of the most recent

Troubles in Northern Ireland. At that time, no one could have realised that the case for internal reform would soon be replaced by quite a different political agenda.

Harold Wilson summoned O'Neill to London to explain his government's response to the events in Derry. O'Neill reported back to his cabinet that Wilson had threatened to take over the governance of Northern Ireland if they could not manage to gain control of the situation. It seems that Wilson had expressed the sort of weary exasperation with Northern Ireland that would become all too characteristic of English politicians in the coming years.

Over the following months, a five point reform programme was introduced by the Stormont government. But, crucially, O'Neill did not agree to any change in the local government franchise. This had been the primary objective of the Civil Rights Association, which was expressed in their effective slogan of 'one man, one vote'. In retrospect, this concession could also have been made without any serious consequences for the constitutional position of Northern Ireland. But, once again, it seemed to represent a symbolic defeat that the unionist government was not yet prepared to countenance.

During the next few months, the political situation continued to deteriorate. A group composed primarily of student Trotskyites in an organisation called the People's Democracy decided to turn up the heat. They embarked on a protest march from Belfast to Derry that was designed explicitly to mirror Dr Martin Luther King's famous march from Selma to Birmingham, Alabama.

Marching has a historic significance for both of the major communities in Northern Ireland since it has often been used to mark out or challenge the ownership of territory. The organisers of this march planned to take a route that would lead them through villages that were predominantly Protestant, where their presence would be regarded as inflammatory. For that reason, NICRA considered the march an act of reckless provocation and refused to participate. But, as Martin Dillon has commented, provocation was a deliberate tactic of the People's Democracy leaders. The march went ahead but gained little media coverage until it was close to Derry. Then it was ambushed by a large group of loyalists on the bridge near Burntollet village. RUC officers were present during this brutal attack, but they failed to intervene effectively to protect all of the marchers or to ensure their safe passage.

One of the marchers attacked that day at Burntollet bridge was a young woman called Dolours Price. In the following years, she would come to play an indirect but critical role in the events that surrounded the disappearance and killing of Thomas Niedermayer. Price later claimed it was at Burntollet bridge that she first realised she would 'never convert these people'. She said she had 'looked deep into their eyes' and made her mind up 'to fight for what was rightfully mine'. She concluded that, if 'these people' (by which she meant unionists) were not open to the force of argument, then they would have to reckon with the argument of force.

According to the historians Paul Bew and Gordon Gillespie, this was the 'pivotal point' where the Troubles shifted from being primarily about civil rights and became linked to 'the most ancient disputes concerning religious and national identities'. The ambush at Burntollet received extensive media coverage and the student marchers received a tumultuous welcome when they finally reached Derry. As Martin Dillon has observed, 'those who had condemned the march quickly changed sides and applauded the students'. Their arrival in Derry was followed by several days of rioting in the city. On one night, some RUC officers went on a drunken rampage in the Catholic Bogside estate. In the following days, barricades were erected to keep the police out.

As the violence intensified, it began to impinge on the Niedermayer family. Writing to his brother, Alfred, Thomas told him that the previous night he had to pick up his daughter Gabriele from a party 'because either Protestants or Catholics were involved in street fighting'. He had already become reluctant to venture out of his home at night because 'if you don't want your car burned, you stay off the streets' and added that he had learned 'that three more people were shot during the night' by local paramilitaries.

In response to this escalation of civil unrest, the Stormont government seemed indecisive and racked with internal divisions, leading to a series of dramatic resignations and sackings from the cabinet. This was the context in which Terence O'Neill decided to call a general election in January 1969. It became known as the 'Crossroads Election', which he called in the confident expectation that he would receive a popular mandate for his reform package. That proved to be a serious miscalculation on his part.

9.
Yesterday's Man

In 1964, Thomas Niedermayer was able to tell a German newspaper that both the size and capacity of the plant in Dunmurry were about to double. 'It's necessary,' he told *Die Zeit*, '[because] the factory was only intended for 500 workers and we already employ 800.' He also claimed that Grundig had a 40 per cent share of the tape-recorder market in the UK and that his plant was responsible for 80 per cent of that total. Niedermayer praised the local workforce – whom he compared favourably with their counterparts in Germany – and said he would always recommend Northern Ireland to other German companies.

Grundig's operation in Dunmurry continued to expand in subsequent years. By the late 1960s, the company had become one of the biggest employers in Northern Ireland with over 1,000 workers. The factory even merited a personal visit from Max Grundig who was shown around the factory by Niedermayer and accompanied by Brian Faulkner. By all accounts, Niedermayer was popular with the workforce. He was regarded as exceptionally committed to his work. According to his secretary, June McClinton, 'his business was his life'. Another colleague described him as having 'a typical German's capacity for endless work' and claimed that Niedermayer thought about his job 'day and night'. He had the reputation of being the first to arrive at work in the morning and the last to leave at the end of the day.

As the Troubles began to develop in Northern Ireland, Niedermayer had not permitted any display of sectarian loyalties on the shop floor and there were no obvious signs of conflict. According to one member of his management staff, 'Grundig make tape-recorders. We don't make Protestant or Catholic tape-recorders.' June McClinton recalls that there was at that time 'a scarcity of work in Northern Ireland. But two thousand people found work in the [Grundig] plant and were able to get a living.' She also believes that 'this wasn't the case of a Catholic company or a Protestant company: the two sides of the religious divide were both helped'.

Writing to his family in Germany at this time, Thomas cited some recent difficulties in his relations with shop stewards at the factory. He reckoned that there had been a strike 'about once a week for the past two to three months'. Thomas believed that most of these had been triggered by trivial issues and he acknowledged that they were, for the most part, brief. Nonetheless, he thought that they had contributed to a new sense of 'restlessness' among the Grundig workforce. At that time, Brian Keenan was, by all accounts, the most militant and assertive of all the Grundig shop stewards. June McClinton remembers him as 'arrogant' and a 'trouble-maker'. She recalls that, on some occasions, confrontations between Niedermayer and Keenan became so heated that Niedermayer would 'more or less tell Keenan to leave the room' – a response which June McClinton believes was 'entirely understandable'.

While the majority of the workforce at the Grundig plant was Catholic, there was also a sizeable number of Protestants employed in the factory. In Northern Irish terms, Niedermayer was in a 'mixed' marriage: he came from a Catholic background in Bavaria, while Ingeborg came from Lutheran Prussia. Perhaps he believed that this gave him a particular insight to the religious divisions in Ulster.

While Thomas Niedermayer was successful on a professional level, he and his family were also well-regarded by neighbours and other locals. They appeared to have settled easily into their adopted country; his daughters, Renate and Gabriele, attended local schools and had even developed soft Ulster accents. Maria McCann lived close to the Niedermayers on the Glengoland estate. She was good friends with Renate and visited her house frequently. She remembers that Renate adored horses and managed to get both herself and Maria part-time jobs in a nearby stables. Although Renate was slight in stature, 'she was very strong and would ride big horses'. According to Maria, 'animals came first' with Renate and 'she would always run to rescue an animal in danger'. Gabriele was a few years older than both girls: 'we used to think she was fantastic because she wore make-up and had a boyfriend'. Maria recalls Ingeborg as welcoming and warm, but with a certain formality and reservedness. She regarded Thomas as a 'gentle father' who was 'very involved and interested in everything that his daughters were doing'.

Niedermayer seems genuinely to have believed that, as a neutral outsider, he was safe from the unwelcome attention of any of Ulster's warring factions. According to his brother, Thomas paid a surprise visit to Bamberg in 1973 – just a few months before his disappearance – in order to celebrate Alfred's birthday. When Thomas was leaving, Alfred's wife, Marianne, begged him to stay safe in Northern Ireland and to make sure that he 'avoided the terrorists'. But Thomas only laughed and told her that there was absolutely nothing for him to fear. Despite the scrupulous personal neutrality that he was so proud to have maintained, later events would prove him wrong.

Life in Northern Ireland was not without other strains and stresses. By the late 1960s, Grundig found itself operating in an increasingly competitive international marketplace. Niedermayer was also coping with a wife who seemed to have grown highly dependent upon his constant support. June McClinton remembers Ingeborg as 'a gentle soul – nobody realised just how much she had been through'. It seems that, in moments of emotional crisis, Ingeborg would often phone her husband and, according to June, 'he was always there for her – anytime she phoned. He never rejected the calls.' Ingeborg attended a clinic in Germany in the early 1970s to be treated for depression and, according to June, her emotional condition was often volatile. In fact, Ingeborg later confided in a psychiatrist that she had been suffering from bouts of acute depression since the late 1960s.

The Grundig plant was regarded both inside and beyond Northern Ireland as a highly successful venture. Niedermayer was involved in the local employers' association and, according to a newspaper profile written in 1968, he had become an 'unofficial advisor' to German firms arriving in Northern Ireland. The tape-recorders made in the Derriaghy plant were of high quality and the factory was delivering impressive export figures. In 1970, Niedermayer was rewarded for his efforts by the British government with an honorary OBE: as he pointed out in a letter to the German consul in Liverpool, this was an unusual distinction for any foreign national to receive – 'but [especially] for a German!' This was not the only recognition of his significant contribution to the Ulster economy: the Grundig factory was also conferred with a prestigious Queen's Award for Industry. Niedermayer believed that more companies from Germany would follow Grundig's example and locate in Northern Ireland thanks to the progressive economic policies followed by its new Prime Minister, Terence O'Neill.

At the start of 1969, Belfast and Derry had not yet been convulsed by political violence, and, when O'Neill called a general election in that year, Northern Ireland still seemed a relatively stable political environment. A cornerstone of this apparent stability was the modest economic prosperity that had raised the living standards of both Catholics and Protestants. The Grundig electronics factory in Dunmurry was one of the best examples of the beneficial effects of the foreign industries that had come to Ulster in the 1960s. Terence O'Neill may have helped to promote progressive economic policies, but he was not well-suited to implement fundamental change in Northern Ireland.

O'Neill had been born into the British aristocracy and grew up in England. He was educated at Eton and had served as a junior catering officer in the Irish Guards during the Second World War. Although his family's historic connection with Ulster spanned several centuries, O'Neill only took up permanent residence in Northern Ireland after the war had ended when he was already approaching middle age. A few months after he arrived, he was elected unopposed to the Stormont parliament. Once there, he continued to use the military rank he had held during the war and liked to be referred to as 'Captain' Terence O'Neill.

On the surface, all seemed propitious for O'Neill's regime. But he had certain liabilities in the eyes of some unionists and one of those was that he was considered to be English. Despite their political unionism, Protestants in Northern Ireland often harboured a deep distrust of English politicians, fearing, with some reason, that 'Perfidious Albion' was more than capable of betraying them. O'Neill also lacked the common touch: he did not seem to recognise, let alone appreciate, the nuances of Ulster society and he often seemed to convey an attitude of unconscious condescension. His comments about the Catholic community, which he professed to want to accommodate, were remarkable for their offhand prejudice and casual offensiveness. 'If you give Roman Catholics a good job and a house,' he told one journalist, they would soon learn to 'live like Protestants'. Otherwise, he continued, 'the Roman Catholic' would continue to inhabit 'a most ghastly hovel' and raise 'eighteen children on national assistance'.

O'Neill's patronising attitude also extended to the Protestant community. As Henry Patterson has noted, he made little attempt to disguise 'his low opinion of the quality of the average unionist MP and of many of his cabinet colleagues'. When Seán Lemass, the Taoiseach of the Irish Republic, made a historic visit to Stormont in 1965, O'Neill did not bother to advise some of his cabinet that he had invited Lemass until the Taoiseach was already in the government buildings. His autobiography, which he wrote after his political demise, reveals both an open dislike of the Unionist Party that he had once led as well as a sense of patrician disdain for the wider Protestant electorate.

I remember, when I was working as a television producer in the Current Affairs department of RTÉ, I came across some archive footage that had been filmed during the 1969 general election in Northern Ireland. This was the first election in more than two decades that O'Neill had been obliged to contest. The footage only lasted a couple of minutes and was shot without any sound, but I still found it revealing.

O'Neill lived in an elegant Regency rectory that was located outside the small village of Ahoghill in the rural Bannside constituency that he had represented for more than twenty years. In the first sequence of the RTÉ footage, O'Neill was filmed walking down the main street of this County Antrim village. Two elderly men were standing outside a pub and, as O'Neill approached them, they both doffed their cloth caps respectfully to him and lowered their heads. O'Neill turned back to look into the RTÉ camera and gave a knowing and fatuous smile. The men's gesture of traditional deference could not have been clearer and O'Neill's sense of social superiority could not have seemed more evident and less appealing.

That short sequence of film was followed by one of Ian Paisley – O'Neill's opponent in the election – holding a rally in an open field. There were young women in miniskirts and plastic cowgirl hats; young men wearing denim jackets and waving Ulster flags; a couple of drummers weighed down with huge Lambeg drums; children watching with widened eyes; old men wearing their Orange sashes; and a few grim-faced Free Presbyterian ministers. Paisley was penned in on all sides by the large and excited crowd which he was addressing through a megaphone – hardly necessary, I thought, given the volume and pitch of his normal voice. To outsiders, Paisley may have seemed like a figure from the seventeenth century. The religious tradition that he represented was almost unknown in the Irish Republic, where Paisley tended to be viewed with a mixture of disgust, fascination and incomprehension. Nevertheless, it is clear even from this short film clip that he felt at home among his people in ways that O'Neill never could and was able to communicate with them in a language that O'Neill would never speak.

Paisley was not a member of the Orange Order or the Unionist Party, or even the mainstream Presbyterian Church – the three pillars of the Northern Irish establishment. As Tom Paulin has observed, that establishment despised him as a 'working-class rabble-rouser' and were often embarrassed by his coarse abuse of the Catholic Church and by his unruly antics. Brian Faulkner, who later led the Unionist Party, dismissed him as a 'stage Ulsterman' and as someone who sought 'notoriety by his anti-Papist views'. David Trimble, who would also lead the Unionist Party, recalled that his first impressions of Paisley were of a 'raucous, sectarian and vulgar personality'.

However, Paisley was not the first or last populist to outmanoeuvre a more liberal candidate. He was not a socialist, but he was able to claim, with some justification, that O'Neill had delivered very little of material benefit to his constituents in all the years he had represented the Bannside. Paisley pointed out that a large number of households in Ahoghill still lacked the most basic of amenities such as indoor toilets and that O'Neill had been driven through the village every morning and evening for decades without giving them a second thought.

The Bannside election also served to open up a deeper division within unionism. O'Neill and his supporters tended to present the defining feature of unionism as its loyalty to the British state. However, fear of betrayal by London had been a recurring feature of unionist politics for many years. In fact, the historic allegiance of many Protestants – and, in particular, Presbyterians – to the British state had always been conditional and on several occasions in the past had been withdrawn.

Although Terence O'Neill won the Bannside election in 1969, it was a narrow and a Pyrrhic victory. Paisley had performed much more strongly than had been predicted by the media and it is not hard to see why. O'Neill was bereft of personal charisma: his public speeches were colourless and anodyne and his delivery was ponderous and seemed to lack any real conviction. O'Neill was, no doubt, quite sincere and justified in his belief that Northern Ireland needed fundamental reform and his social ineptitude has sometimes been attributed to extreme shyness. Nonetheless, he tended to lecture and admonish unionists, *de haut en bas*, rather than seek to inspire and lead them at ground level.

Within a few weeks of his humiliation in the Bannside election, O'Neill had resigned as Prime Minister. A number of bombs had been detonated at reservoirs and electricity stations and the IRA was believed to have been responsible. These incidents were viewed as further evidence that O'Neill had lost control of the crisis. In fact, the bombs had been planted by the UVF, a loyalist paramilitary group, as a 'false flag' exercise designed to undermine O'Neill's position. However, there was a sense that he welcomed the excuse they gave him to resign as Prime Minister. In the ensuing by-election, Ian Paisley won O'Neill's former seat in the Bannside in a decisive and symbolic victory.

The following year, Paisley contested the North Antrim constituency in a Westminster election against Henry Clark, the sitting unionist MP. Clark was another product of the English public school system and a relative of O'Neill. Paisley was able to point out that he had barely spoken a word in the House of Commons in the whole of the previous decade. Clark's indignant response – that he had been busy during much of that time chairing the Conservative Party's East Africa Committee and working as an official observer of elections in Uganda and Mauritius – failed to impress voters in rural Antrim, and Paisley won another famous victory.

Within a few years, Terence O'Neill had not only left the Unionist Party but had quit Northern Ireland, preferring to spend the closing years of his life in that part of southern England where he had been born and raised. By then, his political role was confined to occasional and largely unreported speeches in the British House of Lords.

In 1963, O'Neill's position as the leader of the Unionist Party and the Stormont government, seemed utterly secure. The foundations of the northern state also seemed solid. But by the end of the decade, Northern Ireland was approaching a state of near-anarchy and O'Neill had become yesterday's man. His political career was summed up by Robert Ramsay, his principal private secretary, in succinct and severe terms: when it came to the crunch, 'he was simply not the man who could deliver the goods'.

10.
The Honorary Consul

Of all the honours he received, perhaps the one that had the most meaning for Thomas Niedermayer was that which came from his own country: Honorary German Consul. From the detailed application that he submitted in August 1970, and which Ann Marie Hourihane was able to locate in Berlin, it is quite clear that the post was of considerable importance to him. He was advised in making this application by Dr Curt Friese, the German consul in Liverpool. Dr. Friese was a diplomat whose career pre-dated the Second World War, and, although he lived and was based in England, he also held consular responsibility for Northern Ireland. Niedermayer had corresponded with him about the deteriorating situation in Northern Ireland. When Niedermayer wrote (in English) to express interest in the post of consul, he stressed to Dr Friese that he was not politically aligned. 'Here I am,' he wrote – in words to which subsequent events have added a further poignancy – 'a stranger in this country – therefore, I have no right to get mixed up in its domestic politics.'

Dr Friese had already become something of a mentor to Niedermayer and would later feature in the events surrounding his death. In this instance, the advice given to Thomas by Dr Friese proved shrewd and valuable and Niedermayer was appointed honorary consul by the West German government in Bonn. This was not only a source of great pride for him, but one to which he would make a wholehearted commitment over the next few years. Ingeborg later claimed that this led to a 'very full social life' for both of them, which seems to have had the unfortunate effect of increasing her levels of stress and anxiety.

By the early 1970s, Niedermayer had emerged as a leading figure in Ulster's small German community. In the aftermath of his abduction, the diplomatic status that he enjoyed was often overstated in both the Irish and international press. Indeed, as recently as July 2022, he was described in the Irish media as 'Germany's Consul' in Northern Ireland. However, Dr Friese remained the German consul with responsibility for Northern Ireland and Niedermayer was far from being the high-flying diplomat that was often implied in media coverage. In reality, most of his duties as an honorary consul appear to have involved bailing out merchant seamen from Germany who had been arrested for drunkenness or for fighting with local prostitutes.

The German 'colony' in Northern Ireland was then just a few hundred strong. Many of its activities were centred on the only Lutheran Church in Belfast. Thomas

Niedermayer and his wife became part of its congregation, where services were conducted in the German language and expats could make or maintain contact with each other. Although the majority of Germans living in Northern Ireland were Protestants, they did not identify strongly with either of the two principal communities. Some Germans lived in areas where Protestants predominated. Others, like Niedermayer, lived in or close to districts where Catholics formed a majority. As his German relatives have testified, Niedermayer genuinely believed that, as a neutral outsider, he was safe from the unwelcome attention of any of Ulster's warring factions. But even the scrupulous neutrality that he was so proud to have maintained over the previous ten years could not protect him from the fury of the storm that was already breaking over Northern Ireland.

In April 1969, Terence O'Neill was succeeded as Prime Minister of Northern Ireland by James Chichester-Clark. He seemed rather more sociable and at ease in public engagements than O'Neill, but he came from a very similar social background to his predecessor – scarcely surprising, since the two men were relatives. Like O'Neill, he had been educated at Eton and, like O'Neill, he had served in the Irish Guards during the Second World War. Like O'Neill, he was elected unopposed to the Stormont parliament within months of leaving the British army. His political views were also moderate and liberal. But, also like O'Neill, he lacked the grassroots knowledge and political acumen that were needed to lead the Unionist Party and Northern Ireland to a new and more inclusive chapter in its history.

Chichester-Clark's rival in the contest to become Prime Minister was Brian Faulkner, who had been denied the leadership by Terence O'Neill six years previously. This time, O'Neill again frustrated Faulkner's bid for the leadership of his party. O'Neill later described Chichester-Clark as a man 'with a very unpolitical mind'. In light of that opinion, his decision to give his cousin the casting vote that ensured his election as Prime Minister of Northern Ireland seems heedless and irresponsible. Robert Ramsay, who worked closely with both men, conceded that Chichester-Clark had a better personal relationship than O'Neill with his cabinet colleagues but regarded his public performances as 'invariably shaky'.

Whatever hopes there had been that Chichester-Clark, the incoming Prime Minister, would bring a new stability to Northern Ireland were soon dispelled. He did not have long before the crisis he had inherited from O'Neill assumed a new and much more serious dimension. This marked a profound change in its character and would have tested the most adroit of politicians. As O'Neill observed, Chichester-Clark had neither the political experience nor the natural aptitude to deal with this type of exceptional emergency.

In August every year, the Apprentice Boys of Derry – a loyalist organisation – held a march to commemorate the siege that their ancestors had withstood in 1689. Sectarian clashes often followed this annual event. In 1969, more than 40,000 empty milk bottles were stolen from a local dairy in the Bogside, a Catholic housing estate, a few days before the Apprentice Boys' march. They were clearly intended for future use as petrol bombs – a fair indication that further clashes were likely. On this occasion, the usual skirmishes quickly developed into a major and protracted confrontation between the RUC and the inhabitants of the Catholic estate. This became known as the Battle of the Bogside.

For several days RUC officers were subjected to a constant hail of missiles and petrol bombs, which eventually led Chichester-Clark to request assistance from Westminster. Initially, this was denied by Wilson's cabinet and he was advised, instead, to call upon all the security resources available to his government. That was a calamitous decision by the British since it led to a general mobilisation of the Ulster Special Constabulary (otherwise known as the 'B Specials') – an auxiliary part-time police force that operated more or less as a unionist militia. The Specials were recruited almost exclusively from the Protestant community and had no training or experience in crowd control. As William Beattie Smith has observed, the actual role played by the 'B-men' in this police operation was minor but 'their symbolic part in escalating [the disorder] was considerable'.

Once again, the RUC came under gunfire in nationalist areas of Belfast. Some police officers believed that this marked the beginning of an armed insurrection and, once again, the RUC response was reckless and excessive. Armoured cars fitted with Browning heavy machine guns returned fire in the built-up Divis Street area, killing a nine-year-old boy as he slept. Elsewhere, the RUC failed to prevent Protestant crowds attacking and burning down houses in Catholic districts of the city. In three days, eight people were killed in this communal violence and many hundreds more were burned or intimidated out of their homes. The majority of those killed or forced out were Catholics and it seems that Brian Keenan's family was among those compelled to abandon their home after it was attacked by loyalists.

RUC officers were clearly unable to control the situation. This was, in part, a simple question of numbers – which were clearly inadequate – and, unlike other police forces in the rest of the UK, the RUC was unable to call for any reinforcements from elsewhere. In those circumstances, the Westminster government had little option but to order the British army to restore peace and order on the streets of Belfast and Derry. Their deployment was initially welcomed by very many northern Catholics and they were offered endless cups of tea, banana sandwiches and chocolate biscuits. The most recent operation in which the British army had been engaged was an insurgency in Aden, one of Britain's former colonies. In the preceding decade, the army had also been involved in attempting to suppress popular uprisings in Kenya and Cyprus – but it would be a mistake to presume that the British army commanders viewed Northern Ireland as a colonial problem, or that those commanders were inclined to sympathise with the unionist regime in Stormont.

'Operation Banner' was the code name for the army's deployment in Northern Ireland. In July 2007, the Ministry of Defence was compelled, under the Freedom of Information Act, to publish the army's own analysis of its role in Northern Ireland over the previous thirty-five years. From this document it is quite clear that, when the army arrived in Ulster in 1969, its commanders regarded Catholics as the oppressed community and Protestants as their oppressors. The British army's analysis of 'Operation Banner' identifies anti-Catholic discrimination as 'institutionalised' and describes 'deprivation in the Catholic enclaves' of Derry and Belfast as 'appalling'.

A similar attitude was evident in much of the British media. Indeed, throughout the 1970s and into the following decade, the nationalist goal of Irish unity found a good deal of support among influential sections of the British press, while unionism was often portrayed as a particularly Irish form of political psychosis. It would also be quite wrong to assume that British governments were biased in favour of the unionists: if anything, their sympathies inclined to the opposite direction. Indeed, at times, British ministers could seem more responsive to the cause of Irish unity than some of their counterparts in Dublin.

The cabinet minister responsible for Northern Ireland in 1969 and 1970 was James 'Sunny Jim' Callaghan, an avuncular figure at Westminster. Callaghan soon made it clear that the British government wanted a root and branch reform of the northern state. 'There will be no tranquility in Northern Ireland,' he advised the British House of Commons, 'unless there is equality of treatment.'

Callaghan appointed a senior civil servant from Whitehall to report directly to his office. Oliver Wright had been Harold Wilson's private secretary. He had previously negotiated unsuccessfully on behalf of the British government with Ian Smith, the leader of the white settlers in Rhodesia who had declared unilateral independence from Britain, which may give some indication of the perspective that he brought to the crisis. Wright did not work through regular Home Office channels or the Northern Ireland civil service but reported directly to Callaghan.

In his first confidential report, Wright identified the British government's ultimate goal as preparing for 'the inevitability' of 'Catholic rule in Ulster and then a united Ireland ruled from Dublin'. If unionists had been aware of this report, it would doubtless have confirmed all of their worst fears about British intentions. Such fears were about to lead to the first serious rioting in Protestant districts of Belfast in the Troubles – and the first death of an RUC officer at the hands of a loyalist gunman.

11.
Neighbours with Guns

Following the violent disturbances of 1969, the Westminster government appointed Lord Hunt, best known as the leader of the first successful ascent of Mount Everest, to give advice on how 'the efficient enforcement of law and order' in Northern Ireland might be achieved. Early in 1970, the Hunt Report was published and it made a number of critical recommendations. The most controversial of these was the disbandment of the Ulster Special Constabulary, otherwise known as the 'B Specials' and its replacement by a new 'Ulster Defence Regiment' (UDR) that would be subject to British army and not RUC control. The B Specials had been formed in the early 1920s due to the need of the unionist leadership to bring a number of local Protestant militias under some form of central control.

The B Specials were feared and distrusted by much of the Catholic population in Northern Ireland. Seamus Heaney described the underlying sense of menace that the Specials conveyed to many Catholics. In his poem

'The Nod', he recalled 'the local B-Men' who would spend Saturday evenings 'unbuttoned but on duty', swaggering through his hometown of Bellaghy in rural Ulster. They were, in Heaney's telling words, 'neighbours with guns'. In his poem, some of the Specials pretend to take aim with their weapons at their own neighbours with the unspoken but implicit threat that one day they might shoot them for real.

Most Protestants took a very different view of the 'B-Men' to the one expressed by Heaney. They could remember that, in 1921–2, more than seventy Specials had been killed in armed conflict with the IRA. These part-time policemen had helped to establish the northern state and they were regarded by many Protestants as their first line of defence against republican aggression. In that context, the conclusion reached by Hunt in his report that 'a realistic assessment of the future capacity of the IRA to mount serious terrorist attacks' would 'not be very high' seemed to many Protestants to be not only foolish, but dangerously naive. The decision to abolish the Special Constabulary led to serious rioting in Protestant districts of Belfast, where a loyalist gunman shot dead the first RUC officer to be killed in the most recent Troubles.

Harold Wilson's Labour government lost the general election in June 1970 and was replaced by one formed by the Conservative and Unionist Party. Despite its title, the new government did not regard the Ulster unionists with much more favour than the previous one. The new Prime

Minister, Edward Heath, liked to think of himself as a statesman on the world stage. It was clear that he viewed Northern Ireland as a tiresome distraction from what he considered to be much more important matters. In his memoirs, he absolved himself from any responsibility for the Ulster conflict, which he dismissed airily as evidence of a stubborn and self-inflicted 'atavism which most of Europe had discarded long ago'.

Heath's sense of visceral distaste was shared by Britain's new Minister for Home Affairs, Reginald Maudling. On returning from his first visit to Belfast, he was reported to have asked for a large whiskey while expressing his low opinion of Northern Ireland in unambiguous terms: 'What a bloody awful country!' At this critical juncture in the history of the northern state, Maudling was, perhaps, already succumbing to the chronic alcoholism that would later result in his premature death from cirrhosis of the liver. Foolishly, he stated in public that his political ambition for Northern Ireland was merely to reduce political violence to what he described as 'an acceptable level', which was of small comfort to those who were suffering from such violence.

Later, in his *Memoirs*, Maudling lamented in the same passive vein 'the virtual hopelessness of any attempt by reason to bring peace and reconciliation' to the people of Northern Ireland: the inference being that the political violence in Ulster was basically irrational and driven by some innately Irish love of violent conflict.

The presence of British troops and the handing over of operational control of the security forces to the General Officer Commanding the British army in Northern Ireland had greatly reduced the authority of the Stormont government and undermined the position of Chichester-Clark. He was compelled to accept British demands for reform and, as a consequence, was denounced by Ian Paisley as a puppet of Westminster. An extensive package of legislation was introduced. According to one British cabinet minister, more reforms were 'pushed through in fifty days than in the previous fifty years'.

This meant that, by the start of 1971, all of the key objectives of the civil rights movement had either been achieved or were in the process of being enacted. It could even be argued that some of the new reforms actually went beyond the original ambitions of that movement. In that context, John Hume could claim with credibility that the IRA's campaign was utterly redundant. But, by then, the Troubles had already entered a new and more turbulent phase. Brendan Behan had once claimed that the first item on the agenda of any republican group in Ireland was 'the split'. There had been a number of previous schisms within the IRA, but none were as serious as the one that occurred between 1969 and 1970.

12.
The Split

Brian Keenan, Niedermayer's former employee, was already in the IRA when the disturbances of August 1969 took place: he had joined the previous year at the beginning of the civil unrest in Northern Ireland. According to republican sources, he first used a gun during the sectarian rioting that swept through Belfast that summer. From the start, the force of his personality seems to have impressed other IRA members. According to Bishop and Mallie, he was regarded 'by his friends and enemies alike as possessing the best organisational brain in the IRA'.

Before long, Keenan had become the IRA's quartermaster in Belfast. This was a role of critical importance. To put it simply, the IRA could not continue – let alone escalate – its armed campaign without a constant stream of effective weaponry. At the beginning of its campaign, the IRA's arsenal consisted largely of dated armaments such as old Lewis or Thompson machine guns. In his search for arms, Keenan made lasting contacts with other terrorist groups abroad: ETA in the Basque Country; the PLO in Palestine; and Colonel Gaddafi in Libya. In the words of one former RUC detective, he became a 'roving ambassador' for the IRA.

Sean O'Callaghan was at one time a Sinn Féin councillor and a senior figure in the Southern Command of the IRA. He became disillusioned by republican violence, but he still regarded Keenan as someone who had 'enormous ability and charisma, energy and absolute ruthlessness'. He believed that Keenan was motivated by 'gut nationalism' and a visceral hatred of 'Brits and unionists'. O'Callaghan's own disillusionment with the IRA was triggered by a chance remark made in 1975. A female RUC officer had been killed in an IRA gun attack and a senior republican commented, 'With any luck, she'll have been pregnant, and we'll have got two for the price of one.' O'Callaghan's revulsion at such heartless sectarian prejudice eventually led him to volunteer to act as an agent of the Garda Síochána. He was not the only republican in the past to have been repulsed by sectarianism.

The IRA purported to be following in the footsteps of Wolfe Tone, who was considered to have founded modern Irish republicanism in the late eighteenth century. But Tone was a passionate secularist whose stated ambition was to 'substitute the common name of Irishman in place of the denominations of Protestant, Catholic and Dissenter'. The failure of the border campaign of 1956–62 had led some of the IRA's leaders to question their basic political assumptions. This caused the IRA leadership under Cathal Goulding to move gradually away from sectarian animosities, to develop socialist politics and to become engaged in various forms of economic and social protest, such as an involvement in housing action groups.

Goulding and the IRA's leaders in Dublin wanted to build effective alliances with Protestants in Northern Ireland and some of their leading members in the north shared that ambition. They helped to establish new groups, such as the 'Wolfe Tone Directories', in the hope of appealing to both sides of the northern sectarian divide. In 1966, all of the (renamed) Wolfe Tone Societies in Ireland met in Maghera, County Derry, where they listened to a paper read by the writer and broadcaster Eoghan Harris, who would later become one of the IRA's most trenchant critics. At that meeting, it was agreed that a new civil rights campaign should be launched.

NICRA was just the sort of 'popular front' that the IRA leadership thought could attract progressive Protestants as well as Catholics. At first, the goal of constructing a genuinely non-sectarian movement may have seemed ambitious but attainable: members of the Ulster Liberal Party and the Northern Ireland Labour Party as well as a few unionists attended NICRA's inaugural meeting. Of the thirteen members elected to its steering committee, known republicans or IRA members were in a small minority.

None of those republicans involved in NICRA's committee were later associated with the Provisional IRA, but that has not prevented what Henry McDonald has described as a 'growing calumny': the claim that the Provisional IRA's campaign of violence was 'somehow the logical and moral extension of the NICRA'. In reality, the Provisional IRA did not grow directly out of the civil rights movement; its roots are buried deep in Ulster's sectarian landscape, and its true origins can be traced back to a period before the Northern Irish state had even been created.

During the eighteenth century, a number of secret societies developed in rural Ulster. The primary purpose of these agrarian organisations was to protect the interests of their co-religionists, chiefly in relation to land ownership. These conflicts between Protestants and Catholics often ended in violence, bloodshed and death. In several respects, the IRA in Northern Ireland was a rightful heir to that sectarian tradition and some of its members saw themselves primarily as defenders of the northern Catholic community. In some cases, that could express itself in direct hostility and attacks on the Protestant population.

Towards the end of August 1969, a group of Northern IRA members came together to challenge Dublin's authority. Some of these figures, such as Joe Cahill and Seamus Twomey, were active during the IRA's previous 'border campaign' and their opposition to the existing leadership was long-standing. Others, such as Danny Morrison and Gerry Adams, came from families with long republican traditions.

Things came to a head in 1970 when an IRA convention in Roscommon voted to recognise the Irish parliament, to end the IRA's traditional policy of abstentionism and to take any seats they might win in parliamentary elections on both sides of the Irish border. For some IRA members, this meant abandoning a core belief and only confirmed their reservations about the political strategy being pursued by the current IRA leadership.

Within days, some leading figures in Northern Ireland were refusing to take any more orders from Dublin and, in December of that year, the split in the ranks of the IRA was formalised when a new 'provisional' Army Council was formed. The following month, Sinn Féin also split on the same issue when many delegates walked out of the party's annual Árd Fheis (annual conference) in protest at the leadership's attempt to end its policy of abstentionism in Stormont elections. This Provisional republican movement soon established its own news sheet. In its first edition, an editorial blamed the IRA's previous move towards socialist policies on the influence of 'red agents' who had 'infiltrated' the IRA and 'brainwashed' its members.

The new Provisional leadership had very different ambitions to those held by the former 'official' IRA. Their objectives were no longer to agitate for civil rights in Northern Ireland, nor to try to establish fraternal links with the Protestant working class. Instead, the primary objective was to wage war against the British presence and make Northern Ireland ungovernable.

From this point on, the IRA campaign had little to do with equality of citizenship or societal change. The new goal was not to reform the northern state, but to destroy it. To achieve that goal, some of their northern members were even prepared to countenance a full-scale civil war. As a consequence, the 'official' IRA leadership in Dublin became increasingly marginalised from events in Northern Ireland as the violence escalated. In 1972, the Dublin leadership declared a ceasefire which proved to be more or less permanent: one senior RUC officer told me this was because they were 'alive to the sectarianism of the [Provisionals]' and 'refused to sink to [their] level of depravity'.

Given his own claim to analyse politics 'through a class prism' and his avowed secularism, it might have been expected that Brian Keenan would have stayed with the socialist politics of the 'official' IRA leadership when the split in the republican movement took place. Indeed, Keenan would later refer in dismissive and disparaging terms to some of the IRA's leaders as 'good Catholic boys'. Despite his own apparent lack of Catholic faith, Keenan still opted to join the 'Provisionals'. In *Children of the Revolution*, his daughter, Jeanette Keenan, tried to explain the commitment that he made to the IRA. While she acknowledges the emotional pain inflicted by her father's separation from his family due to his IRA activities, she concludes that this was 'a necessary evil' in order to secure basic voting rights and greater access to third-level education for northern Catholics. However, full voting rights for everyone in Northern Ireland had already been secured by the early 1970s and educational reforms were never part of the Civil Rights Association's agenda, since they had already been introduced to Northern Ireland many years before NICRA was founded.

There are other possible explanations for Keenan's decision to join the Provisional IRA. He may have been driven by an emotional reaction to the events of 1969, or he may have been motivated by his personal temperament and his desire for decisive action. He may simply have been prompted, as Sean O'Callaghan has suggested, by his 'gut nationalism'. Whatever the reasons, Keenan soon came to hold a key position within the ranks of the Provisional IRA and he would spend most of the next twenty-five years either on the run in Ireland – or locked up in British jails.

13.

Legitimate Targets

In July 1970, British army patrols came under sustained fire from republican gunmen in the Lower Falls district of West Belfast. The British decided to seal off the area and impose a curfew. Thousands of troops poured into the district and conducted intensive house-to-house searches. These searches were carried out with little regard for the feelings or property of the local population and they caused a great deal of wanton destruction. The British army also engaged in a three-day gun battle with republican gunmen in which four civilians were killed. Substantial quantities of weapons were seized, but the heavy-handed actions of the army led to a serious loss of confidence among the Catholic population and a concomitant surge of support for the IRA.

The following month, the new Provisional IRA claimed its first RUC victims. Two young officers, Samuel Donaldson and Robert Millar, were blown up by an IRA booby-trap bomb. It contained twenty pounds of gelignite and had been attached to an abandoned red Cortina near Crossmaglen in south Armagh. The bomb exploded when one of the RUC men tried to open a door of the car. Fifteen years later, the domestic scale of the northern Troubles was again made evident when Donaldson's brother, Alex, was killed in an IRA mortar attack, along with eight other RUC officers. In 2021, the Donaldsons' first cousin, Jeffrey, became leader of the Democratic Unionist Party (DUP). He was not the first leader of that party to have direct experience of IRA attacks. John Kelly, the father of Arlene Foster – Donaldson's immediate predecessor – was shot in the head by the IRA while tending cattle at his family's isolated farm in County Fermanagh.

In the decades that followed the deaths of Millar and Donaldson, more than 300 RUC officers were killed and more than 9,000 were injured. By 1983, Interpol had designated the RUC as the world's most dangerous police force in which to serve. More RUC officers were murdered in the course of the Troubles than the combined number of police officers who were killed in the line of duty in England, Scotland and Wales throughout the whole of the twentieth century. Very few of the hundreds of RUC officers who died in Northern Ireland were killed in exchanges of fire with the IRA. Instead, they were the victims of booby trap bombs, were caught by other explosions, were abducted and killed, or were ambushed and shot dead before they could draw their own weapons.

Many officers were killed when they were off duty. A high proportion of those who were targeted by the IRA were part-time policemen, some of whom had retired from service several years previously. Apart from their part-time work as policemen, these men led ordinary civilian lives. Such victims were 'soft targets', going about their daily business and unlikely to return fire, which, of course, made them highly vulnerable to IRA attacks.

The IRA claimed that these men and women were killed solely because of their roles, or former roles, in northern security forces such as the RUC and UDR. Indeed, one former member of the IRA later explained why these part-timers were considered prime targets for attack. He suggested this was because they had 'a detailed and comprehensive knowledge of their areas' and could recognise 'instantly if something was out of place'. In their everyday jobs as 'school bus drivers, postmen, [or] refuse collectors', he believed they could act as the effective 'eyes and ears' of the security forces. As a consequence, it was argued that the IRA's decision to identify them as 'legitimate targets' and kill them was not only rational, but essential.

That may have been how the IRA viewed these part-timers, but it is not how their deaths were understood by most Protestants. They saw such killings as plain sectarian murders and the IRA's denials only added insult to injury. The circumstances in which many of the IRA's victims were killed – while serving in an ice-cream parlour, or collecting their children from school, or going into church – were also deeply offensive to most unionists. When IRA communiqués used the jargon of half-digested

Marxism or anti-imperialist clichés to explain and justify such squalid killings, the offence was further magnified.

Republicans sometimes liked to profess their admiration for northern Presbyterians such as Henry Joy McCracken, who had led an armed rebellion against the British in the eighteenth century and had been executed for his part in that uprising. As far as most northern unionists were concerned, any claims by republicans that they were inspired by the example of McCracken and other Presbyterian rebels were disingenuous, hypocritical and repugnant so long as the IRA kept killing McCracken's current co-religionists. In reality, the new Provisional IRA was enmeshed in sectarian conflict from the outset and whether this was deliberate or circumstantial, implicit or explicit, made little practical difference. Perhaps that could not have been otherwise, given the long history of religious division in Ulster.

By 1971, Keenan had established himself as the quartermaster of the IRA's Belfast brigade. This was a key position since – in contrast to the previous border campaign – Belfast was where the majority of IRA activities took place in the early 1970s. Clearly, there could be no IRA operations without a regular supply of weapons and other war materiel. Keenan proved to be highly adept at procuring what was needed for the campaign and he was highly regarded within the IRA. For obvious reasons, his movements at that time are hard to identify, but they involved travelling abroad to acquire arms and arranging for them to be smuggled into Ireland.

During this period, Brian Keenan is believed to have made his first contacts in East Germany, Syria and Libya. However, in these early years of the Troubles, most of the IRA's weapons came from the USA and, in particular, from the established centres of Irish immigration: Chicago, New York and Boston – where an enthusiastic supporter of the IRA campaign was 'Whitey' Bolger, the notorious leader of the Winter Hill Gang. (Many years later, Bolger would be convicted of the murder of a gang member who had informed the FBI of a shipment of arms to the IRA.) The first US shipments that arrived in August 1970 included hundreds of Armalites: the assault rifles that would become one of the IRA's signature weapons. The Armalite was valued not only for its lightness and powerful impact but also because the rifle came with a retractable stock that made it easier to conceal. Thanks to sympathisers in New York's Longshoremen's Association, a steady supply of these guns made their way to Belfast by a variety of routes. Once there, they were distributed to different IRA units in the city by Keenan. Throughout 1971, this supply of weapons allowed the IRA to step up its campaign and many of its members seemed confident that the following year would be even more successful. In fact, the IRA leadership identified 1972 as 'The Year of Victory'. They were proven right in that 1972 marked a turning point in their campaign, but not in the direction they had expected.

14.

No Half-Measures

As it turned out, the large number of operations mounted by the IRA in 1972 was never equalled in the decades that followed. In fact, it became progressively more difficult for the IRA to engage directly with the British army. This was, in part, because intelligence gathering about IRA operations had greatly improved through the extensive use of RUC and British army agents and informants. In response, the IRA was re-organised on a cellular structure that made it harder – at least initially – for the RUC to penetrate its command structure. As the IRA's chief quartermaster, Brian Keenan played a key role in this process.

As it became more difficult for the IRA to engage with the serving members of the security forces, the concept of 'legitimate targets' was progressively expanded to include new categories of people. Retired members of the RUC and UDR were among the first to be considered 'legitimate' but, in the years that followed, the IRA's targets came to include prison officers, judges, builders, civil servants and even the manager of a firm that had supplied apples to the RUC. In one case, the IRA in Derry killed a young woman who was simply collecting census forms. Initially, the IRA again denied any involvement in this murder, but the weapon used to kill Joanne Mathers was revealed by forensic evidence to have been used before by the IRA in so-called 'punishment shootings'. Many years later, the IRA finally admitted responsibility for her death.

The extension by the IRA of what constituted 'legitimate targets' held long-term implications for the conflict in Northern Ireland. It had a particular impact in some areas close to the Irish border where Protestants were often isolated and in a minority. The IRA could argue that there were good tactical reasons for clearing these border regions of people whom they suspected might sympathise with the security forces, since it would give IRA units greater freedom of movement. In practice, this meant that virtually all Protestants living in those regions became potential targets for the IRA. This process might now be considered a form of 'ethnic cleansing'. That is a label that some, notably the IRA, would dispute, but there is little doubt about the sectarian nature of the republican strategy.

One example of this strategy can be found in the small village of Rosslea, which stands beside the River Finn, just on the County Fermanagh side of the Irish border. When the Troubles began, there were five Protestant-owned businesses in the village. By 1977, there was only one: a shop owned by a man called Douglas Deering. He was a member of the Brethren, a small Christian sect founded in Ireland by John Nelson Darby in the 1830s. The Brethren shunned all 'worldly' activities such as dancing, movies and secular music. They did not engage in any form of politics, declining even to vote in elections. On 12 May 1977, a gunman entered Deering's shop and shot him dead in front of the two women who worked with him. The gunman then drove across the border, and the IRA did not acknowledge responsibility for the murder. However, bullet casings left behind established that the Colt 45 revolver that killed Deering had been used in previous attacks claimed by the IRA. No one was ever charged with his murder and, from the IRA's point of view, this was a successful operation. When inoffensive men like Deering were killed, the message was clear to their co-religionists.

The effects of such attacks went beyond the immediate families of victims and encouraged other unionists to leave the area. By the end of 1977, there were no Protestant businesses left in Rosslea and nobody who might be considered as a possible sympathiser with the RUC or British army remained in the village. Between 1971 and 1989, there were 203 murders in this part of Northern Ireland. Republicans committed 178 of these murders, but there were only fourteen successful convictions. That represented another kind of victory for the IRA: the gunman sent to kill Douglas Deering knew that there was very little chance he would ever be caught.

The wider IRA offensive had gathered momentum throughout 1971. In February, a British soldier was killed in an exchange of fire in north Belfast. Gunner Robert Curtis was the first British soldier to die in Ireland since the War of Independence in the 1920s. A few days after he had been shot dead, an IRA land mine killed five men near a BBC transmitter in County Tyrone. Two of those killed were BBC engineers and the other three were construction workers. This may have been the first occasion in which a group of civilians became the victims of the IRA's indiscriminate violence, but it would not be the last.

The week after the killings in Tyrone, three Scottish soldiers were shot dead by the IRA. The soldiers had been off duty and drinking in a pub in the centre of Belfast when they were lured to their deaths by an invitation to a party. They were all very young – two of the three were still teenagers – and they were shot while urinating beside the road. As Bishop and Mallie have observed, there was 'something particularly repulsive in the way the young Fusiliers had been tricked to their deaths by promises of a party', and their deaths produced widespread feelings of disgust and anger.

The killing of these soldiers was technically in breach of the IRA's own supposed rules of engagement. The Green Book specified that soldiers should only be attacked when they were on duty. That constraint would very soon be abandoned, but it may help to explain why the

IRA issued an immediate denial of responsibility for the soldiers' deaths. This was a tactic that usually occurred when, for a range of different reasons, IRA killings or explosions prompted a negative public reaction. The political antennae of the IRA were acutely sensitive to how individual acts of violence might be viewed within the northern nationalist community.

On occasion, the IRA has followed similar tactics south of the Irish border. Ten years after Thomas Niedermayer was abducted, the IRA kidnapped Don Tidey, a supermarket executive, from his home in Dublin. He was held prisoner for 23 days before his whereabouts were discovered by the Irish security services. In the gunfight that ensued, a Garda and a member of the Irish Army were shot dead by the kidnappers. This led to widespread revulsion among the southern Irish population. The killing was also in direct contravention of the IRA's Green Book, which states categorically that 'Volunteers are strictly forbidden to take any military action against 26 County forces under any circumstance whatsoever.' ('26 Counties' is a derogatory term used by the IRA to describe the Irish Republic.) That may explain why a rumour was circulated by the IRA and its sympathisers that both men had actually been killed by accidental 'friendly fire' from their own colleagues. It was not until 2022 that forensic evidence conclusively established that could not have been the case.

The presentation and disinformation skills that were honed during the Troubles have proved invaluable to Sinn

Féin elsewhere in the world. They have enabled the IRA to gain support from diverse and apparently incompatible sponsors: money and guns, for example, were solicited from both conservative Irish-American communities as well as from Gaddafi's anti-American regime in Libya.

For obvious reasons, the deaths of British soldiers could more easily be accepted by some members of the nationalist community than the killing of random civilians. Similarly, bombing businesses owned by Protestants might be considered more acceptable than bombing those owned by Catholics. In some cases where there was widespread and cross-community revulsion at particularly horrific acts of violence, the IRA could claim that its bomb warnings were deliberately ignored by the security forces in order to damage the IRA's reputation.

Sometimes the IRA adopted a much simpler tactic: to issue a complete denial of their involvement. This was what they did after the Scottish soldiers were killed, although the identities of those involved were soon fairly common knowledge in Belfast. Such denials proved to be very effective from the IRA's point of view: they muddied the waters and sowed confusion even in situations when there was overwhelming evidence of their involvement. This tactic was often followed by the IRA during the course of the Troubles, and, was precisely the one that was followed in the case of Thomas Niedermayer.

In the wake of the shooting of the Scottish soldiers, Chichester-Clark flew to London to ask the new British

Prime Minister, Edward Heath, for more troops to be sent to Northern Ireland. A few days before their meeting, Heath sent a personal message to Taoiseach Jack Lynch in Dublin. Heath had informed Lynch that he believed Chichester-Clark's resignation was imminent and urged Lynch to take some action that would signal his government's determination to move against the IRA. Lynch felt unable to assist and, at his subsequent meeting with the Northern Ireland Premier, Heath also proved reluctant to meet Chichester-Clark's requests for a sign of Westminster's own resolve. Two days later, Chichester-Clark resigned, saying he believed that the measures taken by the Westminster government were 'unlikely to effect a radical improvement' in the security situation.

Brian Faulkner was elected as the new leader of the Unionist Party and Prime Minister of Northern Ireland. For many unionists and non-unionists such as Niedermayer, he now seemed the person most capable of reversing the drift into civil war. It was clear that his political understanding and emotional connection with Northern Ireland ran much deeper than either of his previous rivals for the party leadership. Unlike his two predecessors, who were members of the Church of Ireland and whose families were part of the former Anglican Ascendancy, Faulkner was a Presbyterian. Although Presbyterians did not suffer to the same extent from the application of England's Penal Laws as Roman Catholics, they were also excluded from many areas of Ireland's political and social life for most of the eighteenth and part of the nineteenth centuries and they were not considered part of the former Ascendancy.

Faulkner was also one of the few unionist politicians who knew the back streets and housing estates of Belfast where many Catholics lived. Thanks to his previous business career, he was familiar with some of those districts that were later to become strongholds of the IRA. These were the same streets and estates where Brian Keenan now operated. He had left the Grundig factory in 1970. According to some accounts, he had been fired by Niedermayer because of his prolonged absences from work. That seems credible because Keenan was by then fully occupied with his IRA activities.

In an interview with the republican newspaper, *An Phoblacht* (The Republic) given shortly before he died, Keenan listed the qualities that he thought were essential for any successful guerrilla campaign: 'There cannot be any self-doubt,' he said, 'no half-measures or any holding back.' He followed that principle throughout the 1970s. That perspective may also reflect the implacable nature of Keenan's character, which was described by one of his IRA colleagues as 'very intense and authoritarian'. He seems to have become the sort of leader who was admired and respected, but also feared by his subordinates. Indeed, one former member of the IRA told me that young volunteers were often more afraid of Keenan's disapproval than they were of the British army.

Faulkner began his new administration by making some small but encouraging signs that he was prepared to introduce change, declaring that he looked forward to the day 'when my unionist colleagues on this front bench will be Protestant and Catholic and no one will even think it worthy of comment'. His new cabinet included, for the first time, a member of another political party as well as the first Roman Catholic to be part of any Stormont government.

Faulkner's election coincided with the enactment of the Local Government Boundaries (Northern Ireland) Act. This provided for the appointment of an independent commissioner to assess the boundaries of district councils and ward areas so that future gerrymandering would no longer take place. Faulkner also proposed setting up a system of all-party parliamentary committees to oversee control of key government departments. He proposed that two of these three committees would be chaired by nationalist MPs.

This would have meant the first practical involvement of opposition parties in the business of government since the inception of the northern state. His proposal was initially welcomed by the Social Democratic and Labour Party (SDLP), which was then the main political party representing northern Catholics. Faulkner was described by Paddy Devlin, one of the founders of the SDLP, as having made a 'brisk and encouraging start'. These initial moves could have led to significant developments. However, for some disaffected nationalists, they were merely token gestures – too little and too late to have any real impact. And, for all his previous experience and astuteness, Brian Faulkner was about to make the biggest mistake of his political career.

15.
The Wrong Thing

By 1971, Brian Faulkner was (just about) the only acceptable face of unionism in the opinion of most members of the British cabinet. As far as Lord Carrington, the astute but somewhat cynical Minister for Defence, was concerned, Faulkner was 'a real politician, flexible, ambitious and unscrupulous'. British ministers regarded Ian Paisley, the other major figure in unionist politics, as an antediluvian character who was quite simply beyond the pale in every sense of the term. British ministers believed that it would always prove impossible to deal with him and those he represented in Ulster. (They were eventually proven wrong on that score.)

But if Faulkner enjoyed the initial support of the British government when he became Prime Minister, then his political honeymoon in Northern Ireland was over almost as soon as it had begun. In the months that followed his election, the IRA's offensive gained further momentum and began to acquire the characteristics of a full-scale insurgency. In his autobiography, Faulkner described the relentless build-up of pressure for him to take decisive action. British army commanders had advised him that the IRA was now well-armed and about to launch a major escalation of its campaign. RUC chiefs told him that their small force had been stretched to breaking point.

According to Robert Ramsay, his private secretary, Faulkner was deeply affected by the visits he paid to the families of RUC officers who had been killed by the IRA. Faulkner claimed that demands for action against the IRA also came from many ordinary Catholics who, he said, were appalled at the rising level of violence. 'You can do three things in Irish politics,' he later wrote, 'the right thing, the wrong thing, or nothing at all.' He concluded that he had 'always thought it better to do the wrong thing than to do nothing at all'. In the eyes of many, Faulkner did the 'wrong thing' when he decided to introduce internment without trial.

Faulkner had first introduced internment to Northern Ireland during the 1950s as the Minister for Home Affairs. At that time, it played an important part in defeating the IRA's border campaign. In 1957, internment was introduced on both sides of the Irish border and, with most of its leadership imprisoned, the IRA found it impossible to maintain its campaign. However, the situation in 1971 was radically different to what it had been in 1957. For a start, the mood of the northern Catholic population was not the same. To many Catholics, it appeared that the political unity of the Ulster Protestant community had finally been breached and the unionist regime was falling apart. The morale of the Catholic population was, therefore, buoyant: in a profoundly polarised society, it seemed that their 'side' was winning.

Internment had been used by Irish governments with considerable effectiveness on several occasions in the history of the southern state. Indeed, Taoiseach Jack Lynch had made a public statement in December of the previous year in which he threatened to introduce internment again in the Irish Republic. But the political situation had changed significantly in the months since he made that threat. Two days before internment was introduced in the north, Sir John Peck, the British Ambassador to Ireland, called upon Lynch to ask if his government were prepared to instigate the same measure in the south. He reported that Lynch had given him 'the most solemn warning that the consequences [of internment] would be catastrophic'. But, by then, the die was cast. Lynch's fears proved to be justified, but his position effectively meant that for the next few years the IRA could count upon a place of refuge south of the border, and that proved to be a critical advantage in its subsequent campaign.

What made matters immeasurably worse for the Stormont government in the days that followed the introduction of internment was the obvious lack of political balance in the selection of those who were arrested in 'Operation Demetrius'. More than 300 men were caught up in the early morning raids of 8 August 1971. Only two of these were Protestants – both of whom were republicans – and it was more than a year before the first loyalist paramilitaries were interned. It was also reported that British soldiers had smashed their way into many houses and assaulted, abused and threatened Catholic families. This was compounded by early reports that the British army had subjected some of those whom they had arrested to what the European Court of Human Rights would later judge to be 'degrading and inhuman treatment'.

Faulkner later tried to justify his one-sided actions on the basis that the only real and present danger came from republicans and the IRA. It is true that the Ulster Defence Association (UDA) – the largest loyalist paramilitary group – was not formed until September of the following year. It is also true that the UDA's tactic of killing Catholic civilians in retaliation for IRA actions had not yet commenced in earnest. However, the other major loyalist paramilitary group – the Ulster Volunteer Force (UVF) – was already in existence in 1971. Indeed, the UVF had begun to kill innocent Catholic civilians as far back as 1966. Even if it were true that loyalist paramilitaries did not pose the same type of threat to state security as the IRA, it was still a grave political miscalculation on Faulkner's part only to intern northern republicans.

It soon became clear that Operation Demetrius might have damaged the IRA, but it had certainly not put the organisation out of business. Around half of those arrested by the British remained loyal to the 'official' IRA leadership in Dublin, including some of those subjected to brutal treatment, and they did not pose a serious threat to the security of Northern Ireland. It was also obvious to the Provisional IRA leaders that there was a likelihood that internment would be introduced at some stage, so they were already prepared to take evasive action. They had even received an advance warning from one of their informants in Stormont's Ministry of Home Affairs to that effect.

Republican spokespersons soon claimed that only a small number of those caught in Operation Demetrius had been active Provisional IRA members and most of their key operators – including Brian Keenan – had evaded capture. The most obvious indication that internment had failed in its principal objective of reducing violence was the dramatic rise in violent incidents that followed its introduction. In the space of three days, twenty-four people were killed and the dead included Catholic and Protestant civilians as well as IRA members and British soldiers. The violence abated somewhat in the weeks that followed, but it still represented a sharp increase on preceding levels. In the eight months before Demetrius, there had been thirty-four deaths as a result of political violence. In the four months following internment,

140 people were killed. One of those shot dead was a unionist senator. A few years later, a nationalist senator was murdered by loyalist gunmen. They were not the last Ulster politicians to be assassinated by republican or loyalist gunmen in the most recent Troubles.

Increased activity by the IRA had been accompanied by growing violence from loyalist paramilitaries. The aftermath of the introduction of internment also witnessed the large-scale exodus of Protestant and Catholic families from districts of Belfast that were 'mixed' between different denominations to those where they could live exclusively among their co-religionists. These territories were later formalised by the construction of many so-called 'peace walls' which would in time become a powerful symbol of the sectarian divisions in Northern Ireland. In this context, it may reveal the strength of Niedermayer's confident belief in his own 'neutrality' that he did not consider moving his family further away from Andersonstown. He decided to remain, even though Andersonstown had already emerged as one of the centres of civil disturbance and IRA activity in Belfast. It was also an area in which Brian Keenan had begun to direct IRA operations.

There were clear political implications stemming from the introduction of internment. The main party supported by Catholics, the SDLP, had given a cautious welcome to the package of reforms that Faulkner had proposed. The nominal leader of the SDLP remained

Gerry Fitt but John Hume had already emerged as the dominant intellectual force within the party, and he was the one who determined party strategy. Under Hume's influence, the SDLP announced that, as a protest against internment, it was withdrawing from a number of public bodies. The move effectively shattered the hope of Faulkner's proposals for reform gaining any purchase. This development also advanced another of Hume's political objectives: the collapse or dissolution of the unionist administration at Stormont.

The British Prime Minister continued to give support to Faulkner's government in public, but in private he instructed Reginald Maudling, the Home Secretary, to draw up plans for the direct rule of Northern Ireland from Westminster. In October 1971, Heath established a small cabinet sub-group consisting of four cabinet ministers and himself to develop a new policy for Northern Ireland. Apart from Maudling, the other ministers were Willie Whitelaw, the Lord President of the Council; Lord Carrington, the Defence Minister; and Sir Alec Douglas-Home, the Minister for Foreign Affairs. None of those Ministers might have been considered to be sympathetic to the cause of Ulster unionism. In that regard, their feelings might best have been summed up by Douglas-Home in a letter he wrote to the British Prime Minister in which he expressed the view that the unionists did not properly belong in the United Kingdom: 'I do not believe they are like the Scots or Welsh,' he wrote to Heath, 'and doubt if they ever will be.'

In November, Heath stated in public that if a majority in Northern Ireland ever wanted political reunification with the rest of the island, then the Westminster parliament 'would not stand in their way'. His comments may now seem to be a statement of the obvious. Similar sentiments had been expressed by other senior British politicians in previous years. But some Irish republicans preferred to believe that it was only the presence of a British army of occupation that prevented the reunification of Ireland and that partition was maintained simply because it was in the strategic and economic interests of the UK. But Heath and most other senior British politicians recognised that, since the end of the Second World War, the strategic value of Northern Ireland to the UK had been minimal. Despite the claims of the IRA, it was also of negligible, if any, economic value to the British exchequer. Indeed, the Northern Irish economy was highly dependent on large financial subventions from Westminster in order to remain viable, and it continues to remain so.

In May 1971, a special committee chaired by the civil servant who was head of the British Home Office considered a number of options for the constitutional future of Northern Ireland. This committee explicitly identified the long-term objective of British policy as 'the creation of a united Ireland' and recommended that 'in preparation' for that development, the UK government should encourage the Irish Republic to 'adapt itself politically and socially to accommodating the Ulster Protestants'. One member of the Committee even advocated expelling Northern Ireland from the Union because of the 'disproportionate amount' of financial support it received from the British Exchequer.

Heath's public statements generated an amount of unease within the Protestant community: they did not, after all, manifest any great enthusiasm for the continuing union of Northern Ireland and Great Britain. But Heath was not yet ready to administer the *coup de grâce* to the Stormont government. This would not come for some months. And, when that blow was finally delivered, it was caused by the indiscriminate violence and lack of discipline shown by an elite regiment of the British army.

16.
Dead Man Walking

The march set off from the Creggan housing estate in Derry at about 2.45 p.m. on Sunday, 30 January 1972. It had been planned as a protest by NICRA against internment and was technically illegal. On 18 January, Brian Faulkner had announced a ban on all marches and parades in Northern Ireland. His ruling was intended to impact on both communities and it included those traditional Orange parades that were regarded by many Ulster Protestants as central to their cultural identity.

NICRA, however, was determined to defy Faulkner's ban. Faced with that challenge, he decided that it would be prudent to allow the march to proceed through the Catholic districts of Derry but to prevent it from reaching loyalist areas. British army commanders recognised that there was a strong likelihood that some rioting would take place and Major-General Robert Ford, who was in charge of all land forces in Northern Ireland, decided to send the 1st Battalion of the Parachute Regiment to impose order on any civil disturbances that might arise.

That was a fateful call: the paratroopers were regarded as an elite regiment, trained for combat and with a well-deserved reputation for aggression. During Operation Demetrius the same battalion had killed nine civilians in the Ballymurphy district of Belfast, including a Catholic priest, when they were allegedly returning fire from IRA gunmen. To put it mildly, the paratroopers were not the ideal soldiers to be used in a low-key policing operation.

Several thousand people assembled in the Creggan that January afternoon and the majority of those present accepted Faulkner's decision to reroute the march and restrict it to Catholic areas of the city. However, as expected, a relatively small number of youths began to stone the soldiers and a minor riot soon developed. About an hour after it started, some paratroopers opened fire with live rounds on the rioters and others began to chase and arrest them. By the end of the afternoon, twenty-six people had been shot by British soldiers. Thirteen civilians died that day and one more died some weeks later. This became known to the world as Bloody Sunday and it marked a critical threshold for both communities in Northern Ireland.

The British army released a statement that claimed the paratroopers had only returned fire in self-defence. Within hours of the killings, Brian Faulkner issued a statement that appeared to give support to the army's version of events in Derry. However, Faulkner's true feelings were revealed some years later to an official inquiry by his former private secretary. According to Dr Robert Ramsay, Faulkner did not believe the army's claims. He had chaired the Joint Security Committee at Stormont, and knew that there had been no advance intelligence about an IRA threat; he doubted that those shot by the paratroopers were terrorists. Faulkner was also aware of the likely political implications of the killings. 'This is London's disaster,' he told Ramsay, 'but they will use it against us.' His prediction proved more accurate than even he might have imagined.

The events of Bloody Sunday proved a landmark in the Troubles for all of those involved. Indeed, it is sometimes treated as if these killings led directly to the outbreak of the Troubles and the formation of the Provisional IRA. That was clearly not the case since the IRA's campaign was almost two years old at that stage. However, twenty-six years after the events in Derry, Tony Blair established a new commission of inquiry. This was chaired by Lord Saville and became the most extensive (and expensive) investigation in British legal history. After seven years and the evidence of more than 900 witnesses, Lord Saville's conclusions were utterly damning of the paratroopers' conduct. He judged that all the civilians they had killed were unarmed and posed no danger to the soldiers' safety. Gerry Adams has claimed that 'money, guns and recruits' flooded into the IRA in the weeks that followed Bloody Sunday, allowing it to embark on just the type of escalation of conflict that had been feared by Faulkner. There is a grim irony that indiscriminate acts of violence committed by the British Army would later be cited by the IRA to justify its own – often indiscriminate – acts of terror.

According to Bishop and Mallie, Brian Keenan travelled to Tripoli on a false passport in the aftermath of Bloody Sunday to meet with the Libyan leader, Muammar Gaddafi, in search of arms. Gaddafi, who took political control of Libya in a 1969 military coup, viewed the IRA as his revolutionary comrades. It seems that the Libyans eventually found Keenan a difficult person to deal with, but that did not deter Gaddafi. He was not only prepared to give significant financial support to the IRA, he also supplied much of its modern weaponry. He was to play a long-term and critical role in the future of the IRA – and may even have contributed, albeit indirectly, to the kidnapping of Thomas Niedermayer.

Libya was able to provide mortars and Rocket Propelled Grenade (RPG) launchers for the IRA. Gaddafi was also prepared to supply Semtex, a plastic explosive that is highly malleable, waterproof and, until recently, extremely hard to detect. Semtex was to become another of the IRA's signature weapons. The scale of the war materiel that Gaddafi provided became evident in 1973 when the Irish navy boarded a ship called *Claudia* off the Irish coast and seized five tonnes of armaments that had originated in Libya. This haul included almost 1,000 rifles and anti-tank guns, 100 cases of landmines, 5,000 lbs of explosives and 500 hand grenades.

One former IRA member told me that Gaddafi was dismayed by this seizure and thought it reflected badly on the professional competence of the IRA. The IRA therefore felt the need to demonstrate just how effectively it could operate. That would result in a renewed bombing campaign in London. It seems that this restored the Libyan leader's confidence in the IRA, and in the years ahead Gaddafi would ensure that further large consignments of modern weaponry were delivered safely to Ireland. In fact, his supply of armaments became essential to the continuation of the IRA campaign.

Bloody Sunday marked a turning point for British policy in Northern Ireland. Until then, one of Westminster's priorities had been to protect the position of Faulkner. In the immediate aftermath of the killings in Derry, Heath was at pains to assure Faulkner of his continuing support. 'I've told you, Brian,' he had said when they met in early February, 'we are in this together and we'll support you all the way, however long it takes.' The truth was that, by then, Britain's government had lost all confidence in the unionist administration and had long since drawn up detailed plans for direct rule from Westminster. When he met Heath the week after Bloody Sunday, Faulkner was already, in political terms, a dead man walking.

He believed that his next meeting was simply for further consultation and he was not aware of what was really on the British Prime Minister's agenda. But, when he met Heath on the morning of 22 March 1972, it soon became clear to Faulkner that what the British Prime Minister intended to do was already beyond negotiation. Heath presented Faulkner with proposals he knew would be unacceptable since they divested Stormont of any meaningful executive powers. When Faulkner returned to Belfast, he advised his cabinet of the latest development and they resigned en masse. They were quickly replaced by a new government department, the Northern Ireland Office, and a new cabinet portfolio. The first Secretary of State for Northern Ireland was Willie Whitelaw.

It could be argued that, in proroguing Stormont, Heath had acted illegally, since the terms of the Government of Ireland Act had specified that such action could only be taken with the agreement of the Northern Ireland parliament. Whether that is true or not, what is clear is that the IRA believed it deserved primary credit for the fall of Stormont. This may help to explain why their leaders felt so confident that victory was within their grasp. There were other reasons why they might have thought so.

17.

Blood on the Streets

In the weeks that followed Bloody Sunday, the IRA offensive took on new and terrifying forms. In the first week of March, a bomb was planted in the Abercorn restaurant in the centre of Belfast. It was a Saturday afternoon and the restaurant was crowded with weekend shoppers. An anonymous caller issued a warning but did not give a precise location. Two minutes after the phone call, a handbag containing 5 lbs of gelignite exploded under a restaurant table. Two young women were killed instantly. Many other people were badly injured: limbs were lost and some shoppers were permanently blinded by flying glass. One young woman, about to be married, lost both legs, her right arm and one of her eyes.

Many of those who were horribly injured – as well as the two young women who died – were Catholics. That may explain why the IRA denied responsibility for the explosion and, for some years after the atrocity, continued to plead innocence. Ivor Bell, a senior figure in the Belfast IRA of the 1970s, claimed to believe that 'some right-wing unionist group' or the British army were responsible for the bombing.

Both Protestants and Catholics in Northern Ireland were often ready to attribute particularly heinous atrocities to the 'other side', even when that seemed to fly in the face of all available evidence or probability. Sometimes, such claims were cynical and driven by immediate political exigency; at other times, they represented a more profound form of denial and a reluctance to believe that their own communities were capable of any such depravity. However, it is now generally accepted that two young female members of the IRA planted the bomb that destroyed the Abercorn.

A few weeks after that atrocity, the IRA introduced a new weapon to its armoury: the car bomb. The first ones were used in the mainly Protestant town of Bangor. There were no fatalities on that occasion but, before long, the car bomb had become another of the IRA's signature weapons. According to Seán Mac Stíofáin (otherwise known as John Stephenson), an Englishman who was then the IRA's Chief of Staff, car bombs were both a tactical and a strategic weapon. He believed that they could disrupt the ability of the Stormont government to administer Northern Ireland and also damage the state's economic viability through the sheer scale of their destruction. He did not acknowledge another integral feature of car bombs: their everyday and innocuous appearance greatly increased the terror they generated in the civilian population.

The primary targets of these bombs were not supposed to be civilians. The IRA usually claimed to have given enough warning to allow the affected areas to be cleared. However, there were inevitably many incidents when – due to the absence of timely warnings, inadequate information being provided, or devices exploding prematurely – civilians were killed and grievously injured. On such occasions, the IRA usually denied responsibility or claimed that their warnings had been ignored deliberately by the RUC or British army in order to damage the reputation of republicans. There were always some who were prepared to believe, or who wanted to believe, such claims.

All of these ominous developments might have caused growing concern to Ingeborg Niedermayer – particularly as she and her family lived on the outskirts of Andersonstown. The district had become home to the 1st Battalion of the IRA's Belfast Brigade, which was one of its most active. Once again, it is a measure of the confidence Niedermayer felt about his own 'neutrality' that he continued to live there without any special security arrangements. Perhaps in comparison to the conditions that he and Ingeborg had endured at the end of the Second World War, he regarded the Troubles as relatively minor. Perhaps he felt optimistic that the British would be able to defuse the political situation; in 1973, many people believed that the Troubles were only temporary. Few could imagine that they would continue for the next twenty-five years. At any rate, in the autumn of 1973,

Niedermayer announced that Grundig intended to open a large new factory in Newry that would give employment to a workforce of around 1,000 people.

Newry is a town close to the Irish border that had suffered high unemployment for many years. It was also a town where Catholics formed a large majority and where the Provisional IRA was active in the 1970s and beyond. Senior Grundig executives were understandably wary of the implications of the increasing violence for their business in Northern Ireland and were reluctant to countenance any future investment. Niedermayer had somehow managed to overcome their opposition and convince his colleagues – including Max Grundig – that they had nothing to fear from the worsening situation. He was able to cite the impressive productivity of the Dunmurry plant, but his success in persuading Grundig to make this commitment is also evidence of the high regard in which he was held in the company as well as the confidence he was able to inspire.

The objective of IRA policy was to turn Northern Ireland into an economic wasteland and promote the 'climate of collapse' that Brian Keenan had found such an appealing scenario in Robert Taber's *War of the Flea*. The prospect of a new factory with new jobs coming on stream in one of the republican heartlands was anything but welcome to him or to the IRA's Army Council. At that time, the IRA's leaders also felt supremely confident. With an influx of new members, with unprecedented support from the northern Catholic community and with an array of new weaponry at their disposal, they could claim that, in the space of just a few years, the IRA had been instrumental in causing the collapse of a regime that had managed to survive more or less intact for the previous half-century. IRA leaders believed that they could emulate the short, sharp campaign that Michael Collins had led during the Irish War of Independence. Some of the reasons the IRA believed that was possible came from the signals they thought they had received from the British government.

In early 1972, Heath sent a high-ranking officer from MI6 called Frank Steele to talk to the IRA and identify any common ground for negotiations. MI6 is supposed to deal with security matters outside the UK, while MI5 deals with internal security – so the choice of Steele had its own significance. Steele had previously carried out secret talks that had led to Britain's withdrawal from its former colony of Kenya. For the leaders of the IRA, it seemed that this sort of endgame had now begun in Northern Ireland. In June 1972, the British cabinet had privately agreed that 'no solution was possible unless [the IRA's] point of view was represented'. The following month, Heath authorised the Secretary of State for Northern Ireland, Willie Whitelaw, to hold unofficial talks in London with an IRA delegation led by Seán Mac Stíofáin, which included Gerry Adams. The latter had been interned in March 1972 but was released so that he could participate in these discussions.

In that context, and perhaps for understandable reasons, the IRA held inflated and unrealistic expectations of what Britain was prepared, or able, to deliver. Those expectations led the IRA leadership to declare a brief ceasefire.

When this truce broke down after just ten days, the IRA reaction was to step up its bombing campaign. On 21 July, twenty-one bombs exploded in Belfast within minutes of each other on the day that became known as Bloody Friday. Nine people were killed, and that evening's television news showed disturbing footage of human remains being scraped off pavements with shovels and dropped into plastic refuse sacks. One RUC officer who helped move some of the mutilated limbs did not realise that they belonged to his own brother.

In the immediate aftermath of Bloody Friday, the British army launched 'Operation Motorman', regaining effective control of those so-called 'no-go' areas of Belfast and Derry that had been held for most of the previous year by the IRA. In response to Motorman, the IRA planted yet more bombs – including three car bombs in the small village of Claudy in County Derry. This attack was organised by a Catholic priest, Fr James Chesney, who was in charge of all IRA operations in that part of County Derry. His bombs killed nine civilians that summer morning, both Protestant and Catholic, including an eight-year-old girl. Once again, the IRA followed the tactic which, as Henry McDonald has observed, 'they would return to again and again and again': they issued an immediate denial of responsibility for this atrocity and claimed that an 'internal court' had absolved its members of any involvement. With the collusion of William Whitelaw, the Secretary of State, and Cardinal Conway, Primate of the Roman Catholic Church in Ireland, Fr Chesney was never charged but simply moved to a parish outside Northern Ireland.

The talks that Whitelaw conducted with IRA leaders in 1972 and the concessions he offered through the creation of 'Special Category' status allowed IRA prisoners to wear their own clothes and enjoy 'free association' with each other. Whitelaw later regretted these concessions, and they reinforced republicans' belief that a quick and comprehensive victory was more than likely. However, there were significant obstacles to what the British were able to deliver and the biggest of these was the Ulster Protestant community.

If the British government had agreed to IRA demands and signalled their intention to withdraw from Northern Ireland, it would have meant, in effect, the unilateral expulsion from the UK of around one million of its own citizens against their expressed wishes. It is doubtful whether such a measure has ever been implemented in any state, democratic or not. In other words, it was always highly unlikely that any UK government could have delivered the IRA's core objectives, even though British ministers, and senior officials in the British Home Office and the British Treasury might well have wished that they could.

That may explain why the IRA's own narrative began to change slowly from the notion of an imminent victory to one of a 'Long War' of attrition that would eventually grind the British down – 'sickening the Brits' (as the objective was once described by a member of the IRA's Army Council) – with a stream of coffins travelling back to England that would eventually compel the UK government to force the unionists to accept a united Ireland. The underlying sectarian nature of the conflict in Ulster was also becoming more obvious as the months passed. By mid-1972, loyalist paramilitaries had stepped up their bloody campaign of killing random Catholic civilians as a response to IRA actions. Over the same period, the IRA's definition of 'legitimate targets' had been expanded to include almost anyone who might be considered sympathetic to the security forces. The promised 'stream of coffins' to England never materialized: instead, the British policy of 'Ulsterisation' ensured that most of those who died were local members of the security forces – and their coffins were buried in Northern Ireland.

In subsequent years, the IRA would assassinate both elected and retired representatives of the unionist community, including members of local county councils, the Northern Ireland Assembly and the Westminster parliament. One of the most significant of these killings was that of Edgar Graham, a member of the Northern Ireland Assembly. He was a young lecturer at Queen's University who was within weeks of completing his doctoral thesis at Oxford. Graham was considered a rising star and a likely future leader of the Unionist Party – which, it seems, was the precise reason he was targeted by the IRA and shot in the head as he stood chatting to a friend outside the university's law faculty.

In a communiqué admitting responsibility for Graham's killing, the IRA described his murder as 'a salutary lesson' for unionists. Gerry Adams declined to condemn the killing, claiming that Sinn Féin was not prepared 'to join the hypocritical chorus of establishment figures' who had done so. No one was ever charged with Graham's murder, but Eamon Collins, a former IRA member (subsequently beaten to death by his erstwhile comrades), informed the RUC that Graham had been set up for assassination by a fellow law lecturer at Queen's.

Niedermayer believed that he was perceived by the workforce in Dunmurry to be 'fair and neutral' in his political attitudes, and that he and the company he represented were therefore safe. In 1973, this belief seemed to be confirmed in dramatic fashion. He was driving home from work one evening when he was confronted by a group of armed members of the IRA who intended to hijack his car. When Niedermayer explained that he was the German consul and that most of the workers in his factory came from Catholic districts of Belfast, he was allowed to drive home unharmed.

The IRA's 'anti-capitalist' attacks on the northern economy in the 1970s meant that foreign businessmen and their companies fell within the category that republicans liked to describe as 'legitimate targets'. Brian Keenan would soon identify Thomas Niedermayer – someone he knew personally – as one of those targets. The reason that he chose to identify Niedermayer as a target was not simply because of conflicts in their past relationship. It was also due to an IRA operation in England that had gone badly wrong.

18.
The English Campaign

Irish republicans first detonated bombs in England in the 1860s. The first of these occurred at Clerkenwell Prison in 1867 when a barrel of gunpowder was exploded by members of the Irish Republican Brotherhood, otherwise known as the Fenians. Their bomb was intended to blow up a wall of the prison so that Richard O'Sullivan Burke, a Fenian prisoner, could escape. Instead, the explosion killed twelve civilians, injured many more and no prisoners were set free.

What distinguishes this bombing from subsequent ones was that it was not intended to induce terror in the civilian population, nor to strike at a symbolic or a strategic target. Instead, it was simply designed as the means by which an Irish prisoner might be liberated. Two decades later, the objectives had changed. The 'Dynamite Campaign', which was launched by Fenians in the 1880s, targeted a number of specific government, military and police buildings in a more deliberate and systematic way. The first explosion in this campaign killed a young boy. The only other fatalities were three Fenians who blew themselves up under London Bridge. It was this dynamite campaign that led to the establishment of a new police division called the Special Irish Branch, later known simply as 'Special Branch' (SB).

The third major IRA campaign in England was code-named the 'S Plan' – the 'S' stood for 'sabotage' – and was launched shortly before the start of the Second World War. On 12 January 1939, an ultimatum was delivered to Lord Halifax, the British Foreign Secretary, demanding the complete withdrawal of Britain's armed forces and civilian representatives from every part of Ireland. Three days later, the IRA issued a formal declaration of war and over the next few months there were several dozen explosions in London, Manchester, Birmingham and Liverpool. The objective was, apparently, to paralyse Britain's transport systems and power supplies. However, the IRA's campaign included less ambitious targets, such as a number of high street cinemas and even Madame Tussaud's famous wax works. Then, in August, a bomb concealed in the basket of a bicycle exploded without warning in the centre of Coventry. The bomb killed an 82-year-old man, two shop assistants, a road sweeper and a schoolboy.

One of those implicated but not charged in this bombing was an IRA member called Dominic Adams who is believed to have been in overall command of the IRA unit in Coventry. Thirty or so years later, his nephew, Gerry Adams, would become the long-term President of Sinn Féin and, allegedly, a Chief of Staff of the IRA. Another of those involved in the IRA's England campaign of those years was a Belfast republican called Albert Price. He was subsequently interned by the Fianna Fáil government in Dublin in the Curragh camp in County Kildare. After his release from the Curragh, Price returned to Belfast and raised a family between further spells in prison for his IRA activities. The living room of the Price home seems to have resembled a shrine to IRA militarism and included a wooden replica of a Thompson sub-machine gun hanging above the fireplace. According to one of his daughters, Albert Price inculcated his political views in his children from a very early age. 'Growing up,' his daughter, Dolours Price, recalled, 'we did not have normal bedtime stories of *Little Red Riding Hood* or the like. My father used to sit us on his knee and tell us stories about how he had gone off to war in 1939, aged 19, to bomb the English.'

One former RUC Special Branch officer compared the radicalisation that Dolours Price and her sister received from their father to the process by which Islamist terrorists have been groomed for future martyrdom. Certainly, the concept of martyrdom – or 'blood sacrifice' with its quasi-Christian associations – is deeply embedded in the ideology of Irish republicanism. According to Patrick Pearse, one of the leaders of the Easter Rising, 'bloodshed is a cleansing and a sanctifying thing', and the apparent willingness of Dolours Price to sacrifice her own life led to the IRA's abduction of Thomas Niedermayer.

Her father was not the only member of Price's family to have been involved with the IRA. Dolours' aunt, Bridie, had been handling an IRA bomb when it exploded prematurely, blinding her and blowing off both her hands. Dolours Price seems to have felt some sort of obligation to join the IRA's campaign because of the sacrifice she believed her aunt had made for the republican cause. When the IRA split in 1969, it was not surprising that Albert Price sided with the Provisionals. According to Ed Moloney, he was also one of those who argued that the IRA should begin a new campaign in England. Two of his daughters would play a prominent role in that campaign – which would contribute, in turn, to the circumstances in which Thomas Niedermayer lost his life.

The journalist Kevin Myers worked both for RTÉ and the *Observer* in the early years of the Troubles. He first saw Dolours Price at a political rally in Belfast in 1971 and described her as 'one of the most enchanting, beautiful, bewitching women' he had ever met. It was clear that the Price sisters were regarded with a mixture of awe and respect within the IRA. They were considered to be 'republican royalty' because of their family's long association with the IRA. Indeed, Dolours Price is said to have been the first woman allowed to become a full member of that organisation. In 1971, she had approached Seán Mac Stíofáin, one of the founders of the Provisional IRA, and asked to become a member. He advised her to join Cumann na mBan, the women's wing of the IRA, since he apparently regarded military action as 'men's work'. But Price 'wanted to fight, [and] not make tea' or 'bandage IRA men's wounds'. She told Mac Stíofáin she would settle for nothing less and, eventually, he agreed. Her younger sister, Marian, soon followed her into the ranks of the IRA.

According to her own testimony, Dolours Price became a member of a special unit of the IRA called 'the Unknowns'. Its name may have been rather theatrical, but its purpose was deadly serious. Price claimed that this unit was established by Gerry Adams and was used to 'disappear' certain individuals by killing them and burying their bodies in secret. The IRA would then profess to know nothing about the whereabouts of the victims. There were a number of reasons why the IRA leadership did not want to claim responsibility for particular deaths but, usually, it was because such an admission might prove unpopular or reflect badly on the IRA itself.

Price later admitted to having been personally involved in four of these 'disappearances'. These all took place in 1972, and one of them involved the killing of Jean McConville. She was a widow, a Protestant who had converted to Catholicism (which might have made her suspect in nationalist West Belfast) and a mother of ten children. She was alleged to have supplied information about IRA activities to the British army. Dolours Price subsequently claimed that McConville had been abducted on the direct orders of Gerry Adams and was driven by her across the border to the Irish Republic where she was told she would be reunited with her children. Instead, McConville was shot dead a few days later and buried among sand dunes on an isolated beach in County Louth. For many years, the IRA claimed to have no knowledge of what had happened to her and a rumour was circulated that she had abandoned her children and run off with a British soldier.

It was not until 1998, twenty-six years after her murder, that the IRA finally admitted that she had been killed as an alleged informer. It was not until 2003 that her body was discovered by accident when a severe storm washed away part of the Louth beach where she had been buried. And it was not until 2014 – forty-two years after her disappearance – that Gerry Adams was questioned by police about his involvement in Jean McConville's killing. Ultimately, in 2015, the Northern Ireland Director of Public Prosecutions decided that the evidence available was 'insufficient to provide a reasonable prospect of obtaining a conviction'. Subsequently, Adams was not charged. He was, perhaps, fortunate that he did not face the same court as Jean McConville, since an independent investigation conducted in 2006, which was allowed unprecedented access to all the relevant RUC and British army files, discovered no evidence that she had passed any information to anyone. The conclusion reached by Nuala O'Loan, who chaired the investigation, was that Jean McConville was 'an innocent woman who was abducted and murdered'.

Some republicans are still convinced of McConville's guilt and Dolours Price remained unrepentant of her role in her murder. More than thirty years later, she told the journalist Ed Moloney that she still regarded informers as 'the lowest form of human life' and that 'death was too good for them'. Even if the allegations against McConville were true, Paul Bew has noted that she could hardly have been a significant source of information for the security forces – unlike the senior IRA figures later revealed as long-time agents of the RUC or British army.

'To disappear' is normally used as an intransitive verb, but it acquired a new tense during the Troubles: Jean McConville 'was disappeared' – and so was Thomas Niedermayer. It is estimated that between fifteen and twenty individuals were 'disappeared' by the IRA during the Troubles.

In March 1972, Dolours Price is reported to have travelled to Milan, Italy, for discussions with Lotta Continua (Continuous Struggle), an ultra-left-wing group that advocated a policy of 'general conflict' with Europe's 'bourgeois states'. Such conflict involved armed bank robberies and physical assaults on those judged by the members of this small faction to be 'collaborators' with capitalism, such as factory foremen and managers. Lotta Continua was believed to have contacts with arms suppliers in the Middle East that the IRA wanted to exploit. However, Price was deported by the Italian government soon after her arrival in Milan and returned to Belfast.

As Martin Dillon has pointed out, it was a measure of the 'sad state' of British Intelligence in Northern Ireland that she was not questioned on her return. Apparently, MI5 officers were reluctant to believe that women could become actively involved in paramilitary operations.

Two months after Price's visit, members of Lotta Continua assassinated Luigi Calabresi, the Police Commissioner in Milan. The group's understanding of Ireland can be guessed from the title of a collection of essays that was published by them in the early 1970s – *Ireland: Europe's Vietnam*. Some years later, a gunman from Lotta Continua arrived in Dublin to link up with local sympathisers. These Irish sympathisers belonged to another far-left group whose members would later help the IRA liaise with FARC, the Revolutionary Armed Forces of Colombia. While in Dublin, the fraternal visitor from Lotta Continua shot and seriously wounded a businessman who was delivering a guest lecture in Trinity College. The would-be assassin was later deported from Ireland back to Italy. The Irish sympathisers who had assisted him were never charged and went on to pursue successful careers in the media and academia.

According to Dolours Price, Gerry Adams asked for volunteers at the beginning of 1973 to take part in what was regarded as a particularly hazardous operation. This involved planting a number of bombs in England and both Dolours and Marian Price were more than happy to volunteer. Perhaps it reminded them of similar missions their father had once undertaken. The IRA leadership determined that the bombs would explode on 8 March of that year: a date with particular significance in Northern Ireland.

19.
Happy about Dying

The date of 8 March 1973 was chosen by the IRA to launch their new English campaign because it was the day on which a border poll was due to be held in Northern Ireland.

British government ministers had expressed some concern that the imposition of direct rule might lead to a violent backlash from unionists. As a result, the Joint Intelligence Committee at Westminster had recommended, in a confidential report, that measures should be taken to reassure Protestants that the Union was not in danger. A border poll was designed for that purpose. This public referendum asked voters to indicate a preference for their constitutional future. There were two options available: either Northern Ireland could remain as part of the UK or it could become part of a united Irish state. Since a clear majority of the electorate were Protestants, the result of the poll seemed to be a foregone conclusion.

For that very reason, this referendum was unpopular with nationalists. Soon after the poll was announced, the

SDLP called upon their supporters to 'ignore completely the referendum' by boycotting the vote. At the same time, the IRA determined to distract the attention of the world's media from the poll's likely result by staging a rival 'spectacular' event. As Gary McGladdery has noted, this decision also illustrated the IRA's 'contempt for the idea that unionist consent should be a precondition for Irish unity'.

The IRA's plan was to undermine the impact of the border poll by exploding bombs at a number of locations in England. According to Dolours Price, who was one of the bombers, the idea to target London originated with her. She later explained that she believed 'a short, sharp shock, an incursion into the heart of the Empire, would be more effective than twenty car bombs in any part of the North of Ireland'. This assessment – with its anachronistic (and self-dramatising) reference to 'the Empire' – has often been treated as if it were a simple statement of self-evident fact. However, the effectiveness of this strategy is open to question and so is the thinking behind it.

It is certainly true that, by then, bombings or killings in England resulted in more coverage by the British and international media than bombings or killings in Northern Ireland. It is also true that the London bombs of March 1973 drove the results of the border poll off the front pages. Violence in Belfast had already become 'old news' due to its frequency, while deaths and injuries in the heart of London were sufficiently few and far between to generate newspaper headlines.

The IRA may have claimed that their purpose was to 'take the war to the Brits', no doubt with the intention of raising morale and giving some grim satisfaction to republicans. But the essential appeal of such actions was dependent on their coverage by the mass media. In other words, the IRA bombs that brought death and serious injury to London were essentially publicity stunts. They represented a tactic popular with some nineteenth century anarchists of spreading 'propaganda by the deed' and even the IRA's fondness for the grossly inappropriate term 'spectacular' is revealing in that regard.

In reality, the IRA's England campaign of the 1970s was not on a scale that was ever likely to produce a significant impact either on British government policy or on British public opinion. Republican paramilitaries were responsible for around 2,000 deaths in Northern Ireland during the course of the Troubles. Thousands of individual injuries were also sustained – many of a horrific nature – and there are reckoned to have been more than 10,000 explosions in the same period. Each of those incidents caused their own individual traumas to friends and families as well as to those directly affected and there is no doubt that their steady accumulation made a substantial impact upon the political landscape of Northern Ireland.

In the course of the IRA's English campaign during the recent Troubles, 115 deaths and just over 2,000 injuries were reported. Once again, each of those statistics represents an individual case, a family's grief and a particular trauma, but the scale of their impact is radically different. To put it crudely, for the IRA's attacks in England to have been comparable to those in Northern Ireland, there would have needed to be tens of thousands of dead civilians and hundreds of thousands more injured, and that was clearly beyond the IRA's capabilities.

The IRA had assured their supporters that 1972 would be the 'Year of Victory'. When they failed to achieve that objective, they decided to raise the stakes. A few weeks before the attacks in London were due to take place, four cars were hijacked in Belfast, fitted with English number plates, packed with explosives and driven to Dublin. An IRA unit travelled by ferry to Liverpool and then drove straight to London. The unit was joined there by Dolours Price, travelling under the assumed name of Una Devlin, who later claimed that she had been chosen by Adams to command the whole operation.

The night before the car bombs were planted and their timers set to detonate, the Price sisters went to see a play at the Royal Court Theatre in Chelsea. The play was *The Freedom of the City* by the Northern Irish playwright Brian Friel. This is usually regarded as the most explicitly political of all Friel's work. It features three Catholic civil rights protesters in Derry who are murdered in cold blood by British soldiers. The soldiers are later exonerated of their crimes by an official tribunal. Friel rejected interpretations of his play as a direct commentary on the events of Bloody Sunday, but there are some obvious parallels and, for many, the work represents a powerful critique of Britain's contemporary role in Ireland. One of the cast in the Royal Court Theatre was a young actor with nationalist sympathies who had attended Queen's University at the same time as Dolours Price. His name was Stephen Rea and he would later play a major role in the life of Price, since, ten years after that night's performance, he would become her husband.

Early on the morning of 8 March 1973, the cars containing the IRA bombs were parked in position with their timers set to detonate. By ten o'clock all of the IRA team were at Heathrow Airport. Their explosives were primed to detonate in the mid-afternoon and they had booked morning flights to Dublin so that they would be safely back in Ireland before any of the bombs exploded. Some of the bombers had already boarded and were waiting on the runway for their plane to take off when they were arrested by the British police. It seems that the RUC Special Branch had been tipped off by one of their agents in the IRA. By midday, ten of the IRA's unit were in police custody. At two o'clock, the IRA phoned a warning from Ireland, but the details were vague and imprecise. Two of the car bombs were defused but, at three o'clock that afternoon, two of them exploded. This led to the death of one civilian, an elderly shopkeeper called Fred Milton, and the injury of more than 200 others, some seriously.

Dolours Price later expressed her indifference towards those who were injured by her bombs, claiming that any casualties were not victims of the IRA but of their own stupidity. 'There were warnings phoned in, but people had stood about, curious to see,' she claimed. 'Some had even stood at office windows and been sprayed by broken glass when the car went up. In Belfast, everyone is well enough up on their explosives to know you always open windows to minimise the shock waves. Well, this was London and its people were only novices. If people ignored the warnings and stood around gawking, they were stupid. The numbers of injured came about through curiosity and stupidity.' Her comments are remarkable for their crude and callous nature. As well as the sense of self-congratulation implicit in her reference to those in Belfast 'knowing their explosives', there is, perhaps, also an element of bravado in her denial of any personal responsibility and in the attempt to distance herself from the consequences of her own actions.

The IRA bombs certainly achieved part of their objective. Almost 99 per cent of those who voted in the border poll that day were in favour of maintaining the Union with Great Britain. However, this overwhelming majority was eclipsed on the front pages of the next day's newspapers by extensive coverage of the bombs in London. Despite that, the IRA failed in its other critical objective, which was to ensure that the London bombers would evade arrest and return safely to Ireland.

Those arrested included Dolours Price and her younger sister, Marian. This attracted immediate press attention, partly because their father, Albert Price, was a well-known IRA veteran who had been active in previous campaigns. However, it seems rather more likely that the Price sisters caught the attention of the British media because they were both attractive and intelligent women in their early twenties and appeared quite unlike the stereotypes of fanatical bombers.

The sisters were tried at Winchester in September 1973 along with six men. The trial lasted for ten weeks and saw some of the strictest security in British legal history. The court was heavily guarded throughout and, when the verdict was announced on 15 November, four rows of armed detectives sat behind the dock while fifteen uniformed prison officers surrounded the prisoners. They were all found guilty, which was hardly surprising since Dolours Price had admitted that she supported the 'aims and principles' of the IRA and the IRA had already claimed responsibility for the bombs. One member of the IRA unit – a young woman of 18 – had cooperated with the police. She was acquitted and left the court under police protection. As she left, the other defendants began to hum the 'Dead March' from *Saul* and one of them threw some coins at her, shouting, 'Take your blood money with you.' She was given a new identity by the police and advised never to return to Northern Ireland.

One of the IRA defendants had already pleaded guilty. After the verdicts were given, the remaining eight gave clenched fist salutes to their relatives and friends in the public gallery. It was an ironic indication of the changes that education reforms had made for the Catholic population of Northern Ireland that three of those found guilty had attended third-level institutions and were training to be teachers. The longest sentences given were to those who were deemed to have played the most important roles in the planning and execution of the bombings. Dolours and Marian Price each received twenty years.

Both of these women immediately went on a hunger strike, seeking removal to a prison in Northern Ireland where they could claim the practical benefits of the 'Special Category' status conceded by William Whitelaw, which would allow them to wear civilian clothes and enjoy 'free association' with other IRA prisoners. As the Price sisters' hunger strike progressed, they were force-fed by the prison authorities. This was a distressing and painful procedure and stirred memories of the treatment of those suffragettes who had campaigned for women's voting rights at the start of the century. This helped to generate some sympathy for these young women in Ireland and elsewhere because their status now seemed to become that of victims and not perpetrators of violence. There were public demonstrations in support of the sisters and Albert Price, their father, led one of these in London, the city that his daughters had bombed.

Price was interviewed by the media outside Brixton prison, where he assured journalists that his daughters were 'happy about dying'. He said that all that worried them were 'the excuses that will come when they are gone'. For me, there is something perverse in the pride that Albert Price appears to take in this film interview in the willingness of his own children to sacrifice their lives for the IRA. It may provide some insight into the ways in which they had both been radicalised by him from an early age and the psychological impact that had on their subsequent adult lives.

By this stage, Brian Keenan was director of IRA operations and he had identified England as 'a very important theatre of war' that provided the IRA with an opportunity to 'extend and expand' its campaign. 'All modern states', he claimed, 'rely on transport, communications and power' and he defined these as 'the targets of the English campaign'. In reality, the IRA's subsequent attacks in England bore little, if any, connection with the ambitious strategic targets Keenan had named. Instead, those attacks included bombs tossed into crowded restaurants or bars, planted in department stores and thrown at queues at bus stops. It was clear, however, that any further operations in the UK would not take place on the same 'in and out' basis as the one led by Dolours Price. From now on, IRA members in England would be 'sleepers' – living as unobtrusively among the enemy population as Dominic Adams had done thirty years before.

On the same day that the Price sisters were sentenced, the IRA issued a statement which promised that 'in due course, retribution will be exacted from the people who inflicted such callous punishment on Belfast youth in London today'. An extensive bombing campaign was launched in London, designed to restore the IRA's reputation. Shane Paul O'Doherty was a young volunteer dispatched from Derry to take part in this campaign. O'Doherty went on to serve more than fifteen years in an English prison for the terrorist offences that he committed. In the aftermath of the Price sisters' convictions, he sent numerous letter bombs and planted others in England during 1973.

In the course of my research I met with O'Doherty. He told me that, soon after returning to Ireland from his bombing campaign, he attended a meeting of the IRA Army Council held in the back room of a confectionary shop in Finglas, Dublin. He was warmly congratulated by all those present for the damage and disruption his bombs had caused in England. He also told me that he witnessed Seamus Twomey, who was then the IRA's Chief of Staff, moved to tears while discussing the Price sisters' hunger strike. O'Doherty said that – even then – he found it jarring that no such compassion had been extended a few minutes earlier to the hapless victims of the bombs that he had sent and planted. It became clear to him then that there would be some sort of violent response to the capture of an entire IRA unit and one of Brian Keenan's first priorities was to devise what form the promised 'retribution' would take.

Keenan began to think of ways he could help the Price sisters and restore the reputation of the IRA at home and abroad as an effective fighting force. There was one idea in particular that appealed to him. Admittedly, it did not involve 'inflicting punishment' on any of the people who were involved in the capture or imprisonment of the Price sisters, but it was something that might grab more attention from the media – and which might also give Keenan some personal satisfaction. He decided to kidnap his former boss and hold him to ransom for the transfer of the Price sisters and the rest of their IRA unit to a jail in Northern Ireland.

20.

Kidnappers Always Ring Twice

Kidnapping has long been considered to be one of the most odious of crimes. It works as a particularly cruel form of blackmail or extortion and is designed ruthlessly to exploit the emotional bonds that connect human beings. It involves a deeply disturbing form of psychological terror because it plays upon the tantalising hope that the kidnapped person might somehow be saved and brought home alive and unhurt.

All the available evidence indicates that kidnapping causes profound and long-term emotional damage both to those who have been abducted and to those who wait helplessly for their return. Psychologists have recognised a number of personality changes that can occur as a result of the traumas induced by abduction. These can include a reluctance or inability to trust other people; a profound sense of social isolation; and a recurring state of deep anxiety.

Kidnapping has been described by Paul Howard as 'the crime of the 1970s'. It might be more accurate to say that political kidnapping was the crime of that decade. These abductions began in South America in the late 1960s, but soon spread to different countries and continents. On 5 October 1970, members of the Front de libération du Québec (FLQ) kidnapped James Cross from his private residence in Montreal at gunpoint. Cross had been born and raised in Ireland but, like many thousands of other Irishmen, he had joined the British army during the Second World War. He subsequently settled in the UK and became a Foreign Office diplomat.

Pierre Laporte, a Québec politician, was kidnapped by the FLQ a few days after Cross. He had been playing football with his young nephew and was also taken at gunpoint. His kidnappers demanded the release of twenty-three alleged political prisoners. The Canadian Prime Minister, Pierre Trudeau, responded by ordering mass raids and arrests of possible FLQ sympathisers. Seven days after he had been taken, Laporte's body was found in the boot of a car. It was later claimed that he was killed by his kidnappers in a moment of panic after he had tried to escape. Cross remained a hostage of the FLQ for over two months before his kidnappers were granted safe passage to Cuba and he was released.

In early 1973, there were rumours that a member of the Dublin government was about to be kidnapped by the IRA or a republican breakaway group. The security around Irish ministers was tightened and armed guards were detailed to accompany them at all times. According to Garret FitzGerald, all the Irish ministers agreed that, in the event of any of them being abducted, their colleagues would not negotiate with the kidnappers. It was also agreed that if one of their family members were abducted, then the minister affected 'would resign from cabinet and no concessions would be made'. The steps taken by the Irish government were not unreasonable. Before the decade was over, there would be more high-profile political abductions: Aldo Moro, a former Prime Minister of Italy, was taken by the Red Brigades and later killed, and Hanns Martin Schleyer, a German businessman, was abducted by the Red Army Faction and shot dead.

Brian Keenan had helped to forge close links between the IRA and the Basque terrorist group ETA (Euskadi ta Askatasuna). According to General Valentin Diaz Blanco who led Spain's counter-terrorism operations, 'ETA gave money to the IRA and the IRA provided weapons and explosives for ETA.' Both groups also trained and supported other terrorist groups around the world.

ETA had considerable experience of using kidnapping as a means of furthering its political goals. One kidnapping, in particular, may have influenced the IRA's decision to abduct Thomas Niedermayer. In December 1970, ETA kidnapped Eugene Biehl. Like Thomas Niedermayer, Biehl was an honorary German consul, and, in exchange for his release, ETA demanded clemency for some of its members who were in prison and awaiting execution. The Spanish authorities quickly gave way: the prisoners' sentences were commuted and Biehl was subsequently released. If nothing else, this indicated to the IRA that the kidnapping of consular representatives of Germany could prove highly effective from the kidnappers' perspective.

The terrorist group most associated with kidnapping for political reasons was FARC, which waged an armed campaign against Colombian governments for many years. From the early 1960s, this group carried out abductions on what approached an industrial scale. According to a recent report, more than 2,000 of those who were kidnapped died in captivity. What became of more than 10,000 others is still unknown. Brian Keenan helped to establish the first contacts between FARC and, according to General Blanco, both ETA and the IRA helped train FARC is the use of explosives. As recently as 2004, three men associated with Sinn Féin were convicted by a Colombian court of training FARC guerrillas. They fled the country and returned to Ireland, which has no extradition treaty with Colombia.

This was the context in which Brian Keenan decided to order the kidnapping of Thomas Niedermayer, his former boss at the Grundig factory. Keenan's intention was to ransom him for the Price sisters' transfer to jails in Northern Ireland. He reckoned that Niedermayer's status, both as a leading businessman and as an honorary diplomatic representative of Germany, would compel the British government to concede to his demands.

In recent years, Gerry Adams and other leading members of Sinn Féin have often been seen in the company of millionaire industrialists and entrepreneurs on their regular visits to the USA. 'We can't be getting support from US businesses on the one hand and then be bad for business on the other,' Adams told journalists in 2007. 'That's an oxymoron if you don't mind me saying so.' He may now attempt to joke about this matter but, back in the early 1970s, Sinn Féin supported the IRA's policy of killing businessmen and women in Northern Ireland and blowing up or burning down their businesses.

At that time, the IRA identified foreign companies and their managers as 'agents of multi-national capital' and of 'Imperialism' and, therefore, regarded them as legitimate targets of their campaign. This was an integral part of the IRA's operations in Northern Ireland and led to a number of business managers being assassinated. A gleeful headline in *Republican News* captures the callous attitude of the IRA towards such attacks: 'Panic Hits Local Capitalists as IRA Attacks Grass-Roots Imperialism'. It was from this period that Brian Keenan's reputation as a committed and hard-line 'Marxist' appears to date.

The IRA's targets included 'local capitalists' such as Jeffrey Agate, Managing Director of the DuPont chemical factory in Derry. This company had been encouraged to come to Derry by the same economic strategy followed by the Stormont government that had led Grundig to establish its factory in Dunmurry. Over several decades, DuPont had become part of Derry's industrial landscape. Agate was shot dead as he made his way home after a day's work. The IRA later issued a statement that sought to justify the killing: 'Those involved in the management of the economy serve British interests,' the statement read. 'They represent and maintain economic interests which make the war necessary.' (It might be worth noting that DuPont is, of course, an American and not a British company.)

Other casualties in the IRA's 'economic war' of that time did not even have the same high profile as Jeffrey Agate. These included James Nicholson, the director of a small audio firm. His company was one of the few to locate in those disadvantaged parts of West Belfast that the IRA counted among their principal strongholds. Nicholson was shot in the head by the IRA as he left his factory one evening. An IRA spokesperson later outlined the remarkably crude and feeble thinking behind the decision to kill him. 'England takes out Irish wealth,' he said. 'She is here for a profit. What the IRA can do is cut that profit. Instability creates a lack of confidence in capital here. People are not interested in investing if they know their investment is going to run dry on them.' The notion that the UK's involvement in Northern Ireland was driven by a desire for financial gain is clearly risible since the northern economy had been dependent for decades on large subventions every year from Westminster in order to remain solvent. But, no doubt, the IRA thought their mission to 'cut profits' had been accomplished when Nicholson's company went out of business and closed a few years later.

Further victims of this strategy included Robert Mitchell, an elderly retired businessman who was shot dead while at his home in County Armagh. Joseph Glover, the director of a family timber yard, was shot nine times by two gunmen when he answered the door of his home in Derry. He was due to appear on stage later that night in an amateur drama production of a Gilbert and Sullivan operetta.

Yvonne Dunlop died when the IRA fire-bombed the small clothing shop in Ballymena, the Alley Katz Boutique, which her father owned. She was checking a shopping bag that had been left in the shop by two young women when the bomb exploded. Her 9-year-old son was with her, and she had just enough time to shout a warning to him before she died. Donald Robinson ran a ceiling repair business and was serving a customer when two IRA gunmen arrived at his place of work. They made Robinson and his assistant lie on the floor and then shot Robinson three times in the head.

Whatever claims the IRA might make, these people hardly represented the cutting edge of 'grassroots imperialism' (whatever that means). However, judged by the political criteria that led to their deaths, Thomas Niedermayer could also be considered a 'legitimate target' by the IRA.

Soon after the trial of Dolours and Marian Price, Keenan decided to abduct his former boss at Grundig and hold him as a bargaining chip to secure the sisters' repatriation. He reckoned that Niedermayer's status both as a leading businessman and as a diplomatic representative of

Germany would compel the British government to concede to his demands. According to Alan Simpson, an RUC officer who later played a key role in resolving the mystery of Thomas Niedermayer's disappearance, Keenan's decision was also fuelled by 'a personal grudge' that he harboured against his former boss. This may have been caused by confrontations between the two men when Keenan was a shop steward at the Dunmurry factory, or may have been due to Niedermayer's decision to fire him.

By mid-December 1973, Keenan's plans had been laid, but in order to gain the maximum media coverage of the event – always one of the IRA's primary concerns – it was decided to wait until just after the Christmas festivities. The kidnapping of a well-respected figure was clearly a high-risk gamble for the IRA and reflected the single-mindedness of Keenan's character. But, if it proved successful, it could also be regarded as a major coup for the IRA – one that would resonate far beyond Northern Ireland.

On the night of Thursday, 27 December 1973, at around eleven o'clock, a car pulled up outside the Niedermayers' modest bungalow at Glengoland Gardens near Andersonstown in Belfast. Two men got out and rang the doorbell. It was opened by the Niedermayers' 15-year-old daughter, Renate. She was one of two family members in the house that night: the other was her father, Thomas. Renate's elder sister, Gabriele, was staying overnight with a friend and her mother, Ingeborg, had been admitted to the Musgrave Park Clinic in south Belfast on Christmas Eve.

Thomas and Ingeborg on their wedding day, 1952.
(*Photo courtesy of Tanya and Rachel Williams-Powell.*)

Ingeborg with daughters Renate and Gabriele (l-to-r).
(*Photo courtesy of Tanya and Rachel Williams-Powell.*)

From a young age, Renate showed an affinity for animals. *(Photo courtesy of Tanya and Rachel Williams-Powell.)*

Thomas, Renate and Gabriele feeding pigeons outside Belfast City Hall in the early 1960s. *(Photo courtesy of Tanya and Rachel Williams-Powell.)*

Thomas with his daughters on a family outing. He enjoyed exploring Ireland, especially trips to the seaside. (*Photo courtesy of Tanya and Rachel Williams-Powell.*)

The Niedermayers' two daughters, Gabriele and Renate, in the mid-1960s. (*Photo courtesy of Tanya and Rachel Williams-Powell.*)

The Niedermayer family in happier times. (*Photo courtesy of* Belfast News Letter.)

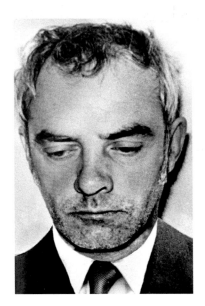

Brian Keenan, a former shop steward at the Grundig factory, was never charged for his part in the Niedermayer kidnapping. (*Photo courtesy of Alan Lewis Media.*)

Brian Keenan's funeral in 2008. Pall-bearers included former Republican comrades, the Balcombe Street Gang, and Mary Lou McDonald, who would go on to lead Sinn Féin in 2018. (*Photo courtesy of Alan Lewis Media.*)

The Grundig factory at Dunmurry, where Thomas was General Manager from 1961. (*Photo by the author.*)

The current entrance to Colin Glen, where Thomas's body was recovered in 1980. It is now a public park. (*Photo by the author.*)

Ingeborg places flowers on the grave of her husband.
(*Photo courtesy of* Belfast Telegraph.)

Ingeborg, supported by her daughters Gabriele and
Renate, at Thomas's funeral in 1980. (*Photo courtesy of*
Belfast Telegraph.)

Tanya Williams-Powell is the elder daughter of Gabriele Niedermayer and Robin Williams-Powell.
(*Photo courtesy of Shane Deasy.*)

Rachel Williams-Powell is the younger daughter of Gabriele Niedermayer and Robin Williams-Powell.
(*Photo courtesy of Haydn Keenan.*)

One of Renate's friends, Maria McCann, had been at her house that evening and they had chatted over tea and biscuits. She remembers that Thomas was in his study when she went home that night. Renate had spent some time watching television but was already in bed when she heard the doorbell ring twice. When she went to open the door, she saw two men standing outside. They told her that there had been an accident that had resulted in some damage to her father's car, which was parked outside their house. Thomas was already asleep, so Renate woke him and he went outside to inspect his car. He had dressed quickly and was still wearing his slippers when he left the house. Across the road, Herbert Hoech, a German national who also worked in the Grundig factory, happened to be awake. He was getting a glass of water when he saw the brake lights of a car on the road opposite his house. He went into his living room to take a closer look and so witnessed what happened next.

Hoech noticed that a third man was already in the driver's seat of the other car. Niedermayer inspected the alleged damage to his Ford Granada. He was making his way back to his house when Hoech saw him being grabbed from behind by the two men. A brief struggle took place before Niedermayer was bundled into the back of the men's car. Hoech shouted to his wife that two men were fighting with Thomas. He pulled on a tracksuit and ran out to help, but the car had already been driven off at speed. Thomas Niedermayer was never seen alive by his family or friends again.

In the minutes that followed the abduction, Hoech was unsure about what exactly he had witnessed. He knew that Ingeborg was in hospital, and thought there might have been an emergency that had necessitated Thomas's presence. He also thought that the struggle might simply have been some friends forcing Thomas to go to a Christmas party. Hoech went back inside and phoned the security officer for the Grundig factory who lived nearby. He then called at the home of another Grundig employee who lived next door to Thomas. Together, they decided to call the British army base at Woodbourne near Andersonstown.

An army patrol arrived a short time later, but by then it had been almost an hour since the abduction. Another hour passed before the army rang the RUC and reported what had happened. By then, Niedermayer had already been moved into a house that had been commandeered by the IRA, and the room where he would be kept as a prisoner for the remainder of his life.

In the immediate aftermath of the kidnapping, there was a good deal of press speculation about which group might have been responsible. Within days, the initial assumption that Niedermayer had been taken as a prelude to political bargaining was, according to David McKittrick writing in *The Irish Times*, 'beginning to give way to speculation concerning his financial and domestic situation'. Such speculation might seem somewhat puzzling. The German businessman had been kidnapped close to a nationalist area that was regarded as a stronghold of the IRA. It may have seemed obvious who the likely culprits were, but a range of alternative theories were soon being advanced.

The Ireland correspondent of the London *Times*, for example, informed his readers that it was 'unlikely that the IRA were responsible' for Niedermayer's disappearance. It appears that this journalist had been personally assured by the 'Provisionals in the IRA battalion in Andersonstown' that 'they knew nothing about it'. He was also prepared to accept the word of the IRA leader, 'Mr Seamus Twomey', that 'his organisation had nothing to do with the kidnapping'. With a breathtaking degree of cynicism, the IRA not only denied having anything to do with the abduction but claimed that their own volunteers had joined in the search for the missing businessman.

Perhaps the explanation that the IRA had abducted Niedermayer seemed just too obvious for some journalists. The *Times* man in Belfast was certainly not the first nor the last reporter who was tempted to look for some hidden narrative or unexpected reasons that might have motivated the kidnappers. Perhaps some journalists wanted to signal to their readers that they had an exclusive inside track on this story. The obvious explanation may not have been exciting; nonetheless, it happened to be true. British cabinet ministers were made aware of that fact when they met the following morning: Although the IRA had claimed responsibility for the abduction in an initial phone call to the British authorities, the British government chose not to reveal that information either to the public or to the Niedermayer family. Instead, they claimed to have an 'open mind' about who Niedermayer's abductors might be. Perhaps, they were simply waiting for a subsequent phone call that would confirm IRA involvement – after all, kidnappers are always supposed to ring twice. Or perhaps this was because they had their own specific reasons to allow the public to believe that someone else may have been responsible for the abduction. Either way, a second call never came and, as it turned out, there were good reasons for that silence.

21.
The Edge of the World

Government papers that were recently released show that Niedermayer's abduction was discussed by the British cabinet the morning after he was kidnapped. It was immediately assumed by the British that responsibility lay with the IRA. That may have been confirmed by more than one phone call from the IRA. One of those believed to have been involved in the abduction was an IRA member called Roy McShane. He was a trusted figure within the IRA who later became Gerry Adams' personal driver, but in 2008 McShane was revealed to be a long-term agent of MI5. He was taken into protective custody and quickly removed from Northern Ireland.

The German government was immediately advised of Niedermayer's abduction and so was Max Grundig. At first, he assumed that this was a simple shakedown and a case of paying a hefty financial ransom to the IRA for Niedermayer's release. Grundig immediately indicated he was prepared to pay whatever the cost and the company Chairman, Adolf Wohltraub, was sent to Belfast from the head office in Nuremberg to assess and negotiate the situation. A German detective who was reported to be 'a specialist in kidnapping cases' also arrived in Northern Ireland, leading to speculation in *The Irish Times* that 'some new turn of events has emerged'. Meanwhile, Ingeborg Niedermayer was released from the Musgrave Park Clinic and had returned home to be with her daughters.

Although the British Government denied at first that they had received any ransom demand from the IRA, that claim was quickly exposed as false. The first public indication of what might have happened came three weeks after the abduction when Ian Paisley, speaking from the pulpit of his church, claimed that Niedermayer had already been murdered by the IRA. He also claimed that the IRA had sent the British an ultimatum which had been ignored.

In response, the new Secretary of State for Northern Ireland, Francis Pym, reaffirmed his government's determination not to negotiate under threats. He believed that such negotiations would only encourage more kidnappings. He did, however, concede that the British had received a demand for the transfer of the Price sisters three days after the kidnapping and accepted that their initial denials had not been entirely accurate. He claimed this was because there had been no further call from the kidnappers – which might reasonably have been expected.

This admission – and the glaring conflict between the two versions of events that the British had circulated within a matter of days – led some to conclude that the public had still not been told the whole truth. Since the British had an obvious interest in portraying the IRA as nothing but common criminals who were prepared to resort to kidnapping an innocent man, some journalists suspected that neither version of this story was credible.

The fact that the British had heard nothing more from the IRA after their first demand also aroused suspicions: kidnappers, after all, need to make sustained contact if a ransom is ever to be paid. The repeated and apparently sincere denials from the IRA that they had anything to do with the abduction further convinced some journalists that there was more to this kidnapping that met the eye. That assumption was not confined to the mainstream media. One left-wing magazine in the UK even claimed that the real 'brains' behind the kidnapping was Herbert Hoech – the neighbour who had witnessed the abduction and had tried to help Thomas Niedermayer. It was claimed that the delays in alerting the RUC to the kidnapping constituted proof that Hoech was either working for British Intelligence or loyalist paramilitaries,

In the immediate aftermath, the leaders of the major Christian churches described the kidnapping as 'an exceptional social case' since Niedermayer was both a 'foreign national and an official representative of the German people'. At Stormont, Brian Faulkner said that it was 'nothing short of a tragedy that a guest in our land, a good friend of our people and indeed a consular representative of his government should now be the cause of such justifiable concern'.

The shop stewards at the Grundig factory in Dunmurry issued a joint statement the morning after the abduction in which they pleaded for his release in the interests of all working people in Northern Ireland. One of them told a television news reporter that Niedermayer had been held in great respect by his workforce, who regarded Grundig 'as a model factory' and one 'where Catholics and Protestants can work together equally'. In their statement, the shop stewards called 'on all trade unionists to join with us in condemning this callous act and to use all their strength to show the world that we will not tolerate it'. They were not aware that the person who planned the kidnapping had once been one of their fellow shop stewards.

Everyone awaited the first contact from the kidnappers, but no sustained contact was ever made and no formal ransom demand was ever received by Niedermayer's family. In any event, both the British and German governments were opposed to meeting any demand from the kidnappers. The Irish government also signalled through diplomatic channels that it 'understood and sympathised with the British position'. Edward Heath, the British Prime Minister, sent a private message to the

German Chancellor, Willy Brandt, in which he stated his unequivocal belief that, if Niedermayer's kidnappers 'appeared to achieve success', it would put 'other innocent lives' at risk and 'particularly German nationals'. Once again, the question of Heath's own political priorities arises. In the lengthy memoirs which he published some years later, Heath fails to mention Thomas Niedermayer or his kidnapping. He does, however, devote considerable space to his efforts at that time to shepherd the UK into the European Economic Community.

Initially, as the London *Times* reported, the IRA denied any part in the abduction. This was not because the abduction was an 'unofficial' action that was unauthorised by the IRA: given the number of IRA members involved in the abduction, it would have been highly improbable that the Army Council was not aware of what was planned. Indeed, it later emerged that the IRA's leadership had been advised in advance and approved of the decision to kidnap Niedermayer. That decision may have only been known to a relatively small number of individuals, but the real reason for the IRA's denial of involvement was because Keenan's ransom plan had quickly run into unforeseen difficulties. The intention had been to use the German businessman to secure the transfer of the Price sisters and other prisoners to jails in Northern Ireland, but within three days of Niedermayer's abduction, he was already dead – and unable to be used in any future bargaining.

The first public indication of what might have happened came three weeks after the abduction when Ian Paisley claimed that Niedermayer had already been murdered by the IRA. He also claimed that the IRA had sent the British an ultimatum which had been ignored. In response, the new Secretary of State for Northern Ireland, Francis Pym, reaffirmed his government's determination not to negotiate under threats. He believed that such negotiations would only encourage more kidnappings. He did, however, concede that the British had received a demand for the transfer of the Price sisters three days after the kidnapping and accepted that this had not been acknowledged by the cabinet. Niedermayer's family in Germany deplored this refusal to negotiate. His brother, Alfred, and sister, Hertha, said that they had learned 'with great shock' that the life of their brother had been put at risk because of the 'unyielding stance' of the British.

Paisley also claimed to have sent a telegram to the German Chancellor, Willy Brandt, but complained that he had not received a reply. Paisley's interventions were not well received by other parties. The SDLP believed that his comments had only 'added to the confusion'. The Labour Party spokesperson for Northern Ireland, Merlyn Rees, expressed his displeasure at Paisley's 'antics'. Francis Pym claimed that 'everything was being done that could be done' in relation to Niedermayer's kidnapping. He also pointed out that the citizens in Northern Ireland currently enjoyed 'a favoured position' in relation to financial subventions from Westminster but in a veiled threat to the sustainability of the Union, added that he 'could not speak for the future'.

However, Pym was not able to deny all of Paisley's claims, and it was obvious that Paisley had been leaked confidential information from sources within the British Home Office. When Pym's admission was made public, the RUC had still not been advised of such a development. This left the detectives working on the case bewildered as to why they had been kept in the dark. They had by that stage spent valuable time pursuing false leads and felt understandably aggrieved. Grundig also questioned whether the British authorities were investigating this kidnapping with sufficient urgency. The company announced that it intended to open its own investigation – despite being asked by the West German government not to 'hamper the official search'.

It was assumed at first that the IRA intended to move Niedermayer to a safe house somewhere south of the Irish border. As a result of increased security, the Gardaí arrested two men as they attempted to drive across the border from County Donegal into Northern Ireland. Their car was found to contain 250 pounds of explosives along with several thousand rounds of ammunition. One of the men arrested was Martin McGuinness, who would later become the Deputy First Minister of Northern Ireland. McGuinness commanded the IRA in Derry when the commercial centre of the city was bombed so frequently that it looked as though it had experienced an aerial bombardment. In the early 1970s, McGuinness dismissed the civilian casualties caused by these explosions in similar terms to those used by Dolours Price when she was asked about the bombs she had planted in London. 'We've always given ample warnings,' McGuinness told one American journalist. 'Anyone hurt was hurt through their own fault: being too nosey or sticking around the place where the bomb was after they were told to get clear.' A court in Dublin jailed him for six months for membership of an illegal organisation, a remarkably lenient sentence given the circumstances of his arrest.

The last time Ingeborg had seen her husband was on the night of his abduction. He had visited her in hospital and brought a bunch of red roses to her bedside. Soon after his disappearance, she pleaded with his abductors. 'Please let me know what has happened to my husband,' she begged in a television broadcast. 'Give me peace within myself. No one can appreciate the agony and strain you are putting me and my daughters through. I pray that you will show me some human compassion.'

A few weeks later, advertisements were placed in local newspapers, begging for information, and she issued a further desperate appeal: 'Please give me some sign to put an end to this dreadful uncertainty.' If her husband were still alive, she told his kidnappers, they 'could ask for anything and we would get it'. She added that, if Thomas were not alive, 'then at least give me some information of where his body may be found, so that he can be decently buried and can rest in peace. I beg of you let me know soon. You have been silent long enough.'

In the immediate aftermath of the abduction, the Niedermayer family seems to have become isolated – even from some of their neighbours and friends. Maria McCann remembers the sense of mystery that surrounded Thomas's disappearance. 'Nobody was saying what had happened,' she recalls, 'but nobody wanted to intrude on the family.' There was a fear that asking questions might be unwelcome or 'overstepping the mark', and Maria's father said that the Niedermayers 'needed their privacy'. Perhaps some of the neighbours also feared that they might somehow be drawn into the web of violence that had claimed Thomas. Maria began to grow distant from her friend Renate, and she recognises that 'as time went on, that gap grew'. Eventually, too much time had passed and there was no way for either of them to reclaim their former easy friendship.

The pressure on Ingeborg was increased by the extent of press speculation about where her husband might have been taken. Stories were published that suggested he had been moved to England or America. One article claimed that he had been taken prisoner by arms traffickers. It was claimed that he had been taken out of Ireland on a yacht which had been blown up close to the Isle of Man after Niedermayer had been shot dead. The German magazine 'Bild am Samstag' even published an interview with someone who claimed to have been present on the boat when Niedermayer was murdered. As events subsequently proved, this was a complete fantasy, and it seems remarkable that this account was treated as credible by any reputable journalist since there was not a shred of corroborative evidence.

Equally distressing were the anonymous letters which Ingeborg received claiming that her husband had simply run off with 'another woman'. This 'other woman' was sometimes alleged to be his secretary June McClinton, who remembers one instance of this baseless rumour being circulated. 'I was in the supermarket one day and I was behind these two ladies,' she recalls, 'and their attitude was "he's not killed. He's away off with his secretary." That was when I jumped in. I tapped one on the shoulder and said, "Excuse me, but I'm the lady you're talking about." I said, "The next time you're discussing somebody, make sure you've got the proper measure of that person." They were very embarrassed.'

There were also a number of hoax calls demanding cash payments, threatening that Ingeborg would never see her husband again. A self-styled clairvoyant from County Kerry offered to assist the investigation. He claimed to have been responsible for locating where Ronnie Biggs, the Great Train Robber, was hiding out in Brazil. This gentleman sat for four hours moving a hawthorn stick between photos of Niedermayer and a map of Ireland before announcing that the German businessman was being held in a house twelve miles outside Belfast. Over the following months, more than half a dozen clairvoyants or spiritualists – including one in Holland who claimed to have 'seen' Thomas's corpse while in a trance – suggested different locations where Thomas would be found. A spokesperson for the RUC assured the press that all leads – even those from clairvoyants – would be considered. It is, perhaps, not surprising that all of these and similar 'leads' proved quite worthless.

The RUC also received a large number of tip-offs from its various informants within the IRA. While these provided a valuable source of accurate intelligence, they were short on details. Their value was also compromised by a number of deliberately false calls made to the RUC's confidential telephone service that were designed to lure police officers into IRA ambushes.

One of their informants inside the IRA led the RUC to conduct a substantial search of the Colin Glen area of west Belfast within a few days of the abduction, This included the actual location where Thomas's body had been buried and where it was eventually found. The RUC officers were supported by soldiers with tracker dogs, and the area was also scanned by an army helicopter. However 'nothing of significance' was detected, and the search was called off. Two further searches of Colin Glen took place in 1974, and in one of them some blood-stained sheets were found. Once again, tracker dogs were deployed, but, once again, the conclusion reached was that 'nothing of significance' had been found and the search was abandoned.

An anonymous caller to the confidential telephone service in May 1974 told the police that Thomas had been held in a specific house in Andersonstown. The caller named the owners of the house, and said that they had recently seen blood stains in the spare room. The Army conducted a search of the house identified but concluded that there was no substance to the anonymous allegation. It was another six years before it was established that the information provided by this caller had in fact been accurate.

In June of that year, six months after the abduction, Ingeborg issued what she said would be her 'last and final' appeal. 'It is terrible living like this and never knowing,' she said in the radio broadcast, her voice breaking with stress and pain. 'I beg these people to let me know – my life has been shattered.'

There was no response from the IRA to any of her appeals. Instead, Ingeborg and her family were condemned for years to what Judith Herman has aptly described as 'a kind of limbo'. They were unable to grieve for the loss of Thomas, or to accept that he might be dead 'because that would feel like a betrayal', and so they 'clung to hope even when that hope (was) unrealistic'. If the first crime committed by the IRA was the abduction of an innocent man, then the second was their deliberate withholding of information from his innocent family.

In fact, as Kevin Myers has pointed out, the IRA did not simply claim to have no knowledge of Thomas's fate; they insisted in the strongest terms for most of the following decade on their own innocence, repeatedly swearing that they had absolutely nothing to do with Thomas's disappearance. As a result of their repeated denials, Judith Herman believes the Niedermayer family were prevented, in several ways, from getting on with the rest of their own lives. According to one of the RUC officers investigating the case, 'It was as though a man walked twenty-five yards to his front door and fell off the edge of the world.'

22.
The Awful Reality

Niedermayer's kidnapping came at a critical time in the history of the Northern Irish state, and one which would impact on the public perception of what had occurred. In March 1973 – just days after the border poll in Northern Ireland and the IRA bombs in London – the British government published a White Paper that proposed the establishment of a new devolved Assembly and Executive at Stormont. It was proposed that this new Assembly would be elected by proportional representation, which, it was believed, would make it less likely to be dominated by unionists. The White Paper also proposed the creation of a new Council of Ireland, which would include elected representatives from both sides of the Irish border.

An election to the Northern Ireland Assembly took place in June and those parties in favour of the new dispensation won a comfortable majority of seats. They included the SDLP, the Alliance Party and the Northern Ireland Labour Party. They also included the Unionist Party, since Brian Faulkner had displayed his essential pragmatism by throwing his weight behind the British proposals. The unionists who supported him won twenty-four seats in the new Assembly. However, unionists who opposed the White Paper proposals won twenty-six. This left Faulkner politically exposed and unable to speak with authority on behalf of the unionist population as a whole. Unionist fears of British betrayal were further heightened by the irredentist rhetoric used by some SDLP politicians and by the apparent momentum of the nationalist political agenda.

In March 1973, the Fianna Fáil government in Dublin, led by Jack Lynch, had been replaced by a coalition of Fine Gael and the Irish Labour Party. The new Taoiseach was Liam Cosgrave, the son of the President of the first Executive Council of the Irish Free State. Like his father before him, Cosgrave loathed the IRA, which he described as 'a conspiracy of hate and evil'. Even so, he seemed much less interested in Northern Ireland than his predecessors and his principal concern was that violence should not be allowed to spill over the border. This allowed the SDLP to exert considerable influence and, some might say, even to dictate the Irish government's northern policy. That led Dublin to support an ambitious agenda for its future negotiations with Faulkner and the unionists he represented. And, as the IRA continued to escalate its campaign throughout the remainder of 1973, Protestant opposition to the British proposals grew in strength and determination.

The discussions between the various pro-Agreement parties and the British and Irish governments took place at Sunningdale House, Berkshire, in the south of England. The main items to be negotiated were internment, policing and a new all-island authority: the Council of Ireland. On 21 November, an agreement was reached to establish a voluntary coalition with Faulkner as its Chief Executive and Gerry Fitt of the SDLP as his Deputy. This was the first power-sharing regime in the history of the Northern Irish state and the new Executive met for the first time on 1 January 1974, just a few days after Niedermayer's abduction. According to Kenneth Bloomfield, a senior civil servant present, the kidnapping focused the minds of the Executive's members and 'reminded us of the awful realities of continuing violence'. Six years later, Bloomfield would play a critical role in the recovery of Herr Niedermayer's body.

Edward Heath's intention was clearly to marginalise those unionists who had not been invited to take part in the Sunningdale negotiations. However, as William Beattie Smith has observed, they did not simply disappear. In fact, they gathered strength and were able to persuade increasing numbers of their community that they were about to be betrayed by the British government and be pushed into a united Ireland. Sir Arthur Galsworthy, the British Ambassador to Ireland, noted that Faulkner had 'made more concessions than anybody else at Sunningdale' and that the southern government 'had conceded hardly anything'. Gerry Fitt, the leader of the SDLP, later blamed the Irish government's stubborn insistence on the Council of Ireland for the subsequent downfall of the power-sharing Executive.

That view came to be shared by more than one member of the Irish delegation at Sunningdale. Garret FitzGerald, the Irish Minister for Foreign Affairs, later admitted that some of the reservations expressed about the Council by his cabinet colleague, Conor Cruise O'Brien, proved to have been justified. According to O'Brien, at the time of the Agreement, FitzGerald showed 'no understanding of unionist feeling' and told him in a tone 'of cold superiority' that 'the Protestant population would accept the Council of Ireland without difficulty'.

It soon became clear, however, that unionist opposition to the Agreement would focus on the proposed Council of Ireland. The original council had been established under the terms of the Government of Ireland Act in 1920. It had been intended as an all-Ireland legislative authority that would have roughly equal representation of both unionists and nationalists. However, in 1922, Michael Collins and James Craig – the *de facto* leaders of the two nascent Irish states – met in London. They agreed that they would work together to 'devise a more suitable system than the Council of Ireland for dealing with problems affecting all Ireland'. Sadly, Collins was assassinated later that year and no alternative system was ever devised.

This Council of Ireland was effectively abolished in 1925. When it re-emerged in the Sunningdale Agreement, many unionists feared it would be used as a stepping stone to an all-Ireland state. Their fears were exacerbated when some nationalist representatives claimed in public that this was precisely what had been achieved at Sunningdale. John Hume, in particular, made it clear that he viewed the Council as the political mechanism through which Irish unity could be achieved. He believed that the Council would be instrumental in removing any 'problems in the way of unity' and would 'have the power to plan a constitution for a new Ireland'. And there were other developments that seemed to give credence to those unionists who opposed the Agreement when they claimed that 'Dublin is only a Sunningdale away.'

The ink, so to speak, was hardly dry on the Agreement before the Irish Taoiseach, Liam Cosgrave, gave an interview to the *Sunday Press* in which he claimed that a united Ireland would be delivered as a result of Sunningdale. Cosgrave stated in unambiguous terms that there was 'no question of changing our Constitution with regard to our claim of sovereignty over all of Ireland'. The Irish Attorney General, Declan Costello, confirmed that the reunification of Ireland was still a 'constitutional imperative'. Anti-Agreement unionists were able to quote statements such as these as concrete proof that the assurances made by the Irish government at Sunningdale were worthless and that Faulkner had been duped.

Cosgrave's interview with the *Sunday Press* was followed by a challenge in Dublin's High Court to the constitutional legality of the Sunningdale legislation. The Irish government felt compelled to deny in court that the Agreement had recognised Northern Ireland's status as an integral part of the United Kingdom. It was also claimed by the Irish government that the Sunningdale Agreement had not conceded the right of consent to unionists. Instead, it was argued that the Agreement had merely acknowledged the right of unionists to negotiate the ways in which a united Ireland might be created.

Against this background, it soon became clear that the internal divisions of unionism were growing deeper. The Standing Committee of the Unionist Party voted to participate in the new Executive, but Faulkner and his supporters were only able to win a narrow and precarious victory. And, in an ominous development for the future of the new administration, all of the major loyalist paramilitary groups came together on 10 December 1973 – the day after the Sunningdale Agreement had been formalised – to establish an 'Ulster Army Council'. Its sole stated purpose was to frustrate British and Irish policy and bring down the incoming Executive.

This was the context in which British Military Intelligence tried to sow distrust and suspicion among the dissenting unionists in the hope that such division would damage and disrupt any plans they might form to collapse the Executive. Military Intelligence used off-the-record briefings to the press to suggest that Niedermayer's kidnappers were not IRA members, but loyalist paramilitaries. There proved to be no shortage of journalists who were eager to swallow that lure – hook, line and sinker.

23.

Fake News

In the early 1970s, British Military Intelligence was embedded in the Thiepval Barracks in Lisburn, some miles to the south of Belfast. A stream of deliberate disinformation flowed out from that location to both the local and international press. Some of these stories were so far-fetched that it is hard to believe that anyone ever took them seriously. In one of these, fake 'black magic' altars were built by a serving member of the British Ministry of Defence and doused in chicken blood. They were then presented to the press as concrete evidence that the IRA was actively engaged in witchcraft. Another bogus story was circulated that IRA detonators hidden in women's knickers could explode prematurely due to the static electricity generated by the friction of their legs. The *Sunday Mirror* published this nonsense under the enticing headline, 'Danger in those Frilly Panties'.

Much of this 'black propaganda' was directed against republican terrorists, but it was also used by Military

Intelligence to discredit loyalist paramilitaries. For that reason, bogus communiques had been written in the Thiepval Barracks and issued in the name of a purported 'Ulster Citizens' Army'. This 'Army' only existed in the minds of those in Thiepval who had written the communiqués, but this fictitious entity issued statements naming prominent loyalists who were allegedly embezzling funds from their organisations – a very dangerous accusation to make in Belfast at that time.

In this context it is not surprising that, within days of Niedermayer's kidnapping, journalists were being fed a range of often contradictory theories about the reasons for his disappearance. According to *The Irish Times*, there were 'mysterious references to non-political motivations' behind his abduction. Some of the sources for these rumours were members of the IRA who wanted to conceal their involvement in the abduction. That may explain the scurrilous suggestion that Herbert Hoech, the only witness to the kidnapping, was connected with the UVF and had helped to set up Niedermayer's abduction. This rumour, which had been spread by British Intelligence sources, was picked up by several far-left groups in the UK and treated as if it were credible.

Following the abduction, journalists were given off-the-record briefings from MI5 officers that suggested alternative reasons for what had happened. In two of these scenarios, loyalists were blamed for the kidnapping. According to Robert Fisk, who was then the Belfast correspondent for the London *Times,* journalists were told that 'a prominent Protestant politician was involved in the murder of the former West German Honorary Consul to Belfast'. The reason given was that the politician's wife was allegedly having an affair with Niedermayer. The woman in question was supposed to be Doris Hilgendorff. Her husband was William Craig, the anti-Sunningdale unionist politician. The obvious reason that she had been chosen for the role of Niedermayer's lover in this version of events seemed to be simply that, like him, she was German.

In an alternative version of this story, it was Craig who was having the affair with Ingeborg Niedermayer – since, it was claimed, he had a preference for German women. In both versions, Craig had apparently asked his loyalist paramilitary pals to dispose of Niedermayer and the German businessman had been abducted and murdered by them. According to another scenario, loyalists were smuggling arms into Northern Ireland, concealed in Grundig containers. Niedermayer had found out about this and threatened to go to the police: he was murdered by loyalists to prevent him from doing so. Neither of these stories gained much traction within Northern Ireland but they were picked up and given credence by some mainstream British newspapers, including the *Observer.* These rumours even reached the headquarters of Interpol, who asked the RUC to investigate if they had any substance. It did not take long for that possibility to be discounted.

From an early stage in the Troubles, the conflict in Northern Ireland had attracted foreign reporters. Perhaps it was the exoticism of having murder and mayhem on Europe's doorstep that drew some (mainly male) journalists: they could hop on a plane in Berlin or London and within hours be discussing military tactics over a pint with a real (or pretend) paramilitary commander. Perhaps they were seduced by what Ian McBride has described as the split personality of Ulster and its 'unsettling combination of humdrum provincialism with the twisted glamour of guerrilla warfare'. In this instance, the IRA's strategy was to direct foreign journalists towards those IRA members who were genuinely unaware that Niedermayer had been kidnapped by members of their own organisation. The palpable sincerity they displayed in denying any IRA involvement convinced some journalists that they had access to the inside track on this story.

In Dublin, the *Irish Press* published what purported to be an exclusive interview with an unnamed loyalist 'commander'. He claimed that his organisation had killed Niedermayer because he 'knew too much'. He also boasted that the body would never be found: 'I can guarantee that,' he told the *Irish Press* journalist, claiming that Niedermayer's corpse had already been incinerated. In reality, the loyalist 'commander' interviewed by the *Irish Press* journalist was working to a script that was almost certainly prepared by British Intelligence. The editorial stance taken by the *Irish Press* at that time was one of strident nationalism, and the newspaper may have been predisposed to absolve republicans from involvement in the kidnapping. However, the account published was completely untrue and little if any thought appears to have given – either by intelligence officers or by the responsible editor – to the disturbing effect this bogus claim might have had on Niedermayer's surviving wife and children.

Similar fictions were also embraced with enthusiasm by some elements of the German press. In 1974, the German tabloid *Bild* had the largest circulation of any newspaper in Europe. *Bild* chose to follow the 'cuckolded husband' storyline with a front-page splash that posed the question, 'Did the Consul die because of a Romance?' The accompanying article suggested that loyalists had murdered Niedermayer because of his alleged affair with William Craig's wife. There was no truth in this story and Doris Hilgendorff appeared on German television to deny its veracity. *Bild* was subsequently sued for defamation by Craig. In November 1975, he was awarded a five-figure sum in damages by the High Court in London.

Der Spiegel is often regarded as one of continental Europe's most influential news magazines and currently claims a readership of several million. The magazine has prided itself on the quality of its investigative journalism and the role that *Der Spiegel* has played in uncovering some major political scandals. *Der Spiegel* has disdained what it has termed the 'nonsense threshold of American and British tabloids' and has deplored the 'daily dose of high-resolution soft porn' provided by *Bild*. However, that did not mean *Der Spiegel* was not prone to publishing its own sensational stories about Northern Ireland.

In 1973, Seamus Twomey, who was then the IRA's Chief of Staff, and two other leading IRA figures escaped from Mountjoy prison in Dublin. A helicopter landed in the exercise yard of Mountjoy, and Twomey and the two others were airlifted out. Their escape made headlines across the world. Shortly after it occurred, Twomey gave an interview to a *Spiegel* journalist who congratulated him warmly on his 'daring escape', and informed him that people all over Europe were 'joking about the incident.'

This interview took place at a time when the 'economic war' being conducted by the IRA in Northern Ireland involved bombing small businesses and killing their managers and owners. Twomey supported the IRA's strategy of targeting high-profile civilians such as Thomas Niedermayer, as he believed that 'hitting that type of person' would result in 'putting more pressure on the British government'. However, he was not pressed – or even questioned – on this belief by the German journalist. That may have been because, according to Kevin Myers, who was well-acquainted with the journalist in question, his political views were sympathetic to the IRA.

In early 1974, the same *Spiegel* journalist claimed to have conducted his own thorough investigation – which included further 'information' supplied by Seamus

Twomey – and to have uncovered the 'real' truth about Niedermayer's abduction, which had taken place just five weeks previously. The journalist did not question Twomey's motives for supplying this 'information' and neither did his editors. In the article, Niedermayer's previous career was described as reading like a 'picture book'. The article recounted how he had worked his way up 'from mechanic to factory director'. Now, the magazine stated, that rosy picture was about to be shattered.

A member of Ireland's Department of Foreign Affairs (DFA) met the *Spiegel* journalist at a drinks reception in Dublin while the story was being researched. The next day, the DFA man reported their conversation to his superiors, revealing that the journalist had told him Niedermayer had been having domestic difficulties at home because his wife had become an alcoholic. The journalist also claimed that Niedermayer had been having 'a number of liaisons with girls working in his firm'. According to the *Spiegel* journalist, Niedermayer had known his abductors and they were not members of the IRA. Instead, it was suggested that the explanation for Niedermayer's disappearance could be found in his numerous adulterous affairs. This false information was passed on to the DFA man's senior colleagues without any critical comment or any reservation expressed about its accuracy or truthfulness.

Some of the same groundless rumours surfaced in the *Spiegel* article when it published the following week

– though now it was Niedermayer and not his wife who was an alcoholic. The article began by mentioning that the 'fanatical Protestant leader', Ian Paisley, had claimed that Niedermayer had been murdered by the IRA. 'But that is only how it seemed,' *Der Spiegel* informed its readers. This journalist claimed to have discovered that 'it was not the IRA, but militant Protestants who kidnapped Niedermayer'. *Der Spiegel*'s journalist included both the 'arms smuggling' and the adultery scenarios in his article and claimed that Niedermayer had been killed because he knew of loyalist plans to use Grundig containers to ship arms to Northern Ireland. It was 'not clear', the article stated, 'if he had been told of the plan, or learned of it by chance'. The answer to this imaginary conundrum was – neither.

Kevin Myers told me that he had played an inadvertent but significant role in the development of this bogus story. He described his role as that of a 'useful idiot' – a term allegedly coined by Lenin to describe those who were objectively helping the Bolsheviks without realising the full implications of their actions. Myers says he was approached by a *Spiegel* journalist and asked if he could verify that loyalists had been involved in smuggling arms to Ireland in Grundig containers. Myers approached one of his regular contacts in the UVF, the loyalist paramilitary group. Jim Hanna was a senior figure in that terrorist organisation and he 'confirmed' the truth of the rumour of loyalist involvement in the abduction. The actual reason why Hanna chose to verify a story that he must have known was untrue may have been revealed the following year when he was executed by his own comrades in the UVF because they had discovered he had been operating as an agent of British Intelligence.

When Myers passed on what Hanna had told him, the journalist from *Der Spiegel* regarded it as confirmation of what he had been told by the IRA and wrote his article with the apparent conviction that it was the unvarnished truth. There is an extraordinary amount of detail in the *Spiegel* article about arms smuggling from Germany. While there are only vague references to the unnamed loyalist group behind this alleged smuggling, there are elaborate and breathless descriptions of the circuitous routes that the Grundig containers holding the loyalists' weapons had allegedly taken. The article claimed they were moved from Dusseldorf to Nuremberg, then to Rotterdam, then to Hull – a port that is apparently situated just 'north of London' and not over 200 miles away – then to 'Haysham' [*sic*] and, finally, on to Belfast. Precise dates are provided by *Der Spiegel* on which payment for the arms were supposed to have been made. Even the serial number of one of the containers – TW1221 – is given.

The article includes references to a sinister loyalist figure named 'Andrew Carter' with whose wife Niedermayer was having an affair. *Der Spiegel* acknowledges that 'Carter' is not his real name but claims that the true identity of this man is known to their journalist. In fact, 'Carter' is easily identifiable as William Craig, and *Der Spiegel*'s use of a pseudonym is obviously intended to avoid the sort of legal action that *Bild* would later face.

All of this may have given readers the impression of painstaking and thorough research on the part of *Der Spiegel*'s journalists, but this wealth of detail only serves to conceal the spurious nature of their analysis and claims. Throughout the article, hearsay information and unsubstantiated rumours are treated as if they are incontestable facts. What is more, as we now know, *Der Spiegel*'s central assertion – that Niedermayer had been abducted by loyalists – was entirely without foundation. In fact, almost nothing in this article is corroborated by any hard evidence, and much of it rests on a series of apparent coincidences, wishful thinking and naive assumptions. The reality is that no *Spiegel* journalist could have conducted the high-powered investigation that they claimed to have carried out, or they would have quickly discovered that IRA members were the much more probable suspects. Instead, these gullible reporters swallowed and reproduced what they had been fed, directly or indirectly, by British Intelligence sources, or by the IRA, or by both.

That was not the last time that *Der Spiegel* published articles that proved to have no basis in reality. In December 2018, the news magazine admitted that one of its star reporters had falsified many of his stories. Claas Relotius had written for the magazine for years and had won numerous awards for his investigative reporting, including the prestigious Deutscher Reporterpreis on no less than four occasions (for the 'lightness, density and relevance' of his work). He also was awarded the CNN Journalist of the Year in 2014, and the European Press Prize in 2017. The following year, *Der Spiegel* was compelled to apologise to its readers for publishing the fake articles he had written for years, and to anyone who had been the subject of his 'fraudulent quotes, made-up personal details or invented scenes at fictitious places'. The magazine described the episode as a 'a low point in *Der Spiegel*'s 70-year history'.

It could be argued that a similar low point was reached in *Der Spiegel*'s coverage of the Niedermayer abduction. In this instance, the failure was not only of basic journalistic standards. We cannot expect journalists to be infallible, but what jars with me is not only the self-regarding assurance with which *Der Spiegel* announced the results of their 'investigation'; for me, what is most remarkable – and shocking – is that it was written with no discernible sympathy for Niedermayer or recognition of the dreadful ordeal that his wife and children were experiencing. By any reckoning, Niedermayer was the victim of a brutal and unjustified crime that had caused intense suffering to his family. Instead, he was portrayed by the *Spiegel* journalists in just the sort of sensationalist terms that their magazine professed to despise. Niedermayer is described as deeply unhappy in his marriage, mentally unstable, prone to uncontrolled violence, and as a chronic alcoholic and serial adulterer. It is even suggested that Niedermayer was himself involved in running guns to loyalist paramilitaries, but had become scared and 'wanted out'.

Once again, this crude, fictitious and melodramatic portrayal can only have added to the misery of Ingeborg and her children. Given Ingeborg's delicate psychological condition, such coverage seems particularly cruel. However, unlike *Bild*, the *Spiegel* magazine managed to avoid paying any damages for the elementary and shameful mistakes made in its coverage of the Niedermayer case; loyalist terrorists could hardly sue for the loss of their reputation – and, for obvious reasons, neither could Niedermayer.

It is part of the modus operandi by which false news is spread by intelligence agencies that they should include a sprinkling of truths and half-truths in their off-the-record press briefings. This is the sugar, so to speak, that allows some journalists to swallow total fabrications. It may well have been true that the Niedermayers had experienced some recent difficulties in their marriage. Even so, the purpose of the rumours that were spread by both British Intelligence and the IRA was utterly cynical – not to cast light on the real circumstances of Niedermayer's abduction but to spread deliberate confusion.

Fanciful speculations about the German's fate continued for several years. In 1975, the *News of the World* published an article stating that its investigative journalists had uncovered 'the truth' about his disappearance. On this occasion, it was reported that Niedermayer had been abducted by a renegade member of the IRA who had intended to ransom him for personal gain. The newspaper also claimed that the man responsible for the kidnapping had been executed by the IRA for doing so. Once again, this story was completely untrue. Had the *News of the World* journalists bothered to check, they would have discovered that their story of a 'solo run' was contradicted by the direct testimony of Herbert Hoech, the man who had witnessed Niedermayer's abduction. Instead, their story – which almost certainly came from a republican source – enhanced the public image of the IRA as a disciplined military force following and enforcing ethical codes.

Die Zeit is a German newspaper that often publishes learned essays or excerpts of lectures from distinguished authors and the paper is known for its long and erudite articles. In 1977, *Die Zeit* published an article by Rudolph Walter Leonhardt. He was a respected journalist who had worked for the newspaper in a senior editorial role for many years. In this instance, he claimed to have conducted his own investigation into the Niedermayer case and announced that, as a result of his enquiries, he had reached three conclusions.

The first of these was that it was 'very unlikely' that Thomas Niedermayer was still alive. That was hardly news since the previous year a German court had ruled that Ingeborg was legally a widow. The second conclusion Leonhardt reached was that the reasons for Niedermayer's abduction and death 'were personal and not political'. It seemed that this journalist had accepted at face value the denial offered by the IRA and, once again, the spectre of

Niedermayer's alleged adultery was conjured up as the real background to the kidnapping.

Leonhardt's third and final verdict followed on from that assumption: he concluded that the IRA 'had nothing to do with' the kidnapping. The reasoning behind this opinion was that he had been persuaded that the abduction was 'really not in their interests' since the IRA wanted to be perceived as 'freedom fighters' and not as common criminals. Leonhardt admitted he had no concrete evidence to confirm his assumptions, but claimed that he still 'felt' they were all entirely true and based on a dispassionate analysis of the situation. Once again, the political naivety (and, perhaps, also the personal arrogance) of a journalist is quite remarkable: Leonhardt was writing about a subject about which he clearly knew very little – although that was not evident in the bland assurance with which he presented his opinions. And once again, a story which we now know had no basis in reality was published without any apparent concern for the impact that might have on the German businessman's surviving family.

All of these spurious 'investigations' seem to have had some features in common. The journalists involved assumed that they were being told the truth by either British Intelligence or the IRA. They do not seem to have considered that both those organisations might have had reasons for wanting to mislead them. There was no actual evidence to support the claims that Niedermayer's alleged adultery had led to his kidnapping and murder being ordered by William Craig. There was also no evidence that guns had ever been smuggled from Germany for loyalists in Grundig containers – given that the workforce in Grundig was largely Catholic, that scenario should have seemed improbable from the start. But that did not prevent some journalists from publishing and disseminating what was essentially idle gossip and a series of unsubstantiated rumours, most of which had been planted by the IRA and British Intelligence.

Beyond that, there is an underlying and disturbing sense of moral judgement in the narrative fashioned by these journalists: the smearing of Thomas Niedermayer's character carries an unspoken implication that he was, to some degree, responsible for his own abduction and subsequent death. And that inference could be seen as letting both the IRA and the British security services off the hook. In spreading these false rumours, members of the press in Ireland, Britain and Germany were, in effect, also fulfilling the role of 'useful idiots'.

The dissemination of false and misleading information about the killing of Thomas Niedermayer continues to the present day. In July 2022, British cabinet papers from the 1970s were released, and some of these referred to the kidnapping. Reporting on these confidential papers on RTÉ's main evening news, Niedermayer's death was described as 'accidental'. RTÉ's online site went even further, attributing his death to 'natural causes'. In his book about IRA prisoners in English jails, Ruan O'Donnell, professor of history at Limerick University, also described Niedermayer's death as being from 'natural causes'. As we now know, there was nothing natural about the circumstances in which Thomas Niedermayer died, yet it seems that has still not been accepted by some journalists and historians.

24.
Breakthrough

Within days of Thomas Niedermayer's abduction, advertisements appeared in the local press offering a substantial reward for information leading to his rescue. They had been placed by Dr Curt Friese, the German consul in Liverpool. Unlike Niedermayer, Friese was a professional diplomat and the German consul with responsibility for Northern Ireland, and he made regular visits to Belfast. Ingeborg Niedermayer made an emotional television appeal for her husband's release as did the West German Chancellor, Willy Brandt. Brandt's appeal was drafted by Dr Friese. He was a highly educated and sophisticated man who had become something of a father figure for Niedermayer and he was clearly deeply moved by his disappearance. The script that Friese wrote for Brandt reveals something of his personal relationship with Niedermayer: he described him as someone who had been 'drafted at 14', who was 'a prisoner at 16' and who had been 'cheated out of [his] youth' by a world war.

Both Brandt's and Ingeborg's television appeals fell on deaf ears. Instead, the attention of the world's media turned to focus on the deteriorating physical condition of the IRA hunger strikers in British jails. Bernadette McAliskey (*née* Devlin), who was then the Westminster MP for Fermanagh and South Tyrone, visited the Price sisters and told the waiting camera crews that she had been 'shocked' by their appearance. The following week, it was reported that the Labour peer and tireless campaigner against sexual pornography, the Earl of Longford, had visited another of the hunger strikers in Wormwood Scrubs Prison. A few days later, the television news covered a visit by relatives of the London bombers to Merlyn Rees – who was soon to become the new Secretary of State for Northern Ireland. Growing concern about the well-being of the Price sisters was also expressed by the Irish government in Dublin. Against this unfolding news story, media coverage of the German businessman's disappearance soon lost its prominence. Indeed, nothing more was heard of Thomas Niedermayer for several years. It was tacitly assumed that he had been murdered and Ingeborg was legally declared a widow by the Nuremberg District Court in 1976.

Meanwhile, events in Northern Ireland followed what seemed like an inexorable course. The week after Niedermayer's abduction, the Ulster Unionist Council voted down the pro-Sunningdale Agreement unionists who were aligned with Brian Faulkner. His position became untenable and he resigned both the leadership and his membership of the Ulster Unionist Party. In subsequent weeks, Faulkner made increasingly desperate pleas to Westminster for some sort of row back on the Council of Ireland or, at least, for some initiative from Dublin on security cooperation. Westminster passed his requests on to the Irish government. At that time, the Fine Gael-Labour coalition in Dublin was heavily influenced by John Hume of the SDLP. Indeed, some thought that Hume was largely responsible for determining the Irish government's policy in relation to Northern Ireland. And Hume was adamant that the Council of Ireland was not open to re-negotiation.

Sir Arthur Galsworthy, the British Ambassador in Dublin, believed that Faulkner needed 'urgent help to fend off the loyalist challenge and sell the Agreement to Protestant waverers'. He also thought that the coalition government in Dublin had to show evidence of a 'more active and visible cooperation' on the security front. However, the Irish government was concerned that, if it were perceived to be helping the unionists, this would prove counter-productive with the Irish electorate. According to Garret FitzGerald, Irish public opinion might have accepted the need for action against the IRA, but 'old attitudes [might] come to the fore if such action demanded collaboration with the British'.

At this critical juncture, a general election was called in Britain and the Conservative government of Edward

Heath was replaced by a Labour administration which was, once again, led by Harold Wilson. The results of that election were decisive in Northern Ireland: all of the eleven unionist seats at Westminster were won by anti-Agreement candidates. Despite this severe blow to the moral authority of the power-sharing Executive, the Dublin government continued to call for the full implementation of the Sunningdale Agreement and blamed Faulkner for his failure to sell the package to the unionist community. In truth, the real failure was the Irish cabinet's inability to recognise the depth and extent of Protestant resistance to the Agreement. But events were about to teach them the full measure of that opposition.

In May, a general strike was called by the Ulster Workers' Council. This was an alliance of anti-Sunningdale unionists and various loyalist groups – some of which were paramilitary organisations. Within days, civil and commercial life in Northern Ireland had been paralysed. The Workers' Council had gained control of the supply of petrol, food and power and had assumed many of the functions and responsibilities of a provisional government. On day eleven of the strike, Harold Wilson chose to make a public address on television. This address was spectacularly ill-judged and only added fuel to the existing flames. In his broadcast, Wilson roundly abused those on strike as people whom, he said, had 'sponged' for years off the British welfare state. Far from defusing the crisis, his insulting, condescending and provocative comments only gave the strike's organisers an added credibility in the eyes of the greater unionist community.

At the end of May, Brian Faulkner and the other members of his party in the Executive resigned and the first cross-community administration in the history of Northern Ireland collapsed. What followed were more dismal years of direct rule from Westminster, a series of failed political 'initiatives' and a further catalogue of violent incidents from both loyalist and republican paramilitaries. It took more than twenty-five years before the next power-sharing Executive took office in Northern Ireland. Writing in 1977, Paul Wilkinson had predicted that 'if and when a new viable framework for devolved government in Northern Ireland does emerge it is likely to very closely resemble the model of Mr Faulkner's administration'. His prediction proved fairly accurate. Indeed, in some respects, the power-sharing administration established in 1998 constituted what Seamus Mallon, the Deputy Leader of the SDLP, memorably described as 'Sunningdale for slow learners'.

For many months after his abduction, Niedermayer's office in the Grundig factory was left undisturbed and unoccupied. It seemed as if he had just stepped out of the room and was expected back at any moment. Republicans continued to deny any complicity in the kidnapping. One senior figure even claimed, in another display of extraordinary cynicism and self-regard, that if the IRA really had been involved, Niedermayer's abduction would have been conducted in a more professional way. 'If we had kidnapped Herr Niedermayer with the purpose of using him to obtain the return of the Price sisters,' he claimed, 'we would not have brought it about in that manner.'

In the years that followed, Niedermayer's name and his ordeal began to fade in popular memory. Perhaps it was because he had always been an outsider in an internal dispute that was peculiar to Northern Ireland, with all the intensity and fixations that such domestic conflicts can generate. Niedermayer was, as he had claimed, not aligned to either of the two warring communities and so neither of them maintained a vested interest in reminding the public of his existence, or in keeping his memory alive.

However, the RUC remained committed to finding Niedermayer's body: indeed, in the words of one officer, 'The investigation had never really ceased.' There were reports that RUC officers knew who had planned the kidnapping – and had identified Keenan as the ringleader – but were unable to apprehend and interrogate him. Meanwhile, in the years that followed the kidnapping, the RUC received a number of tip-offs about where the German businessman might be buried. In 1976, a digger was used to excavate a field near the village of Waterfoot on the Country Antrim coast, but no human remains were found.

Two years later, the RUC were confident that they had new and reliable information. The location they were given was near the village of Cushendun in the Glens of

Antrim. Once again, a lengthy excavation took place but found nothing. The following year, a former member of the IRA now living in the USA told the FBI that Niedermayer had been buried in 'a swamp' near Andersonstown.

This was a promising lead and it was passed on to the RUC. However, the informant could not give a precise location where the body might be found and the lead ended there. In 1978, an SB officer in the RUC discounted press reports that Niedermayer had been buried in County Armagh or County Monaghan. In a confidential memorandum, he recorded that a 'reliable informer' in the IRA had named a number of those involved in the abduction and had told him that the body had been buried in the IRA's '1st Battalion area (upper Andersonstown)'. This was accurate information, but, once again, there was not enough exact detail to locate the grave.

In the years that followed her husband's abduction, Ingeborg continued to live in Northern Ireland for a time in the same home she had once shared with Thomas. To begin with, she worked as a children's nurse. Later, she was employed as a clerk in the Grundig factory that her husband had once managed. In a note to the Northern Ireland Office, an unnamed Grundig executive stressed that Ingeborg was only employed on a 'grace and favour' basis since she was 'without any qualifications'. In 1978, she purchased a burial plot for her husband in the picturesque Church of Ireland cemetery in Derriaghy, where Thomas had once told her he would like to be buried.

She also arranged for a marble headstone to be placed at the grave – although she was still unable to record the date of her husband's death. According to the local Church of Ireland minister, Ingeborg often visited the cemetery and would stand for some time looking down at the empty grave: a resonant image of desolation and unresolved grief.

Then, quite unexpectedly – six years after his abduction – came the breakthrough for which Ingeborg and her daughters had long waited.

25.

A Force Like No Other

A number of secret or secretive state agencies have operated in Northern Ireland. At first, most IRA agents were run
by the Irish section of British Military Intelligence (MI5), or
by RUC Special Branch handlers, or by a combination of
the two. Other agencies included the Military Reaction
Force, the Special Reconnaissance Unit and the Force
Research Unit. They all enjoyed some success in recruit-
ing agents within both the IRA and loyalist paramilitary
groups. All of these agents were taking great personal
risks: both republicans and loyalists did not hesitate to kill
anyone they believed was acting as a 'tout' (informer) and
passing information on to the security forces.

Agents who operated within paramilitary groups were
the principal and most valuable source of intelligence
for the RUC. As well as providing information, their
presence also had a destabilising effect within the various
paramilitary groups. More than 2,500 years ago, the
Chinese military philosopher Sun Tzu wrote that 'nothing

is more demoralising to the enemy than realising that people inside their organisation are providing information to the other side'. British Intelligence and the RUC had an obvious interest in encouraging the belief that both the IRA and loyalist paramilitaries were packed with their agents. Nonetheless, the penetration of both republican and loyalist organisations by the RUC Special Branch was genuinely extensive.

Fr Denis Faul was a well-known priest in Northern Ireland and the principal of a large secondary school in County Armagh. He used to caution his pupils against joining the IRA. 'It will sooner or later emerge that your commanding officer was a tout,' he warned them, 'and that his commanding officer was a tout too. And whilst you're rotting away [in jail], they will be getting off scot-free.' Fr Faul was barely exaggerating. By 1980, the security services were running multiple agents in both the IRA and various loyalist groups. Fr Faul was well aware of the dangers that such agents ran. On one occasion, he showed me photographs of a young man who had been shot by the IRA because they suspected he was an informer. His body had been dumped on a lonely stretch of road in the middle of winter. His eyes had been taped shut before he was shot, and his face was frozen in a horrifying rictus.

It was reckoned by one senior SB officer that, at any one time, there were at least fifteen well-placed and full-time agents active in the IRA. There was also a regular turnover of agents: some only worked for the RUC for a few years and then drifted away from the SB, or the IRA, or both. Some agents were exposed and killed by the IRA's internal security unit: the fearsome 'nutting squad'. Others were kept in place by the RUC for decades and some of these remain undetected to this day.

In 1972, a very valuable agent had been recruited by the RUC Special Branch. His name was Eamonn Molloy and he was a close associate of Brian Keenan. Both men worked as quartermasters for the Belfast IRA, but Keenan was the older and senior of the two. He was not only Molloy's commander but also acted as a kind of mentor to the teenager. Indeed, according to Ed Moloney, when suspicions were first expressed that Molloy might be the source of information passed on the RUC, it was Keenan who defended and protected him. Molloy was eventually exposed as an RUC agent and murdered by the IRA in 1975. Like Thomas Niedermayer, Molloy was 'disappeared' and buried in a secret grave. Nothing more was heard of this young man for the next 24 years and the IRA denied any knowledge of what had happened to him. Eventually, in the aftermath of the Good Friday Agreement, Molloy's remains were recovered by the IRA and left in a coffin that was dumped close to the Irish border.

According to one Branch officer, a high proportion of IRA volunteers passed on information at some point – even if they did not all become full-time 'career' agents. The level of penetration was even greater in loyalist groups, which tended to be less disciplined than their republican counterparts and this was evident in the higher conviction rates for loyalist terrorists, which was almost twice that of the IRA. The relentless search for new agents may explain why there was a degree of competition within the security forces to acquire agents that were thought to be of special importance.

According to William Matchett, a former SB officer, there is a world of difference between running an agent and running an informant. He defines the difference as being that between 'intelligence-led policing and investigative-led policing'. According to Matchett, the SB ran agents – active members of terrorist organisations – while the Criminal Investigation Department (CID) ran informants. For Matchett, the information supplied by the latter usually came 'after the event', was 'seldom life threatening' and only provided 'a minor aid in an investigative strategy'.

Branch officers could be viewed with some suspicion and even, at times, with intense resentment by other members of the RUC. It was rumoured that Branch men had allowed other RUC officers to be attacked and even killed by the IRA in order to protect their high-ranking sources. The identities of those agents were usually restricted to SB officers, which, in turn, led some other members of the RUC to believe that they were not trusted enough to be given such information.

This practice also raised the possibility of CID officers investigating a crime when the SB already knew who was responsible – perhaps even in advance of the crime taking place – but had not shared that knowledge with the CID because it might compromise one of their agents. Colin Breen, a former RUC officer, recorded the testimony of one member of a uniform patrol that was caught by an IRA explosion. According to this officer, SB surveillance had observed the bomb being planted. 'They knew exactly what was going on,' he complained, 'but never bothered to tell us.' Instead, the SB officers had 'fucked off before it exploded'. One of his patrol sustained serious injuries – including the loss of an eye – and he believed that it was 'no thanks to [the Branch] we weren't [all] killed'.

However, SB officers were not immune to attacks from the IRA and a considerable number of its officers were killed and injured during the Troubles. One of those who died was Peter Flanagan, shot dead by Sean O'Callaghan in a pub in Omagh before O'Callaghan became a Garda agent. It seems there were two particular reasons that the IRA wanted Flanagan dead: one was because he was a member of the hated SB; the second reason was because Flanagan was a Catholic and was therefore regarded by the IRA, in O'Callaghan's words, as an 'outcast among outcasts'. Like their colleagues in the CID and uniformed divisions, retirement did not exempt Branch officers from attacks by the IRA. Ivan Johnston had left the SB and the RUC and was driving a lorry when he was abducted in South Armagh in 1973. His body was found a few days later. The RUC discovered that Johnston had been questioned by his kidnappers before he was shot. During this interrogation, a post-mortem revealed that Johnston had been stripped and immersed repeatedly in a bath of scalding water.

Perhaps some of the RUC's internal tension was predictable and even inevitable. When the most recent Troubles erupted in Northern Ireland, the RUC was in some respects typical of a small provincial police service and Northern Ireland had enjoyed, for many years, one of the highest detection rates of crime – and the lowest incidents of murder – in the whole of Europe. But, in other ways, the RUC was already a unique force. Its officers were deployed across a large and varied landscape and had to deal with an unusual range of crime. As well as the common forms of criminal activity found in most urban centres, there was the smuggling that was endemic in the border regions. The RUC also had a paramilitary capability and was armed since there had always been the possibility of violent attacks by members of subversive organisations. That threat advanced and receded at different times, but it remained a constant possibility. This had led the RUC to become, in the words of Colin Breen, 'a force like no other'.

The attitudes of the Northern Irish population to the RUC were often polarised. There were those who regarded the RUC as little more than the armed wing of the Unionist Party, while others regarded them as their lawful protectors. It may have proved difficult to change attitudes towards the police in both communities. However, in the course of the Troubles, the RUC was transformed in several radical ways. As it struggled to come to terms with rapidly changing events, its numbers grew exponentially from a few thousand to more than 13,000. Over the same period, the range and depth of its detective and counter-intelligence work also grew and so did the skills that this demanded.

This was especially true of the RUC's Special Branch. In time, the SB would serve as a model for similar police agencies throughout the world, but it would also become a principal focus for the antagonism of both the IRA and loyalist paramilitaries. The SB was acutely aware of how much the IRA longed to know the identities of RUC agents. Indeed, according to William Matchett, when the SB's main office in Belfast was burgled in 2002, four years after the official end of the republican campaign, it showed just how much the IRA still wanted to know the names of those agents.

The central importance of intelligence gathering to modern counter-terrorism is indisputable. Almost by definition, conflicts that depend on such intelligence will involve deceit, betrayal and moral compromise. This can sometimes involve the loss of innocent lives, but it can also save them. There is no easy answer to that particular conundrum. In the case of Northern Ireland, electronic surveillance and sophisticated technology only seem to have played a limited role in countering the activities of both the IRA and loyalist paramilitaries. The key factor was the use of agents and informants and their effectiveness often depended on the quality of the personal relationship they developed with their handlers.

Of course, the IRA also employed its own agents and informants and often used a harsh mixture of coercion and blackmail to secure their services. In the course of the Troubles, information was passed on to the IRA by members of the civil service, by prison staff, by some loyalist paramilitaries and even by a few RUC officers. The reasons for such collusion ranged from straightforward intimidation to complicated romantic entanglements to resentment or jealousy of work colleagues. The IRA could also count on a flow of information that had been acquired by some ordinary members of the Catholic community. In his book *Killing Rage*, Eamon Collins, a former IRA intelligence officer, provides one example of a television repairman who used his house visits to peek into wardrobes and closets and see if any RUC or UDR uniforms were hidden there.

The running of agents by state security services clearly involves complex ethical questions that are difficult to resolve and the boundaries of what is acceptable were frequently tested and sometimes crossed in the course of the Northern Irish Troubles. There is a balance that is often hard to strike and sometimes even harder to justify in moral terms, but it is a dilemma that other countries and other police forces have also had to face. Clearly, any police service should be held to higher standards of ethical behavior and accountability than terrorist organisations; however, a sense of proportion needs to be maintained. More than 30,000 men and women served in the RUC during the course of the Troubles. The number of officers who observed the correct standards greatly exceeds those found to have betrayed the trust both of their colleagues and the communities they had undertaken to protect and serve.

The RUC's Special Branch no longer exists in the form that it once did. That has been viewed by some of its former officers as a betrayal and by some of its critics as a vindication of their distrust. Whatever its faults, the experience of the SB in counter-terrorism is still well-regarded by many other police forces and the expertise that it developed over the decades of conflict in Northern Ireland has been shared around the world. In the late 1970s, the IRA committed its members to fighting a 'Long War'. But so did the various security agencies that opposed them. Ultimately, the IRA's military capacity was worn down and contained in part through the investigative work of RUC detectives, but also through the cumulative effects of years of intelligence gathering and by agencies, such as the SB, whose resources (and patience) proved to be even greater than those of the IRA.

26.
We All Feel the Shame

CID detectives in the RUC usually received their information from so-called 'ODCs' (Ordinary Decent Criminals). The information often related to small-scale or petty crime. In the case of Thomas Niedermayer's abduction, it was an IRA informant code-named 'Disciple' who provided the RUC with crucial information about the circumstances of the German businessman's death.

Individual relationships between RUC officers and the agents and informants they ran in both republican and loyalist groups proved critical in containing the actions of both organisations. Such relationships not only resulted in the effective gathering of intelligence, but they also helped to undermine republicans' and loyalists' confidence in their own colleagues. The connection between agents and their RUC handlers could sometimes become extremely close. Martin McGartland was an intelligence officer for the IRA who also worked for the RUC Special Branch. In his revealing account of his career as a double agent, McGartland describes 'Felix', his Branch contact, as 'almost family' and his 'closest friend'. At the same time, McGartland also came to believe that senior RUC officers were prepared to sacrifice agents like him for their own motives. 'They encouraged the closest relationships and deep trust to develop between agents and their handlers,' he wrote, 'knowing that, in the end, these relationships count for nothing.'

It should also be acknowledged that these relationships often created great personal stress for the RUC officers involved. It was usually impossible for them to meet with their agents in accessible locations without risking being seen and targeted. For that reason, they normally met in remote and isolated places. One former SB officer told me of the intense feelings of dread and anxiety that he experienced while waiting for such meetings – usually on his own and in the dead of night, and often in a car parked far from any human habitation. He sometimes had to endure agonising hours before his agent would arrive as agreed, and there was always the possibility that his informant had been exposed by the IRA as a 'tout' – in which case, the officer might receive other and less welcome visitors that night.

Dangerous, volatile and unpredictable as these relationships might be, if one had not been established between an RUC detective and the man known as Disciple, then the circumstances of Thomas Niedermayer's death might never have been revealed.

Disciple had played a key role in the IRA's operations in Belfast. His job was to move unobtrusively around the city, co-ordinating the activities of the different IRA units. He had been chosen to do so by the IRA's Army Council because they believed that he was not being monitored by the security forces. In fact, I was told by one former SB officer that Disciple had never been 'Green Booked' – in other words, that he was not a full member of the IRA and had not taken part in any of their operations. This helped to ensure that his identity was only known to a handful of senior IRA members. However, they were unaware that Disciple had been identified by an IRA informant to an inspector in the Belfast Regional Crime Squad called Alan Simpson.

When he joined the RUC, Simpson had thought that the Troubles were 'a passing thing'. He imagined that, if he served 30 years in the police, he might be 'at one or two murder scenes'. Instead, during his first two years in the RUC, he was first officer at the scene of twelve sectarian murders. The same period saw the murder of some of Simpson's colleagues: 'we lost 8 to the IRA and 2 to the UVF'. These killings had a profound effect on Simpson: he simply 'couldn't believe that humans could do what they did'.

Quite often there were deals to be struck with IRA suspects in return for information. One of these informants passed on the name of a man who would ultimately play a crucial role in the discovery of what had happened to Thomas Niedermayer. 'He said to me, "there's a man you should be interested in. He is moving from (IRA) battalion to battalion. He keeps a very low profile, but he's a very important man within the organisation.'" The informant gave Simpson the man's name and, in return, Simpson released him without charge.

Soon after that, the man named by the informant was taken in for questioning. Simpson quickly recognised that the man who became known as Disciple was in a state of emotional exhaustion and was open to being 'turned'. The IRA advised their volunteers that they could expect to be beaten if they were arrested by the RUC, but Simpson was able to work that expectation to his advantage: 'He thought that I was going to kick the crap out of him,' Simpson recalled. Instead, he offered him cigarettes. According to Simpson, that was when Disciple began to talk, because 'he just couldn't cope with the kindness'.

After two nights in a police cell, Disciple finally admitted to the critical role that he had played in co-ordinating IRA operations in Belfast. He had carried messages between the different units 'because it wasn't safe to give instructions by telephone or any other way'. He also told Simpson that he had a lot more information to pass on, but was nervous that he might be betrayed by the RUC and end up in prison.

Disciple was also nervous that he would be questioned by the IRA security team after his release. Simpson advised him to admit nothing: despite the fact that the IRA often promised that no harm would come to those who confessed that they had passed information to the RUC, many of those who believed this promise were ultimately 'executed by the IRA's "nutting squad"'.

Once he had been released, Disciple feared that his life was at grave risk from his former comrades and so he fled Northern Ireland. Simpson had arranged to meet him at a venue in central Belfast, but on the day of the meeting, Disciple never showed. It seemed that he had simply vanished and was no longer prepared to provide RUC officers with any information. But Simpson thought otherwise. He took part in a fake raid on the street where Disciple lived so he had a pretence to give his phone number to Disciple's wife. She passed this on to Disciple and Simpson managed to re-establish contact with him.

The intelligence that Disciple could provide about various IRA operations was clearly of great potential value, but it also raised some thorny issues within the RUC. Because of the threat to witnesses' lives, it could prove extremely difficult to find any who were prepared to testify against republican or loyalist paramilitaries in open court. In that context, intelligence gathering became more important than hard evidence and intelligence gathering was what the SB considered to be its speciality. It became an established procedure in 1981, following recommendations contained in a report by a senior MI5 officer, that CID officers were never to arrest a suspected terrorist 'without first consulting Special Branch'. This was to give SB officers an opportunity to 'turn' the suspected terrorist into one of their agents. All intended arrests also had to be cleared in advance with SB officers to 'ensure that no agents, either RUC or Army, are involved'.

This degree of official protection allowed some of those actively involved in serious crimes to go free, as Fr Faul claimed, or to receive greatly reduced prison sentences. Gary Haggarty, for example, was an SB agent in the UVF. Eventually, he pleaded guilty to five murders and twenty-five conspiracies to murder – among many other serious offences. In January 2018, Haggarty was sentenced to six and a half years in prison. He was released in May of the same year. On his release, he entered a witness protection programme and was quickly moved out of Northern Ireland. Freddie Scappaticci worked in the IRA's 'nutting squad': the unit that was responsible for torturing and killing suspected informers. His code name while he operated as an agent inside the IRA was 'Stakeknife'. Scappaticci is suspected of involvement in at least seventeen murders. He was eventually revealed to be another agent of British Intelligence and was also spirited out of the country. Scappaticci died of natural causes in 2023.

When SB officers discovered that the CID had recruited an important member of the IRA such as Disciple, they regarded this as an intrusion on their turf and reacted with fury. As far as the SB was concerned, its officers should have been informed when Disciple was first taken into custody. SB officers could argue that Disciple was clearly an 'agent' and not an 'informant'. In turn, the CID officers could counter that, since he was no longer operating within the IRA, Disciple should not be considered an active agent. Eventually, it was agreed that Disciple would continue to be debriefed by Alan Simpson, who had already established a relationship with him, and Simpson would be accompanied to their meetings by a British officer from MI5.

Simpson and Disciple met up on the Channel Island of Jersey. Disciple had found work as a cook on a merchant ship that lay at anchor in the Jersey harbour for a few days. Over the course of those few days, Disciple met repeatedly with Simpson and an accompanying MI5 officer. The information that he gave Simpson met all his expectations: 'He knew all the membership of the IRA in Belfast. He knew the identities of all the bombers and he knew which bombs they had made.' By the end of the week, Simpson had filled more than 80 pages of closely written notes. Disciple never returned to Northern Ireland. He is believed to have established a new identity and settled with his wife and children in an isolated part of rural England where he established a new identity. His neighbours – and the local police – are believed to have no idea of the previous role that he played in Belfast.

Some of the valuable information that Disciple passed on to the RUC related to the abduction and killing of Thomas Niedermayer. Disciple told Simpson that he drank regularly with the commander of the IRA in Andersontown. One night he had taken part in a drinking session in one of the IRA's shebeens (illegal drinking dens) when somebody asked 'whatever happened to Niedermayer?' The IRA commander's response was, 'Don't worry about him. He's down a hole and he's only digging himself deeper.' When Disciple asked what that meant, he was told, 'He's buried face down. Just beyond the bridge at Colin Glen.' The account that Disciple gave coincided in several important respects with confidential information that the RUC already possessed, which meant that Simpson could regard what he had heard as credible.

The waste ground at Colin Glen near Andersonstown, which Disciple identified as the location of Thomas Niedermayer's grave, had since become an unofficial dumping ground. Because of the special significance of Niedermayer's abduction, Alan Simpson was authorised by Kenneth Bloomfield – the same senior civil servant who had described Thomas Niedermayer's kidnapping as an 'awful reality' – to invest the substantial funds needed to locate his body. Simpson obtained aerial photos of the area that had been taken in 1973, but that was before more than 2,000 tons of rubbish had been dumped there. Simpson asked himself, 'how are we ever going to find a body in the middle of all this?'

It would not have been possible to use the British army to clear the rubbish as Colin Glen was near the Republican stronghold of Lenadoon where they would have become obvious targets for the IRA. Instead, the

RUC set up a fictitious environmental agency – complete with its own office, bank account, logo and press release – and its officers began the laborious task of clearing Colin Glen of rubbish. In the words of Alan Simpson, the dumping site included everything 'from old fridges to dead animals', with rats scuttling out of the garbage every few seconds. The IRA had been running an illegal fly-tipping scam in the Glen that served a double purpose: it helped to prevent the discovery of Niedermayer's body and it also raised money for the local IRA commander through dumping charges.

The excavation of the Glen was extremely demanding and stomach-churning for those involved: due to heavy rain, the terrain was often reduced to a quagmire of mud and illegal dumping continued during the weekend breaks. The last large pile of rubbish had become a refuge for the remaining vermin on the site and, when this was finally cleared, scores of rats surged out and ran around the RUC officers, squealing 'like dervishes'. Once all the garbage had been removed, the RUC could begin to work their way through the topsoil for evidence of Niedermayer's body. This was the most dangerous part of their mission and their side arms were now supplemented by several Sterling sub-machine guns, concealed in their car.

After almost four weeks of excavation, the RUC officers were on the verge of giving up. They were using a digger excavator on what was intended to be their last day at the site and Simpson was standing guard a short distance away from the excavation. Suddenly, he heard a shout from one of the RUC officers. 'One of them shouted up to me, "We've got him!" I said, "What have you got?" He said, "There's two legs in the (digger) bucket." I ran down and there was a pair of trousers with bones sticking out of them in the bucket. The legs had been bound together with a pair of woman's tights.' Simpson felt a sense of overwhelming relief: 'At the very last minute of the very last day, we had found what we came for.'

Over the next few hours, they uncovered the rest of Thomas Niedermayer's remains. His hands had been bound with a belt, the faded remnant of a red check shirt could be seen and close to his feet were the brown slippers Niedermayer had been wearing at the time he was taken by the IRA. Otherwise, it was just as Disciple had reported: the body had been buried face down, so that he could 'dig himself deeper'. Thomas's granddaughter Tanya still feels disgusted by the circumstances in which Thomas was buried: 'Face down with his arms tied behind his back – I wouldn't call that a burial. I would call that a dumping. What had he done to deserve that?'

Ingeborg Niedermayer was still living nearby and senior RUC officers called to inform her that they believed the body of her husband had finally been located. While she was relieved that her husband's body had been recovered, Ingeborg was extremely distressed that he had been found buried under a rubbish tip. On the day after, the body had been uncovered, Ingeborg went to RUC Headquarters in Belfast. She was shown the brown slippers that had been found at Colin Glen and was sure they belonged to Thomas. She was accompanied by Renate who was also certain that these were the remnants of the clothes that her father had been wearing when he was abducted. Forensic evidence later confirmed that this was Thomas Niedermayer's body.

Renate was very disturbed to learn that she had often travelled past the dump without knowing that was where her father's body was concealed. The process of identification turned out to be a lengthy one since the body was badly decomposed, which also caused Ingeborg further distress. Eventually, dental records established beyond doubt that the body was that of Thomas. Ingeborg placed a notice in a local newspaper in which she thanked the public for the support given to her over the previous years.

A post-mortem examination was conducted by the deputy state pathologist for Northern Ireland. He recorded that there had been 'two depressed fractures of skull due to blows on head from a blunt object'. The X-rays reveal two large depressions on one side of the head. A forensic scientist examined the skull at the request of the pathologist. He compared the profile of the larger depression with the butt and toe of a 9mm Browning pistol and found that the length and unusually large width of the Browning magazine fitted neatly into the depression; in other words, the wounds in Thomas's head were compatible with blows from a particular type of heavy revolver.

The pathologist deduced that the wounds had been inflicted 'relatively soon prior to death' and that it was therefore highly likely the severe blows had led to Thomas Niedermayer's death. However, due to 'advanced decomposition', he found that 'absolute proof was lacking' that such blows were the immediate cause of death. This lack of absolute certainty is what has allowed some – including RTÉ's News department in 2022 – to describe Niedermayer's death as 'accidental', as if he had died as a result of some mishap and had not had his skull broken open in a brutal assault.

In order to conceal the source of their information, the RUC continued to claim in public that the body had been found by complete chance by an environmental group. In March 1980 – more than six years after his abduction – Thomas Niedermayer was buried in a Church of Ireland cemetery in Dunmurry. The burial ground was close to the factory he had once managed, where he had told Ingeborg that he would like to be buried – a further indication of how much the Dunmurry factory had meant to him. His funeral was attended by his widow and two daughters as well as by diplomatic representatives from Germany, the British administration in Northern Ireland and the RUC. Dr Curt Friese – Niedermayer's former mentor – travelled to Belfast for the interment.

A large number of workers from the Grundig factory nearby also attended the service, which was conducted in both English and German. The Church of Ireland minister paid tribute to the way in which Ingeborg had 'come through the sorrow and the suffering with great dignity'. He also referred to the wish that Niedermayer had expressed to be buried in Northern Ireland and how much he had loved the country. 'He ended his life in a dreadful way,' the Rev. Butler told the congregation, 'and we all feel the shame of it.'

In some photos taken at the funeral, Ingeborg seems composed and dignified; in others, she looks distraught and strained; in some, she is clinging to her daughters for support. Renate appears to be hiding her grief behind dark glasses, long hair and a large floppy hat. As the coffin was lowered into the grave, Ingeborg took a red rose from one of the wreaths and threw it into the grave. Perhaps she remembered the bunch of roses that her husband had given her in hospital on the last night she saw him.

In the year before he died, Niedermayer had tried to persuade Grundig to open a second factory in Northern Ireland and, in the month before his death, he announced that he had succeeded in that goal. However, such plans were abandoned not long after his abduction and, a few months after his funeral, the original Grundig plant in Dunmurry closed for good with the loss of almost 2,000 jobs.

It later emerged that Keenan was not the only member of the Grundig workforce to have sympathised with or joined the IRA. Stolen equipment from the factory would turn up in radio detonation devices in IRA bombs throughout the 1970s. Following Keenan's arrest in 1979, the RUC found evidence that revealed the expertise of some of Grundig's workers was also used by the IRA to set up a network of telephone taps – including the private phone line of the British army's General Officer Commanding (GOC) in Northern Ireland – and the electronic components of these taps were also found to have been stolen from the Grundig factory.

A former worker at the Dunmurry plant told me that she was living near Andersonstown in the early 1970s, which was unusual as she was Protestant and it was a predominantly Catholic area. She worked closely with one colleague for several years who was later arrested and convicted for IRA activities. The worker told me that she had felt a profound sense of betrayal: 'I trusted him and thought he was my friend', she told me, 'and all the time he was only laughing at me behind my back.' It was clear that almost fifty years after these events, they still pained her. She left the factory, and moved into a Protestant district soon afterwards.

At the time of Thomas Niedermayer's abduction, Grundig was still one of the biggest manufacturing companies in Europe, with more than forty factories and a workforce of around 40,000 in Germany alone. The huge plant that Max Grundig had built in Nuremberg was known locally as 'Grundig City'. Apart from the factory, Grundig had built two residential tower blocks for his workforce – each sixteen stories high. At the top was an enormous blue sign with the company brand name.

However, the advent of new technology in the 1970s made televisions lighter and, therefore, easier and cheaper to transport. That brought Europe within reach of the Asian entertainment industry. 'Our markets are being destroyed,' Max Grundig told the European Commission in 1979. 'In a decade, Japan will rule the world!' A few months later, he announced that he was selling his majority shareholding in his company and intended to retire. He said later that, when he left the company, he felt that he had 'lost his soul'.

Today, what is left of Grundig's original company is still producing electronic products and is still based in 'Grundig City'. But now it shares the huge site in Nuremberg with the call centre of a clothing chain, the local branch of the Red Cross and a post office. The huge residential towers that once were occupied by hundreds of workers in Max Grundig's factory no longer house any labour force. Instead, they have been used to detain asylum seekers from the Middle East and sub-Saharan Africa.

27.
How He Died

A number of IRA members had been named by Disciple as being involved in the kidnapping, and most of them had already been identified by the RUC as part of the abduction team.. Those named included Brian Keenan, Eugene McManus – who had been adjutant in the IRA's Belfast Brigade – and John Bradley, a lower-level IRA member. Before long, McManus and Bradley were held in RUC custody. When he was questioned by the RUC, McManus at first claimed that he knew nothing of the kidnapping until he heard it reported on the television news. On the second day of questioning, he offered a different response. According to Alan Simpson who interrogated him, McManus said that the Niedermayer 'job' had been devised by Brian Keenan and officially sanctioned by the leadership of the IRA.

RUC officers initially assumed that the IRA had ferried Niedermayer to a safe house in some remote rural area. The RUC now learned that he had been held less than a mile away from his own home. The woman who owned the house in Hillside Crescent in Andersonstown where Niedermayer was held told the police that a group of men had called at her home on St Stephen's Day. They informed her that she would have to vacate her house until further notice. She told the police that she was not a supporter of the IRA, but had been too afraid to refuse their instructions, and the RUC believed her. She was informed by the IRA that she could return on 31 December, at which time she found the house untidy and reeking of cigarette smoke. In the days that followed, more IRA men came to her home and the front upstairs bedroom was completely redecorated, with the existing door handles, bed and carpet removed and replaced.

The RUC also identified the man whose car had been hijacked by the IRA. He told officers that he had been approached by some men who said they needed to borrow his car. He had thought it expedient to give them the keys. Once again, the RUC believed his story and took no action against him.

McManus said he had been told that Brian Keenan had wanted to visit his family over Christmas and, since he was on the run and could not stay at his home, McManus had agreed to house him for the night of 30 December. Around 10.30 p.m., someone knocked at the door and asked to speak to Keenan. Soon afterwards, Keenan grabbed his coat and left. He returned a few hours later in an agitated state and confided in McManus that there had been a 'fuck-up' and Niedermayer was dead. According to McManus, Keenan was concerned about how he would explain this to the IRA leadership since what could have been a propaganda coup for the IRA had turned into a major embarrassment. McManus also admitted that some weeks later he acted as a guide to a German journalist who had come to Belfast to follow up on the Niedermayer story. McManus had ensured that he only spoke to members of the IRA who knew nothing about the crime. This may explain (in part) why the story was misreported in the German press.

Alan Simpson had been surprised when Disciple had given him the name of John Bradley as someone who was involved in Niedermayer's abduction. According to Simpson, Bradley was only 'a small-time player'. Perhaps the reason that he was chosen was simply because he lived in a district close to where other members of the kidnap gang lived and could easily be reached.

Bradley told Simpson that 'out of the blue' someone from the IRA had turned up at his front door. He was informed that he was needed for 'a major operation', and that he was to act as a jailer 'because we're short'. Bradley said the house in Hillside Crescent was in a state of almost complete darkness when he arrived there. Niedermayer was kept blindfolded, gagged and bound on a mattress in the upstairs front bedroom of the house where he was held. Bradley said that Niedermayer was quite calm, and the only light in the room came from one bar of a small electric fire.

According to Bradley, Niedermayer made repeated attempts to engage him in conversation. Perhaps he was attempting to follow the approach later taken by Tiede Herrema, a Dutch businessman, when he was kidnapped by the IRA. Herrema was able to establish a friendly relationship with his kidnappers, which he could work to his advantage. However, Bradley had been instructed not to speak to his captive and neither he nor any of the others proved as susceptible as Herrema's abductors.

When their shifts guarding Niedermayer were over, each IRA member would relax downstairs or sleep in another bedroom. A woman brought fresh food to the house every day. By the third day Niedermayer had become restless. He must have known that he had only been brought a short distance from his home and he may have expected that he would soon be discovered and rescued. However, he was being held in the middle of a district of Belfast whose inhabitants were either sympathetic to the kidnappers or simply too scared to oppose them.

Bradley claimed that on the evening of the third day of his captivity, Niedermayer made an attempt to escape while on his way to the bathroom. He was dragged back to the bedroom where he had been kept. Apparently, he began to shout for help. The four men guarding Niedermayer forced him back to the mattress on which he had slept and tried to subdue him. Bradley claimed that he sat on Niedermayer's back and legs while another of the men clubbed him with the butt of a revolver and the others forced his face into the mattress. The four IRA men pinned Niedermayer down until he stopped moving.

After his body was recovered, it was impossible to say whether Niedermayer had been killed by the blows to his head, or by being suffocated, or whether he had died from a heart attack. The IRA claimed that his death had either been 'accidental' or due to 'natural causes', as if he had not had his skull broken open in a brutal assault. The responsibility for his death clearly rests with those who had abducted and imprisoned Thomas. In this regard, the absence of masks used by his abductors and jailers may also be revealing, since it strongly indicates that they did not think Niedermayer would live long enough to identify them. According to Bill Matchett, a former Special Branch officer, there was little or no chance of Niedermayer ever being released alive: 'He had seen their faces – he was never coming home. No two ways about that.' Matchett cited the cases of most abductions in Northern Ireland – whose victims were very seldom released alive.

Enda O'Doherty has also pointed out the underlying reality: 'kidnappings have to carry the threat that the person seized may be killed: that's the whole point of them'. At the very least, it seems highly unlikely that, if the British had not agreed to the IRA's ransom demands, Thomas would simply have been set free by the IRA and allowed to go home.

What is indisputable, however, is the results of the autopsy. I had the opportunity to view the X-rays of

Niedermayer's skull, and it was quite clear to me that only violent physical force could have inflicted such extreme damages. Niedermayer may have died before the IRA intended, but it seems most unlikely that he would ever have survived for long.

When Keenan arrived at Hillside Crescent on the night of the murder, Niedermayer was already dead. Keenan was apparently enraged that his hostage was now of no practical use to him. According to Alan Simpson, the kidnapping 'would have been a masterstroke of propaganda' for Keenan 'if he could have got the Price sisters moved to Northern Ireland, but now it had all gone terribly wrong and that was bad for his reputation within the IRA'. Keenan told the gang to dispose of the body secretly and the following evening three of them drove to Colin Glen with spades and shovels. Bradley and another man dug the grave while the third IRA member went back to Hillside to collect a fourth member and Niedermayer's body.

They could only dig a shallow grave because they soon hit a bed of rock. In order to conceal the fresh soil, they dragged an old mattress and placed it over the grave. The IRA also allocated £200 to cleaning the house in Hillside Crescent in order to destroy any forensic evidence. Bradley claimed that he was so disturbed by Niedermayer's death that he had to leave the room whenever it was mentioned on the television news. He also claimed that he left the IRA in 1978 because he was no longer able to stomach its violence.

A number of the other IRA members who were involved in the abduction and killing of Thomas Niedermayer were subsequently arrested by the RUC, but they remained silent and, without any corroborating evidence, they were soon set free. One of them is believed to have shot and killed himself by accident some months after the abduction. In 1981, McManus and Bradley were tried in a Belfast court. Bradley's defence counsel was Richard Ferguson, who had already defended a number of republican prisoners, and who was once a unionist MP at Stormont and a liberal supporter of Terence O'Neill's reforms. Bradley pleaded guilty to manslaughter and was sentenced to twenty years in prison – an unusually severe sentence for manslaughter and one that surprised the RUC, who did not regard Bradley as an important 'player' in IRA operations. McManus pleaded guilty to withholding information and membership of the IRA and received five years. Ingeborg and her two daughters attended court for the duration of the trial. According to Renate, when sentence was being passed, McManus caught her eye and began to cry. She said that, for one moment, she felt sorry for him.

No charges were brought against the man whose car had been used in Niedermayer's abduction or against the woman in whose house Niedermayer had died: the RUC accepted that they had only acted under extreme duress from the IRA. Although it is generally accepted that Brian Keenan ordered and planned the kidnapping of Niedermayer, he was never charged in relation to the kidnapping. As it turned out, the abduction of the German businessman was not the only IRA kidnapping intended to secure the transfer of the Price sisters to Northern Ireland.

28.
The Stuff of Martyrs

A few months after Thomas Niedermayer was abducted and killed, there was another attempt by the IRA to force the return of the Price sisters to Northern Ireland. On 26 April, Bridget Rose Dugdale, a former debutante and the daughter of an English millionaire, led three other IRA members on a raid of Russborough House in County Wicklow. Dugdale did not have a similar status to Keenan within the IRA, partly because her privileged background in England distinguished her from other volunteers, and partly because she was considered to be something of a 'loose cannon'.

Russborough House was the home of Sir Alfred Beit, a wealthy philanthropist and his wife. The elderly couple were pistol-whipped by Dugdale's gang, who then stole eighteen valuable paintings. This seemed to be something of a habit for Dugdale, who had previously been found guilty of stealing artworks from her own father in what appeared to be an act of (somewhat delayed) adolescent rebellion. She was given a suspended sentence by a judge who assumed that someone from her social class was 'extremely unlikely' to offend again. Her accomplice, who came from a less privileged background, was not so fortunate: he was sent down for six years. On this occasion, the IRA sent a ransom note offering to exchange the stolen paintings for the transfer of Dolours and Marian Price to Northern Ireland. It did not take long for the Gardaí to trace the upper-class Englishwoman who had led the raid to a house in County Cork, where they were able to recover all the paintings.

In June 1974, the IRA gained entry at gunpoint to Knocklofty House in County Tipperary where they pistol-whipped and abducted Lord and Lady Donoghmore. This elderly couple had no connection with either British or Irish politics, but they were wealthy landowners, which seems to have made them 'legitimate targets' in the eyes of the IRA. Both the Beit robbery and the abduction of the Donoghmores took place south of the border, which had implications that were potentially damaging for the IRA. Not only did they risk negative public opinion, but their actions raised the possibility that the Irish government might introduce more severe security measures such as internment. In this instance, the Donoghmores were released within five days. They were told this was because the Price sisters had decided to end their hunger strike. The reason they had done so was because of a significant shift in the policies of the British government.

At the time the Donoghmores were abducted, the British Home Secretary, Roy Jenkins, was known for his liberal views, and had already indicated that the Prices would be moved to jails in Northern Ireland in the near future. In his memoir, *A Life at the Centre*, Jenkins insisted that his decision to transfer the Price sisters was not made in response to any actions by the IRA. Instead, it seemed he had thought it prudent to concede that the sisters – whom he chose to describe as 'two slim dark girls' – should be moved because he believed that they were just the sort of 'charismatic colleens' who would become 'the stuff of Irish martyrs' if they were left to die in an English jail. In other words, Jenkins claimed that his decision had been pre-emptive of future events and not reactive to current ones. However, he also admitted that considerations for his personal safety had influenced him since he feared he 'might never again be able to walk in freedom and security down a street in Boston or New York or Chicago'.

There was a postscript of sorts to these events. In December 1974, Bridget Rose Dugdale gave birth to a child in Limerick Prison. The father of her child, Eddie Gallagher, was also in the IRA and, in October of the following year, he and one of his associates kidnapped a Dutch businessman called Tiede Herrema (believing him to be German). Gallagher demanded the release of Dugdale in return for Herrema's life. This episode climaxed when the location of Herrema was discovered eighteen days after his abduction.

Like Thomas Niedermayer, he had not been taken to a remote cottage somewhere in rural Ireland, but had been held captive in a terraced house on a local council estate. Herrema had worked with the Dutch Resistance during the Second World War and had been imprisoned in a Nazi slave labour camp. That experience may have prepared him to deal with his captors and he managed to establish some sort of emotional connection with Gallagher. Herrema was released by the Gardaí after a two-week siege of the house in which he had been kept and he later said that he regarded his kidnappers less as calculating terrorists than as 'children with a lot of problems'.

This was not the last instance of kidnapping by republican paramilitaries in the following years. However, it was the last abduction to be connected in any way with the return of the Price sisters to Northern Ireland. In that sense, it marks the end of the sequence of events that had led to the kidnapping and killing of Thomas Niedermayer.

29.
Asking to be Killed

By the end of the 1970s, Brian Keenan had consolidated his reputation within the IRA both in operational and strategic terms. He was summed up to me in four words by someone who knew him in the early 1970s as 'charismatic, driven, intelligent, ruthless'. Keenan had been associated with some of the most notorious and shocking acts of violence in the history of the Troubles. He is believed to have been responsible for planning the assassination of the British Ambassador to Ireland, Sir Christopher Ewart-Biggs, who was killed in 1976 along with his assistant, a young civil servant called Judith Cooke. A massive bomb had been planted in a culvert near the diplomat's residence on the outskirts of Dublin and was detonated as the Ambassador's car drove past.

According to Sean O'Callaghan, an agent of the Garda Síochána, Keenan also planned the 1976 massacre at Kingsmill, County Armagh, when a van carrying a group of textile workers was stopped by a large group of more than a dozen heavily armed men. Eleven workers were identified as Protestants, lined up, and ten of them were shot dead. (The eleventh man survived despite being shot eighteen times.) Keenan had apparently claimed that these sectarian murders would demoralise and 'knock the nonsense' out of any loyalist paramilitaries in the area.

The Kingsmill massacre was subsequently claimed by the so-called 'South Armagh Republican Action Force' and the IRA again denied any degree of responsibility. Few found their denials convincing: it was, to say the least, unlikely that so many armed men could operate in that part of the country without the IRA's active involvement. In 2011, a report by the Historical Enquiries Team established that the IRA had indeed perpetrated this sectarian massacre. The report stated that the ten men had been killed solely because of their religion and that the attack had been planned for some weeks in advance. A few months after the killings, Raymond McCreesh and two other IRA members were captured while attacking a British army observation post. The rifle carried by McCreesh, who later died on hunger strike in the Maze prison, was one of those used in the Kingsmill massacre. Forensic evidence also linked the weapons used at Kingsmill to more than 100 other attacks and thirty-seven murders claimed by the IRA.

The limited resources that were available to the RUC throughout most of the 1970s are also evident in the police response to the Kingsmill massacre. Fewer than thirty officers were assigned to investigate these killings and they were required to work at the same time on many other IRA murders and robberies in that area. This contrasts with almost 1,000 British policemen who were detailed to investigate the IRA's bombing of Manchester in 1996 in which (thankfully) nobody was killed.

In 1974, Keenan was imprisoned briefly in the Irish Republic for IRA membership, but from 1975 he became centrally involved in organising a new phase of the IRA's campaign in England. He had learned from the mistakes of previous years that had resulted in the arrest of the Price sisters and the rest of their unit. This time, the IRA units were smaller and were resident in the UK. They included bomb-makers and did not depend on explosive devices being assembled and transported from Ireland. Between 1975 and 1976, the IRA mounted, on average, one gun or bomb attack in England every three days. These actions might be regarded as more successful than previous efforts – at least, in terms of the damage and disruption that they caused.

However, the IRA was rather less successful in attacking the strategic objectives that Keenan had identified as 'transport, communications and power'. The IRA's targets in England were much more random and lacking in any genuine strategic significance. In reality, their arbitrary nature reflected their underlying purpose since the intention was primarily to generate terror in the general population and headlines in the next day's media coverage. For that reason, the apparently haphazard nature of this unit's attacks was a positive advantage and may explain why the IRA targeted a varied assortment of hotels, restaurants, department stores, pubs, clubs and even pillar boxes.

It is true that IRA units managed to kill dozens of people in this period, but the majority of those who died were civilians who had no connection of any kind with Ireland. They included a young homeless man killed at a bus stop and a telephone operator blown up at his place of work. There were also a number of people killed or injured as a result of mistaken identity. One was an insurance broker shot dead in his car as he waited in traffic. Another was a schoolteacher who was confused with his next-door neighbour. One of those killed by the IRA in this phase of its English campaign was Gordon Hamilton-Fairley – one of the world's leading cancer specialists and Professor of Medical Oncology at St Bartholomew's Hospital in London.

On the morning of 22 October 1975, a man phoned the home of a backbench MP at Westminster and asked what time the MP left for work in the morning. The phone was answered by a cleaning woman who innocently told the caller that it was usually around nine o'clock. The man thanked her and hung up. That night a bomb was planted underneath one of the wheels of the MP's car that stood outside his house. The next morning, his neighbour Professor Hamilton-Fairley was out walking his two dogs when he noticed a strange device under the car. When he bent down to investigate, the bomb exploded, killing him instantly. John Crown, one of Ireland's foremost oncologists and a former member of the Irish Senate, later wrote a moving tribute to Hamilton-Fairley. He described him as 'innocent collateral damage in a struggle that he had no part of'. He pointed out that the IRA bomb that killed him was intended to murder someone else and 'did not even have a military target'. Professor Crown wondered 'how many hundreds, or how many thousands, or more, would have been saved [from cancer] had Gordon been free to live?'

In fact, Hamilton-Fairley's death led directly to another murder. His friend, Ross McWhirter, the co-founder of the *Guinness Book of Records*, led a public campaign to raise a reward for information leading to the capture of the killers. One of those killers later complained that McWhirter 'put a price on our heads. That man thought he was living in Texas. He asked to be killed.' A few weeks later, two members of the IRA arrived at McWhirter's home. Mrs McWhirter happened to arrive at her front door that evening at the same time as the men who had come to kill her husband. They forced her to hand over her front door keys and they entered the house. As Ross McWhirter came into the hallway to greet his wife, he was shot repeatedly in the head and chest with a heavy Magnum revolver. The IRA gunmen escaped in McWhirter's car and he was pronounced dead a few hours later.

The next week, the same IRA members fired a sub-machine gun into a crowded London restaurant as they drove past. They had thrown a bomb into that restaurant a few weeks previously which had killed two of its customers and injured many more. On this occasion, they had stolen a blue Ford Cortina and were spotted driving close to the restaurant. This was not the first time this unit had returned to the scene of a previous attack to mount another one – in fact, it had almost become their modus operandi – but this time the British police were well prepared for that possibility. A patrol car was in the area and gave chase to the gunmen.

The IRA members abandoned their car and were cornered in a flat in Balcombe Street where they took an elderly couple hostage. After a siege that lasted six days, the IRA unit became hungry and demanded food. A meal of sausages, Brussels sprouts, potatoes, tinned peaches and cream was lowered down to the flat where they were holed up. After it had been consumed, the four IRA men – who were by then known as the 'Balcombe Street Gang' – surrendered quietly. In 1977, they were all found guilty of multiple murders at their Old Bailey trial and received lengthy prison sentences.

In 1998, the same four IRA men made a surprise entrance to the platform of a special Sinn Féin conference in Dublin that had been called to ratify the Good Friday Agreement. They were now in prison in Ireland and were given special release by the Irish government to attend the meeting. Gerry Adams introduced them to the delegates as 'our Nelson Mandelas'. According to newspaper reports, their appearance was greeted with 'stamping feet, wild applause and triumphant cheering'.

During their trial in England, the members of this IRA unit had admitted that they were also responsible for bombing pubs in Guildford and Woolwich in which seven people had died and for which innocent Irish people were falsely convicted and imprisoned. It would take many more years before those innocent people were finally exonerated and released.

Brian Keenan was considered to be an active member of the IRA and not someone who only led from a back room. This was in contrast to the role allegedly taken by Gerry Adams. According to Dolours Price, 'Gerry didn't allow himself to be in the presence of guns, or in any situation that would put him at risk of arrest.' It was considered highly unusual for a senior member of the Army Council, like Keenan, to become actively involved in the IRA's day-to-day operations. Perhaps there was, as Ed Moloney suggests, a 'weak spot in his vanity' that led him to want to get close to the action. He was to pay for his active role in IRA operations in 1977 when his fingerprints were found on bomb-making equipment in England. They matched with prints taken from him more than fifteen years before when he had vandalised a cigarette dispensing machine in Corby.

In 1979, Keenan was arrested by the RUC at an apparently random checkpoint near Banbridge in County

Down. It seems certain that the RUC Special Branch had been tipped off about his movements by an agent inside the IRA. Since then, there has been intense speculation as to who that agent might have been. The car in which Keenan was travelling at the time of his arrest was 'clean' and unknown to the security forces. Only a very small number of senior IRA figures knew of Keenan's movements and, at the time of his arrest, he was not only on the Army Council, but was the IRA's joint Chief of Staff.

When Keenan was arrested, the RUC found a number of coded diaries in his possession. It did not take long for cryptographers to crack the code and reveal that Keenan had extensive contacts with sympathetic radical groups overseas. Some of the decoded information also referred to contacts in Northern Ireland and, as a result, RUC officers raided a number of houses, including one in Dunmurry, where, according to Chris Ryder, they found a 'hugely significant horde of intelligence information'. This included electronic monitors that had been used to tune into the frequencies used by undercover police and soldiers, as well as sophisticated bomb-making equipment. Some of this materiel was later traced back to items stolen from the Grundig factory.

Keenan was flown to England where he was charged with multiple terrorist offences. He was considered so important to the IRA that a specially selected team of experienced operatives was quickly dispatched from Ireland to break him out of Brixton Prison. These men planned to use a helicopter in his escape, but all four of these senior IRA members were arrested – in an upmarket flat in Holland Park – before they could put their plan in motion and they all received substantial prison sentences.

Keenan was tried at the Old Bailey where he was defended by Michael Mansfield, the high-profile barrister who had also represented the Price sisters. While the Balcombe Street Four had followed the traditional IRA practice of refusing to recognise the authority of a British court, Keenan was considered of such importance to the IRA that he was allowed to ignore that convention. Instead, he appeared quite relaxed in the dock as he scribbled notes to his legal team and joked with the prison warders. This nonchalant attitude was, no doubt, part of a deliberate strategy to present himself to the jury as a carefree and innocent family man. His wife and mother sat in the public gallery throughout the trial – presumably to reinforce that impression.

On the third day of the court case, one jury member complained that he felt under constant and intimidating scrutiny by Keenan's family and asked for them to be moved. This was the first sign that the defence strategy might not be working and Mansfield immediately asked for a re-trial. That was refused, but the judge ruled that some elements of the prosecution case – including the coded diaries found on Keenan when he was arrested – were not admissible. Despite that, there was other compelling evidence that connected Keenan to the Balcombe Street men. There was a document found in one of their bomb factories with his fingerprints. This document listed dozens of chemicals and electronic parts that the IRA unit needed to acquire in order to manufacture explosives. The basis of Keenan's defence was a direct address by him from the dock to the jury. This address lasted for almost two hours, during which Keenan repeatedly claimed that he had nothing to do with the IRA and was not part of any conspiracy to cause explosions. He began by describing his background in Belfast and said that he lived in a 'nationalist ghetto'. While he acknowledged this was 'nothing like the Warsaw ghetto', he claimed it was an area 'where people made the rules for themselves'. He said that there were no public buses running in Belfast and he had joined in community efforts to run an affordable taxi service. He explained that the false identity papers, which he was carrying when arrested, were to protect him from possible assassination by Ulster loyalists. He suggested that, when the English has passed the Prevention of Terrorism Act, it had served the same purpose and was also intended to protect innocent people like himself from terrorist attacks.

Keenan claimed he had only come to England to have a look at the taxi trade and, perhaps, to buy one of London's black cabs to bring back to Belfast. In the course of his visit, he had looked up an old friend – one of the Balcombe Street Four – but said he had absolutely no idea that his friend was involved with the IRA. Keenan presumed that the visit to his friend explained why his fingerprints had been found in a number of houses used by the IRA unit. He concluded his lengthy speech by saying that his trial had been a nerve-racking experience and that he hoped the British government would soon find a peaceful solution to the political situation in Northern Ireland. His counsel, Michael Mansfield, then rose to say that Keenan's address concluded the case for the defence.

The judge, in his summing up, was often interrupted by shouting from Keenan, who called him 'immoral, twisted and prejudiced'. Perhaps that was just another instance of Keenan's impatience with differing opinions or any other form of dissent. At any rate, the jury did not find Keenan's version of events convincing and the verdict they returned was that he was guilty of involvement in eight murders – including those of McWhirter and Hamilton-Fairley. It was only after the verdict was announced that his previous conviction for IRA activity was revealed to the jury. Keenan was then sentenced to eighteen years in prison: a good deal less than the members of the Balcombe Street Gang had received.

Two days after his arrest, Sir Richard Sykes, the British Ambassador to the Netherlands, was shot dead, along with his young assistant, by an IRA unit. The IRA chose not to claim responsibility for this killing until after Keenan's conviction and sentencing. Sykes had been in charge of an internal inquiry into the killing of Christopher Ewart-Biggs and would, no doubt, have been fully aware of Keenan's role in that assassination. Two RUC officers subsequently travelled to England to question Keenan about his part in Niedermayer's kidnapping. According to Alan Simpson – who was one of those officers – the interview lasted for about two hours: 'I would ask him questions and he would just stare back at us with venomous eyes.' Keenan declined to say a single word for the entire duration of the interview: By the time it was over, Simpson reckons that 'he had probably learned more from us than we had from him'.

30.
Ballot Boxes and Armalites

According to Sean O'Callaghan, the Garda agent who was serving a sentence for murder in the same jail and at the same time, Keenan remained a dominating figure among both the Irish and other prisoners in the Full Sutton Prison. He had apparently become friendly with some members of the Richardson gang, otherwise known as the 'Torture Gang', one of south London's most notorious and violent criminal outfits. One of their members, Eddie Richardson, later claimed that Keenan was his regular bridge partner during those years. He did not rate him highly as a card player, but described Keenan as 'a lovely fellow' and it seems that the English gang was willing to supply any 'muscle' that might be needed by him. O'Callaghan also claimed that Keenan had become 'paranoid and untrusting' and was understandably preoccupied with the presence of real and suspected RUC agents inside the IRA. It appears that he was convinced that his arrest came as a result of information supplied by a highly-placed informer. According to O'Callaghan, he was determined to exact revenge when he was released.

While he was in prison, Keenan corresponded with a small factional group that had split from the Communist Party of Great Britain (CPGB). This faction had founded its own news-sheet, *The Leninist*, and was noted for its strictly orthodox pro-Soviet views and its unremitting opposition to the liberalising tendencies of those who advocated so-called Euro-communism. The group claimed to be engaged in 'an open polemical struggle against the opportunists of the CPGB' in order to 're-forge a principled Marxist organisation'. It is, perhaps, not surprising that Lenin's vision of a vanguard political party, operating according to its own goals irrespective of any popular mandate, would appeal to Keenan's preferences. He and Lenin shared a similar degree of personal ruthlessness, even if he lacked some of the Bolshevik's intellectual and analytical vigour. In his correspondence, Keenan admitted to some confusion about his own politics and asked, 'Have I lost my way a bit? Or am I just a victim of my own isolation? It is difficult for me to take certain steps ... because of my [IRA] roots.' He also expressed his dissatisfaction with what he considered to be the negative influence of nationalist ideology within the IRA – which, given the history of that organisation, seems like a curious reservation.

Despite such apparent qualms, when Keenan was released – after serving twelve years with remission for good behaviour – he soon resumed his position on the

IRA's Army Council. Indeed, according to one of his daughters, he renewed his IRA activities on his first day back in Ireland. This was during the early stages of what became known as the Peace Process and the situation in Northern Ireland had changed a good deal since the years when Keenan had been most active. In the early 1970s, members of the IRA thought they would soon 'sicken the Brits' by sending home their troops 'in boxes'. 1972 and 1973 were the years in which the greatest numbers of British soldiers were killed by the IRA: indeed, close to half of the British army's total casualties across four decades died in just those two years. But the introduction of the policy of 'Ulsterisation' in the mid-1970s – through which security was largely devolved to locally recruited forces – significantly reduced the number of British army casualties and changed the fundamental nature of the conflict.

During the mid-1980s, some of the IRA's leaders realised that their campaign could not be escalated any further, although the existing strategy and its objectives were still being defended both in private and in public. In April 1989, Danny Morrison, a senior figure in the republican movement, gave an interview to *Playboy*, the magazine that has provided 'entertainment for men' since the 1950s. In between nude photos of Jennifer Lyn Jackson, a 'shapely and sexy redhead' from Ohio, and Marilyn Cole, the 'first Briton to be Playmate of the Month', Morrison reiterated IRA strategy and completed the circle of toxic masculinity. 'When it's politically costly for the British to remain in Ireland, they'll go,' he told *Playboy*. 'It won't be triggered until a large number of British soldiers are killed, and that's what's going to happen.' His confidence in that eventuality proved to be misplaced.

At a Sinn Féin Árd Fheis a few years previously, Morrison had asked delegates if they would have any objection to the IRA 'taking power in Ireland' with a 'ballot paper in this hand and an Armalite [rifle] in the other'. Sean O'Callaghan knew Morrison when they were both prisoners in Crumlin Road Jail and considered him 'wonderfully indiscreet'. That may explain Morrison's candid admission of a strategy that was clearly designed to use the democratic process to subvert democracy. But, by the time Morrison gave his *Playboy* interview, the IRA's campaign was already in slow and bloody retreat, and the number of successful attacks it staged had been in decline for several years.

In the early years of the IRA's offensive – when it still merited the title of 'provisional' – the RUC and British army had little intelligence about what was essentially a new paramilitary organisation. This lack of credible intelligence helped to doom Brian Faulkner's internment policy. It also allowed the IRA to inflict the maximum casualties on the security forces in the opening years of the Troubles. The toll of those killed by the IRA reached its peak in 1972–3. But, inevitably, as the campaign continued, some IRA members were arrested and that led to the gathering of new and reliable intelligence. That resulted in a reduction in the level of IRA violence. The republican leadership was compelled to recognise a basic reality: IRA operations had to be better planned and lead to fewer arrests if they wanted to attract new volunteers.

In other words, IRA operations began to be constrained by the limits imposed by the security forces. The IRA was also compelled to reorganise on a cellular basis, which gave its members greater protection. However, as the RUC and British army managed to penetrate the IRA's command structure with more well-placed agents, the IRA was also compelled to divert a good deal of its resources and energies to internal investigations.

After secret negotiations with the British, the IRA declared a ceasefire in 1994. It broke down temporarily in 1996, and Brian Keenan is believed to have organised the IRA's response to that breakdown: the bombing of Canary Wharf in the financial centre of London. This was the last major action taken by the IRA in England and, in some respects, it was also the most successful, since it caused a great deal of damage – both to buildings owned by banks and other financial institutions and to the reputation of London City as a secure investment centre.

Keenan viewed the damage that the Canary Wharf bombing had caused with some regret, but only because a similar attack had not been mounted at an earlier stage of the IRA's English campaign. It was arguable, he lamented, that if only the IRA had been 'able to sustain a bombing campaign in London a lot earlier by using Canary Wharf-type bombs then we might have changed the course of the war decisively in the IRA's favour'. Keenan did not, however, express any regret for the two young men who were working in a newsagent's shop in Canary Wharf when the IRA bomb was detonated. They were blown through two solid walls by the force of the explosion and killed outright. He did not mention the immigrant from Morocco who suffered permanent brain damage, or sympathise with the young woman who was blinded by flying glass.

It might have seemed likely that Keenan would strongly oppose the Peace Process. Indeed, as Henry Patterson has noted, it appeared that when he was released from prison, Keenan emerged 'from a 1970s time warp of fundamentalist militarism'. He made a number of public speeches in which he stated emphatically that the IRA would never decommission its arms. He told one rally in Belfast that nobody should be confused by the 'Staters' – another term used to denigrate those who had accepted the Free State and the Anglo-Irish Treaty in 1922. For Keenan, 'those bastards in power in Dublin' were 'spineless' and he assured his audience that 'the only thing the Republican movement will accept is the decommissioning of the British state in this country'. He also appealed for those present to vote for Sinn Féin while, at the same time, insisting that the IRA 'doesn't really want to get involved' in electoral politics but, due to present circumstances, 'we have to get involved': hardly a ringing endorsement of the democratic process.

Addressing a republican rally in County Armagh in 2001, Keenan told his audience that political negotiations and political violence when pursued concurrently were both 'legitimate forms of revolution'. He concluded by claiming that the Irish conflict would never be over 'until we have British Imperialism where it belongs – in the dustbin of history'. However, it seems that the tide of history was already running in a different direction. In 1980, thirty-seven soldiers were killed by republican paramilitaries; still a substantial number, but a fraction of the peak reached in 1972. By the beginning of the next decade, the number of British army casualties had entered single figures. By then, it was also clear that, despite the deaths of more than 500 members of the local security forces, the resistance of the northern Protestant community had not been broken.

It was true that the RUC, in particular, had paid a high price and not just in the numbers killed by the IRA: over seventy police officers committed suicide in the course of the Troubles. Despite that, applications to join the RUC throughout those years exceeded the number of vacancies by an average ratio of 20 to 1. That was explained to me by one republican activist as simply being due to the money that recruits could earn by joining the police: an eloquent expression of the lack of respect that some IRA supporters felt for the other major community in Northern Ireland.

From the early 1990s, there was also a marked increase in loyalist paramilitary murders. Some of these are alleged – and some are proven – to have involved collusion by the security forces. By the closing years of the Troubles, loyalists were killing more people than the IRA. This prompted the IRA, in turn, to pursue even more explicitly sectarian attacks against the unionist population. One of the most notorious of these occurred in October 1993. The IRA had intended to kill the leaders of the loyalist Ulster Defence Association (UDA) whom they wrongly believed were meeting above a fish shop in a Protestant district of Belfast. Two IRA members entered the shop disguised as delivery men, but the bomb they were carrying exploded prematurely. Ten people were killed. Apart from one of the bombers, all of those who died were Protestants, including two young children.

By the early 1990s, the number of such operations in Belfast had been greatly reduced and a high proportion of IRA attacks now took place in border counties, just as they had in the failed campaign of the 1950s. But, if the IRA offensive was in decline, the fortunes of Sinn Féin were on the rise. Republicans had been able to build in electoral terms upon the political impact of the hunger strikes of 1981 in which ten republican prisoners had died and Sinn

Féin looked well on its way to replacing the SDLP as the principal party representing Northern Ireland's Catholic population.

The IRA may not have been defeated by the British army but, to say the least, it did not look any closer to achieving its ultimate goal of Ireland's reunification. Indeed, it could be argued that the result of a democratic referendum on Britain's membership of the EU did more to raise questions about the political integrity of the UK state than thirty or more years of IRA violence. It is hard to resist the conclusion that the IRA leadership, by the early 1990s, was prolonging the campaign in order to improve the political position of Sinn Féin in any future negotiated settlement.

31.
The Price of Peace

There were two landmark events that signalled the end of the Troubles in Northern Ireland. Both the Good Friday Agreement of 1998 and the St Andrew's Agreement, eight years later, represent, in different ways, very considerable political achievements. Indeed, some of those involved in creating the first of those Agreements have spent a good deal of their time since then travelling the globe, basking in its apparent success. Bill Clinton, who was one of them, has described the Good Friday Agreement as 'a work of surpassing genius'. In April 2019 Nancy Pelosi, then Speaker of the US House of Representatives, claimed that the Agreement had 'ended 700 years of conflict' in Ireland. Even allowing for political hyperbole, that was a boast of remarkable naivety in several different respects. The most telling of these came a few days after Pelosi made the claim, and while she was still in Ireland, when a young journalist, Lyra McKee, was shot dead by the 'New IRA' during a riot in Derry.

It is true that the Agreement was accepted in a referendum by a majority of both sides of the religious-political divide in Northern Ireland – a historic achievement in itself. It is also true that this led to a very substantial reduction in political violence when both republican and loyalist paramilitaries declared (more or less) permanent ceasefires. But anyone who believes that Northern Ireland offers a model of conflict resolution that can be applied on a global scale might be well advised to think again.

The Good Friday Agreement established a new Assembly and an Executive with power shared primarily between the Unionist Party and the SDLP. Both David Trimble and John Hume, the leaders of those two parties, were awarded the Nobel Peace Prize and were embraced (awkwardly) on stage by Bono at a U2 concert. However, this Agreement was sold, in effect, as two different products to two different markets: a strategy that has sometimes been characterised as a case of 'creative ambiguity'.

The Agreement was presented to the nationalist community as a stepping stone on the road to a united Ireland. Some IRA members may even have believed that a secret deal had been done behind the scenes with the British. If they did, they were seriously deluded. According to Ed Moloney, the IRA leadership had lied to and deceived its own membership for years, lulling them into 'a false sense of security until it was too late for them to do anything' about the terms of the ceasefire. It would seem that Brian Keenan contributed to that deception – either deliberately or unconsciously. Addressing a rally in County Tyrone in 1999, he told his audience that the IRA viewed the new Executive, Assembly and other institutions of the Good Friday Agreement merely 'as a method of building more political strength'. This process, he continued, would 'make it harder for British Imperialism to stay in this country'.

For Protestants, the emphasis of the GFA fell on the IRA's acceptance of the principle of unionist consent and the return of a permanent devolved government at Stormont. Both of these concessions by the IRA removed what had previously been considered as the cornerstones of republican ideology. As Ian McBride has commented, these 'unprecedented compromises' by the IRA were presented to their supporters as merely 'transitional arrangements' and as evidence of the continuing 'momentum' towards national unity. Many Protestants, however, regarded the Agreement as a 'final closing of accounts with their Catholic neighbours'.

The announcement of an IRA ceasefire in 1994 was followed by a bizarre and clearly orchestrated episode in which members and supporters of the IRA drove through Catholic districts of Belfast with their car horns blaring, waving Irish flags and loudly proclaiming their 'victory' to the world's media. The obvious intention was to put the best possible spin on the IRA's decision to end its campaign and it showed unmistakable evidence of the IRA's need to reassure its own supporters that the years of armed struggle had all been worthwhile.

Given the price in blood and anguish that had been exacted over the decades from both Catholic and Protestant communities, nobody was eager to question the motives of the IRA leadership too closely. Colin Breen, a former RUC officer, has even cited instances where British and Irish politicians appeared to intervene directly in the judicial processes of their respective countries to ensure that terrorist charges against IRA members were either dropped or the sentences minimised.

It could be argued that it was not only the Irish and British governments, but also the mainstream media in Ireland and the UK that tried to induce a form of collective amnesia. According to the journalist Ed Moloney, many felt that 'telling lies in the quest for peace in Northern Ireland was not only excusable but laudable'. At times, the public response in Ireland to the Peace Process has seemed like a battered wife being grateful that her husband had stopped beating her, but fearful that any complaints about the previous abuse might provoke him into renewing his assaults. This might be described as a state of suspended terror in which the 'prize of peace' has constantly been invoked in order to warrant the turning of blind eyes to both the past and present actions of the IRA.

Nonetheless, it is hard to say that the Agreement represented any real victory for the IRA. The British army may have failed to eliminate all republican paramilitary activity and the IRA continued to recruit, to organise and to commit acts of violence in the run-up to their ceasefire, but by the early 1990s, the RUC and British army were able to contain most IRA operations and restrict the campaign in large part to the border regions of Northern Ireland. No one would have liked to admit it in public, but the security situation approximated to what Reginald Maudling had once foolishly described as 'an acceptable level of violence'. The IRA had been unable to reclaim Ireland's 'fourth green field' and, with the Good Friday Agreement, republicans also abandoned goals that had previously been regarded as sacrosanct and non-negotiable. This was the context in which Brian Keenan urged his colleagues to win what he called (without any obvious irony) the 'savage war of peace'.

The Executive established by the Good Friday Agreement eventually collapsed over the IRA's refusal to decommission its arsenal of weapons. Such intransigence was to change following the terrorist attack on the Twin Towers in New York in 2001. In the aftermath of that attack, the IRA began to give way to increased pressure from the Bush administration – which took a much more robust line than that of Clinton – and commenced the destruction of its weaponry. Despite expectations, Brian Keenan came to play a central role in the process of decommissioning. He also helped to ensure that the political strategy advocated by Gerry Adams and others retained the confidence and support of the IRA and that led to the effective abandonment of the IRA's military campaign.

The rank and file members of the IRA trusted Keenan and believed that, when he promised there would be no decommissioning of IRA arms, he would prove as good as his word. In fact, Keenan ended up acting as the IRA's secret intermediary with John de Chastelain – the Canadian general charged with decommissioning weapon stocks in Ireland. Jonathan Powell, Tony Blair's Chief of Staff, had once described Keenan as 'the biggest single threat to the British State', but he came to believe that if Keenan had remained opposed to decommissioning, then 'it would not have happened'. Powell was aware that Keenan was seriously ill at this time and thought that 'if he had died, then it might have been impossible to persuade the IRA to trade the Armalite for the ballot box'.

Powell's assessment may be overstated and overlooks the central role played by Martin McGuinness, whose credibility as someone who had taken an active part in IRA operations and personal charisma were of critical importance in carrying the IRA grassroots along with the Peace Process and avoiding a serious split in the organisation. There is also a persuasive argument, advanced by Ed Moloney, that the IRA's leaders – and Gerry Adams, in particular – deliberately misled its members for a number of years in the run-up to the Good Friday Agreement. Moloney has argued that the IRA's grassroots had been persuaded that the military campaign was not in its terminal stages and that the whole Peace Process was merely an elaborate tactic on the part of the Sinn Féin leadership to outfox the British. Many people in Northern Ireland can only feel grateful if Adams' opponents were misled so successfully and that he and his supporters were able effectively to outmanoeuvre those who were prepared for the 'armed struggle' to continue indefinitely.

When it became quite clear where the Peace Process was leading, some disenchanted IRA members eventually left the IRA to form their own dissident republican paramilitary groups such as the 'Real IRA'. In that context, the backing given by Keenan to Gerry Adams further helped to avoid a more significant split. In fact, Keenan is said to have shown great hostility to any of those who wanted to break away from the mainstream IRA. According to one of his former colleagues, he wanted all such dissidents to be shot. He is also believed to have visited several homes in south Armagh after the Real IRA's bombing of Omagh – in which twenty-nine people were killed (including a woman pregnant with twins) – and personally issued a number of death threats. Few would have taken such threats lightly, or doubted that Keenan meant what he said.

For some, the apparent contradiction in Keenan's role in the Peace Process is so extreme as to be inexplicable. He had the reputation of being, in Paul Bew's words, 'a manic figure' and 'the militant of the militants'. Keenan spent much of his adult life planning events with similar intent to the Omagh bombing and he is alleged to have been involved in planning IRA operations (such as Kingsmill) that deliberately killed innocent civilians. In his role as Quartermaster General for the IRA, Keenan had also travelled extensively in his search for weapons. This supply of war material helped to ensure that the IRA's campaign could be maintained over three decades. Yet, as David McKittrick has observed, Keenan 'first helped build up the organisation [of the IRA] and then, decades later, helped shut it down'.

Perhaps the reason for this apparent contradiction is that Keenan's personal commitment to the IRA as an organisation was so complete that he was prepared to back its leadership even when he disagreed with their strategy. He is said to have been a forceful advocate of the doctrine of 'democratic centralism'. In practice, the emphasis seems to have fallen rather more on (his) central control than on (others') democratic debate. In his book, *The IRA and Armed Struggle*, Rogelio Alonso interviewed scores of members and former members of the IRA. Apart from the sense of disillusionment expressed by many of those he interviewed, a recurrent complaint was that the hierarchical nature of the IRA and its leaders' rigid control effectively suppressed any dissent, or genuine dialogue, within its ranks.

Beyond that, the IRA had been Keenan's political home for almost all of his adult life. Perhaps this made the prospect of leaving the security of that home and opposing Adams' strategy too hard to contemplate. Perhaps his worsening health was also a factor: there are several references to him looking frail and physically weakened at this time. But Keenan also liked to think of himself as a political realist. 'Revolutionaries have to be pragmatic,' he told *An Phoblacht*, 'wish lists are for Christmas'. Perhaps, by that time, Keenan had concluded that the IRA's military campaign was simply unwinnable.

It is tempting for some to construct an appealing narrative out of the apparent contradictions in Keenan's political evolution: a narrative of how a 'man of war' eventually became a 'man of peace'. However, for me, this is a sentimental, naive and flawed reading of his political commitments. One indication that Keenan – and the IRA – had not undergone a profound moral conversion occurred three years after the Good Friday Agreement had been signed and four years after the IRA had declared its final ceasefire.

In August of 2001, three senior IRA members were arrested at Bogota International Airport in Colombia. They were travelling on fake passports, and the Colombian authorities alleged that they had spent the previous five weeks in areas of the country that were under the control of FARC rebels. The IRA members claimed that they had gone there as simple tourists. However, according to Michael McDowell, the Irish Minister for Justice, their actual purpose was to trade the IRA's expertise in explosive and mortar production in exchange for money. According to the Irish Minister, this exchange was worth 35 million in 'narco-dollars' to the IRA.

According to Dean Godson, the reactions to this news of both John Reid, who was then the Northern

Ireland Secretary of State, and Jonathan Powell, the British Prime Minister's Chief of Staff, were of disbelief. They were quick to assume that the 'Colombia Three' has been acting on their own initiative and that the trip to South America had not been authorised by the IRA's Army Council. It is most unlikely that such a major exchange of money and expertise could have been set up without the prior knowledge and agreement of the IRA's leadership. According to Ed Moloney, Brian Keenan was the Army Council member in control of this ambitious transaction. He had previously travelled to Colombia to prepare contacts with FARC and had also used family links in the USA to facilitate this deal with the Colombians.

Towards the end of his life, Keenan was associated with Coiste na nIarchimí (the ex-prisoners' committee), an organisation that was set up to help former IRA members. Keenan opened the group's Dublin office, which received a substantial grant from an agency that distributes EU peace funds. The EU's peace and reconciliation fund is one of the largest blocks of money handed out by Brussels. So far, it has spent hundreds of millions of euros on a wide range of community projects in Ireland. Coiste is also financed by the Irish government as a consequence of the Good Friday Agreement and, once again, there is an inescapable irony in Keenan supporting an organisation that is also backed by those 'Staters' he once treated with contempt.

Following the IRA's decommissioning of its arsenal, the St Andrew's Agreement restored the Northern Ireland

Assembly. This led to the formation of a new power-sharing Executive in which, for the first time, the DUP and Sinn Féin were the dominant parties. It also marked a decision by Sinn Féin to support the new Police Service of Northern Ireland and to accept the legal authority of the northern state's existing courts and laws. In the following election for the new Assembly, the DUP and Sinn Féin both consolidated their positions as the principal representatives of their respective communities. The Unionist Party and the SDLP, which had held those pole positions in the early years of the Troubles, were firmly relegated to supporting and secondary roles.

Shortly before he died, Keenan sat in the VIP gallery at Stormont – under an assumed name – and watched as Ian Paisley became the First Minister of Northern Ireland. He also witnessed Martin McGuinness – a former colleague of his on the IRA's Army Council – become Deputy First Minister. A devolved administration working within the structures of the British state was, to say the least, not on Keenan's mind in the winter of 1973 when he made those deliberate and calculated decisions that led to the killing of Thomas Niedermayer.

32.

The Prerogative of Mercy

In 1975, less than two years after Niedermayer's abduction, the Price sisters were moved to Northern Ireland. That had been the chief objective of the kidnapping – and it had been delivered without any further threat of murder. In 1980, Marian Price was released from prison on a parole license for life. Subsequently, she was closely associated with those 'dissident' republicans who wished to pursue further armed conflict with Britain. She emerged as a leading figure in the '32 County Sovereignty Movement': an organisation believed to be linked to the dissident paramilitary group, the 'Real IRA'. On 17 November 2009, Marian Price was arrested in connection with a Real IRA attack on the Massereene Barracks at Antrim in which two British soldiers were killed. No charges were brought against her, but her parole license was subsequently revoked and she was imprisoned again in 2011. A campaign to secure her release on the grounds of ill health was successful and she was set free in May 2013.

In 1980, Marian's elder sister, Dolours Price, received a Royal Prerogative of Mercy. She was released from prison suffering from anorexia nervosa. The following year, she married the actor Stephen Rea, whom she had watched perform on the stage of the Royal Court Theatre in Chelsea the night before her IRA unit bombed London. During the 1980s, according to Patrick Redden Keefe, she and her husband were accepted into the mainstream of artistic and intellectual life in Dublin, London and New York. Seamus Heaney, the Nobel Laureate, even wrote an original poem for her children on a Japanese fan that hung on one of their walls. However, Price and Rea separated in 2000 and divorced in 2003.

Like her sister, Dolours Price was strongly opposed to Sinn Féin's involvement in the Peace Process. As far as she was concerned, the party's leaders were not real republicans but 'Stalinists' who were now acting 'as British administrators'. She believed that they had turned 'a once noble Army into an armed militia'. The only role that was left to the IRA, she wrote, was 'to strong arm any opposition to [the leadership's] insatiable political greed and opportunism'.

In 2009, Dolours Price admitted on camera to her involvement in the murders of Jean McConville and three men who were killed as suspected informers by the IRA. In all these murders, she claimed to have acted under the direct orders of the man who was a former Westminster MP, a former MLA in the Stormont Assembly, a former

TD in Dáil Éireann and, for almost thirty-six years, the President of Sinn Féin: Gerry Adams. He has consistently denied ever having been a member of the IRA. This denial – which most observers regard as lacking in credibility – seems to have outraged Dolours Price. '[Adams'] ego has taken him to believe himself above the common people,' she wrote in one of many online comments about her former commander, and she described the substance of his 'present life' as 'a lie'.

She also became alienated from many of those whom she once regarded as comrades: 'You mean nothing to me,' she wrote. 'You people with whom I once shared a dream, an aspiration, prison and pain.' It is possible to understand the reasons for Price's sense of betrayal and to appreciate the high personal price she paid in an armed campaign that she came to see as futile. But it is also possible to feel relief that her intransigent opinions did not prevail in the leadership ranks of the IRA. When the Northern Ireland power-sharing Executive was established in 2008, Dolours Price wrote that she had spent a good deal of the day in tears: 'for myself, my dead comrades, my damaged comrades, for innocents and even for squaddies [British soldiers]'. She concluded that 'none of us, with a soul or conscience, [have] come through without any damage'.

In 2011, Dolours Price was arrested in Dublin and charged with possession of stolen prescription pads and forged drug prescriptions. She was not imprisoned, but was ordered by the court to attend meetings of Alcoholics Anonymous. In January 2013, she was found dead at her home in Dublin. A post-mortem revealed a lethal combination of drugs – antidepressants, sedatives and antipsychotics – in her system. The Gardaí said they were satisfied there were no suspicious circumstances surrounding her death. Dolours Price was buried in the republican plot at Milltown Cemetery in West Belfast, close to the grave of her beloved father. Gerry Adams expressed his sadness at her death, but did not attend the funeral.

33.
Legacies

The ceasefire called by the IRA in 1996 did not mark the end of its violent actions; Gerry Adams was telling the truth when he assured a rally of republican supporters in 2004 that the IRA 'haven't gone away, you know'. Indeed, even the term 'ceasefire' is something of a misnomer: the IRA communiqué of 1994 had only referred to a 'cessation of military operations'. In the years following this cessation, IRA members were implicated in further bank robberies, many so-called punishment shootings and a number of individual murders. One such murder was that of Robert McCartney, who was stabbed to death by IRA members outside a bar in West Belfast following an inconsequential row. Other IRA volunteers then systematically removed any forensic evidence from the scene of the murder. When questioned by police, all of those present in the crowded bar claimed to have been in the toilet at the time of the murder.

It was widely believed that the British authorities were prepared to turn a blind eye to many violations of the IRA ceasefire – both at home and abroad. 'The IRA changed urban warfare on a world basis,' Keenan boasted to *An Phoblacht* shortly before he died. 'Other armed revolutionary organisations have borrowed the IRA's tactics.' There was some truth to his comments. In the years following the ceasefire, the IRA's bomb-making expertise was exported around the world. IRA members were available to give advice to guerrilla groups such as FARC in Colombia, where they were said to have been paid handsomely for their services by a group that had grown rich in 'narcodollars' from the illicit drugs trade.

The armed conflict between the IRA and the British state may have ended in what Gerry Adams described as a 'stalemate'. In several respects, that statement was true. But sometimes even a draw can be interpreted as a defeat for one side or the other and, in this case, it would appear that the IRA was the loser. However, if the Troubles ended with a strategic defeat for the IRA, then, in some ways, it has proved to be a tactical success for Sinn Féin. That party seems to have inverted von Clausewitz's famous maxim, and politics has become the continuation of its war by other means. Cut loose from the anchor of current IRA killings and bombings, Sinn Féin has proved relentless in its determination to establish and preserve its own narrative of what the Troubles signified.

Part of that process has been to stage what seems like an endless succession of ceremonies in which those considered to be martyrs for the republican cause are commemorated. As Ian McBride has commented, what is striking about these events is not just the tendency for 'present conflicts to express themselves through the personalities of the past', but also the way in which these 'rituals have become historical forces in their own right'.

In 2018, these rituals included one designed to honour the memory of Thomas Begley. He was the IRA volunteer who blew himself up in a fish shop on the Protestant Shankill Road – along with nine civilians who happened to be shopping there. At the republican ceremony to mark the twenty-fifth anniversary of his death, there were warm tributes to Begley's self-sacrifice. One Sinn Féin councillor did mention the others who were killed by Begley that day, but he insisted that there should be 'no hierarchy of victims' among those who died in the fish shop.

That phrase has become something of a mantra among IRA supporters, but I would question whether the death of Thomas Begley can really be equated with that of Leanne Murray who was thirteen when she was killed by his bomb, or Michelle Baird who was just seven and who died with both her parents. For similar reasons, I wonder if the loyalist gunmen who were convicted for killing Catholic civilians in the weeks that followed the explosion of Begley's bomb can be considered to be victims of the Troubles in quite the same way as the people they murdered.

There has been an annual memorial lecture run by Sinn Féin in which Brian Keenan is honoured, as well as a 'Brian Keenan Mountain Challenge' to celebrate his 'love of nature'. (Ironically, the organisers of this memorial walk were subsequently accused of 'damaging the protected landscape' of the Cooley mountains.) Keenan's life and work are regularly cited with approval in the republican press and in its various publications where he is described as a 'Republican Legend'. It is also possible to purchase an icon of the IRA leader: the 'Brian Keenan Print' comes in four sizes and two different finishes ('gloss and parchment'). For a 'small additional charge', you can also have a short biography of Keenan printed beside his portrait.

The legacy of Thomas Niedermayer has been rather different. He helped to bring hundreds of jobs to a deprived part of Northern Ireland and he took no role in any political activities. But, in 1973, he was still considered to be a 'legitimate target' by Brian Keenan and his associates. That was, of course, a time before Sinn Féin could cheerfully describe itself as being 'pro-business' and Gerry Adams could boast that Sinn Féin was fully aware of how crucial foreign direct investment was to the Irish economy. Until Ciaran Cassidy and Joe Duffy broadcast their radio documentary in 2013, Thomas Niedermayer was almost forgotten. There were no 'fun runs' to celebrate his life and, if he were recalled at all, it was probably only because his surname was such an unusual one in any part of Ireland. Like so many victims of the Troubles, he 'disappeared' – both literally and figuratively.

When he died of cancer in 2008, Keenan was described in the British press as the 'most ruthless and formidable' of all IRA leaders. His coffin was carried by the man to whom he had given such unstinting and invaluable support, Gerry Adams, who was then President of Sinn Féin. Adams gave a eulogy in which he spoke warmly of how much Keenan had 'loved the IRA'. He mentioned his devotion to all 'natural things' and recalled one 'hilarious' experience that he had shared with Keenan, 'trying to mate one of his dogs with mine'. Another speaker described him as 'a thinker, a doer, an ambassador of the written word, a progressive thinker, (and) a master orator'. The same speaker noted that he had been 'instrumental in taking the war to Britain in the 1970s.'

Keenan's funeral service was without the benefit of clergy and this was hailed by some as proof that he really was a 'secular' republican, following in the tradition established by Wolfe Tone. In reality, it is quite easy to be a convinced atheist in Ireland and also display sectarian prejudice, and it speaks volumes that a non-religious funeral could still be viewed by anyone as some sort of radical political statement.

It is true that Wolfe Tone was both a revolutionary and a republican, but he was also a product of the great European Enlightenment – whereas Keenan belonged to a darker sectarian tradition in Ireland. Unlike Keenan, Tone dedicated his life to abolishing 'the memory of all past dissentions' in Ireland. Although he was raised in the Established Anglican Church, with access to all the privileges that entailed, when Tone founded the Society of United Irishmen in 1791 all but one of the other co-founders were Presbyterian. And Tone also wrote and published *An Argument on Behalf of the Catholics of Ireland* and served as secretary to the committee that worked assiduously for Catholic emancipation.

In other words, Tone consistently sought to find new ways of 'uniting the Catholics and Dissenters' of Ireland. Brian Keenan might have spent considerable time and energy in forging alliances with terrorist groups outside Ireland, but it is clear that he showed little interest in doing the same with the unionist population of his own country. Shortly before he killed himself in 1798, Wolfe Tone expressed concern that his political activities might have 'brought misfortunes upon [Ireland]' and worried that he might have contributed in any way to the United Irish movement 'degenerating into a system of assassination, massacre and plunder'. Keenan never seems to have experienced similar crises of conscience.

According to a news report, there were 'heartbreaking' scenes at Keenan's funeral as his daughters 'kissed and caressed his coffin'. Of course, they were afforded an opportunity to express their grief that was denied to Thomas Niedermayer's daughters for many years. One of Keenan's children later commented upon the emotional pain her father's absences from his family caused her and her siblings. However, she believed that his willingness to sacrifice the happiness of his own family for a greater goal was evidence of his personal integrity. But Brian Keenan had chosen of his own volition to go down a path that led to his separation from his wife and children. Thomas Niedermayer was given no such option. He was abducted by force from his home in the middle of the night and he was killed by men to whom he had done no wrong. Brian Keenan was given a funeral with full paramilitary honours by the IRA, but Niedermayer's body was left under a rubbish dump. Keenan knew the man whose kidnapping he had planned and he was quite prepared to use Niedermayer as a pawn in a bitter conflict in which the German businessman had no direct or indirect involvement.

William Faulkner famously wrote, 'The past is never dead. It's not even past.' He was referring to the former states of the Confederacy in North America, but his words could apply equally well to Northern Ireland. With the effective end of the Troubles, a new type of conflict has emerged. This one involves ownership of the past or, to be more precise, ownership of a narrative that can explain what the Troubles were all about. Given the amount of individual and collective traumas experienced in Northern Ireland over more than thirty years, perhaps that was only to be expected.

In his classic drama about the Irish Civil War, *The Shadow of a Gunman*, one of Seán O'Casey's characters comments that he is sick of the gunmen boasting about 'dyin' for the people when it's the people who are dyin' for the gunmen'. His complaint is pertinent to contemporary Ulster. The IRA was responsible for almost 2,000 deaths in the course of the Troubles, a large number of whom were innocent civilians. In the same period, the IRA lost over 300 of its own members. In three months alone between December 1971 and March 1972, fifteen IRA members blew themselves up. Indeed, almost as many IRA members were killed by their own bombs, or by each other, as by the British army. That equation does not feature prominently in many of the narratives that have found purchase since the end of the Troubles. Henry McDonald has even suggested that the Northern Ireland conflict is unique because 'truth was the last casualty rather than the first'. What is certain is that the victims of both IRA and loyalist paramilitaries are seldom, if ever, memorialised with the same type of elaborate public display as those who killed them. It is also true that the circumstances of their deaths are seldom subject to lengthy public enquiries.

In this context, Chris Ryder identified what he terms an 'underclass of victims' in Northern Ireland: those who suffered in the 'prolonged carnage' and who have received 'little formal justice for their suffering'. The vast majority of murders during the Troubles have remained unsolved. In many cases, as Ryder pointed out, this means that some victims 'see the people responsible for their loss on a daily basis'. That was certainly the case with the family of John Proctor in Swatragh. However,

Ryder identified another group of victims: those who have been organised in 'high intensity campaigns' around a series of 'public enquiries, tribunals or renewed inquests'. Such campaigns invariably involve claims made against the actions of the state's security forces.

Ryder believed this constitutes the real 'hierarchy of victims' in Northern Ireland. He also believed that the practical result of this retrospection is to nourish divisions and to prevent the 'wounds of conflict from ever healing'. For that reason, Ryder has argued that all files relating to the Troubles should be sealed for the next fifty years and that the millions of pounds earmarked for legacy investigations should be redirected to help address the psychological and physical needs of the surviving victims. I do not agree with Ryder's proposals: any sort of imposed silence seems unrealistic and counter-productive to me. Besides, as Edna Longley has pointed out, there is ample room for choice along a spectrum that ranges from cultural 'amnesia' to 'total recall'.

When he was alive, Brian Keenan participated in many similar commemorations to the one that honoured Thomas Begley. In 2003, he addressed a crowd of Sinn Féin supporters who had gathered in Fairview Park in Dublin around the statue of Seán Russell, a former Chief of Staff of the IRA. Keenan praised Russell as someone who had preferred freedom to slavery and he quoted Patrick Pearse, a leader of the 1916 Easter Rising, to the effect that 'there are worse things than bloodshed'. Keenan was joined on the platform by Mary Lou McDonald, the future President of Sinn Féin, who heaped extravagant praise on Russell's memory. McDonald is currently rated as the most popular politician in the Irish Republic.

Sixty years or so earlier, during the Second World War, Russell was also honoured for his role as an IRA leader – on that occasion, it was by the Nazis in Germany where he spent the last years of his life. The Nazis provided him with a spacious villa outside Berlin, a car, a driver and a personal assistant. German Intelligence also trained him in the use of high explosives. Russell died on board a German U-Boat in 1940. He was on his way back to Ireland with the intention of leading a sabotage campaign directed at the Allies. Not surprisingly, none of this was mentioned by either Keenan or McDonald as they stood beside what has been described as the only public statue of a Nazi collaborator to be found anywhere in Europe.

34.

The Deep Dark Wood

Much has changed in Colin Glen since the body of Thomas Niedermayer was found buried under tons of rubbish in this public parkland. It is now officially known as a 'Forest Reserve': the reclamation work that began as an undercover exercise by a team of RUC officers in 1980 has been maintained and expanded. It now includes two sites. One offers an adventure centre which features high wires and an environmental education course. The other site is less than half a mile away and consists of a nine-hole golf course, a driving range, three football pitches and a gymnasium.

The forest park is advertised as 'ideal for Families, Birthday Parties, Hen or Stag do's [sic], School and Youth Groups, Sports Teams, Corporate Team Building and Incentive Days, Scouts and Guides'. The Glen was the first community park in Northern Ireland to be awarded the Green Flag Award – a national benchmark for quality parks and green spaces. It has also become a playground for individuals, families and other assorted groups who are 'seeking some solace from the hustle and bustle of everyday life'. At the entrance to Andersonstown, an arch quotes from a children's book to welcome all those who have come to this 'deep dark wood'. It is claimed that the Glen attracts hundreds of thousands of visitors every year,

Since 1989, thousands of Ireland's native trees have been planted in the Glen and it is now administered by a charitable Trust. The ultimate goal is to create a 'cross-community amenity'. It is hoped that this will link a unionist housing estate in one part of the city with a nationalist one on the other side. In other words, the Glen is intended to become both a genuine recreational resource and a symbol and agent of reconciliation between the two major communities in Northern Ireland. For the time being, that goal remains – both literally and metaphorically – just an aspiration.

Indeed, in some respects Protestants and Catholics have become even more polarised than they were when the Good Friday Agreement was signed in 1998. At that time, the two dominant parties in Northern Ireland were the Ulster Unionist Party and the SDLP. It could be argued that both of those centrist parties were set on a course of long-term decline for years before the Agreement. But that process accelerated in the decades that followed and they have now both been eclipsed by Sinn Féin and the DUP.

The 1998 Agreement was produced by the extra-ordinary efforts of the Irish, British and American governments and the personal commitments of the Irish Taoiseach, the British Prime Minister and the American President. Their objective was to promote reconciliation in Northern Ireland. However, that has not been achieved – or, at least, not in the way that was originally envisaged. Several decades after loyalist and republican paramilitaries declared ceasefires, the political relationships between Protestants and Catholics remain unstable. It seems that the most we can expect in the immediate and medium-term future is a form of grudging cooperation between two hegemonic parties that still do not trust each other.

When the Conservative government of Theresa May became temporarily dependent on DUP votes to stay in office after the election of 2017, the reaction of many *bien pensants* in the UK was one of unconcealed horror and disgust. Ulster's unionists have often been regarded in England with a degree of social embarrassment – rather like distant and disorderly relatives who gate-crash a fashionable wedding and can't be refused admission. As it happens, successive British governments share a considerable measure of responsibility for the rise of the DUP. It was, for example, the former British Prime Minister, Tony Blair, who gave written undertakings to the Ulster Unionist Party, led by David Trimble, that there would be no early release of prisoners and no inclusion of Sinn Féin in government without IRA decommissioning.

Blair may have thought this was necessary to secure the Good Friday Agreement, and he may have been right, but, when decommissioning did not take place, it had the effect of undermining both Trimble's personal standing and the credibility of the party he led in the eyes of many Protestants. This loss of trust helped the DUP to emerge as the dominant party representing unionists in Northern Ireland.

Like similar ethnocentric parties elsewhere in the world, the primary focus of the DUP is on its own backyard and its members appear to care very little about what the rest of the world thinks of them. Although around one-third of the DUP's members are believed to be connected in some way with the Free Presbyterian Church, the entire membership of that Church counts for less than one per cent of the total Protestant population in Northern Ireland. What is more, opinion polls have demonstrated that a large majority of those Protestants who vote for the DUP do not share the views of Free Presbyterians on such matters as evolution or homosexuality. Ironically, those polls also indicate that some Catholics in Northern Ireland share the DUP's conservative position on specific social issues – notably, abortion – yet vote for a party like Sinn Féin that holds opposing views. Indeed, opinion polls have indicated that a surprising number of Catholics who vote for Sinn Féin are actually in favour of Northern Ireland staying within the UK.

That raises the obvious question: why do Protestants and Catholics in Northern Ireland continue to vote for parties whose objectives and beliefs do not necessarily coincide with their own? The explanation may lie in the extreme polarisation of the two communities that has emerged from decades of inter-communal violence. This tends to operate on what has been termed a 'zero-sum game': meaning that, when one side in the conflict appears to have gained something, the other side assumes that it has lost. In other words, as the Northern Irish poet Louis MacNeice once observed, this is a society where 'one man's hope becomes the other man's damnation'.

The Good Friday and St Andrew's Agreements brought peace (more or less) to Northern Ireland, for which all (or almost all) of its inhabitants were profoundly thankful. Despite this, the binding terms of the Agreement could also be said to have formalised and even institutionalised existing sectarian divisions. It would appear this has also worked to the electoral advantage of both Sinn Féin and the DUP. Voluntary segregation between the two major communities in Northern Ireland has not diminished since the Good Friday Agreement: if anything, it appears to have increased. It is reckoned that at least half of the population of Northern Ireland now live in areas that are only shared by their co-religionists. There are still many 'peace walls' in Belfast and in several other towns separating Protestants and Catholics: in fact, there are more now than when the Good Friday Agreement was signed.

This does not mean that the outlook for Northern Ireland remains uniformly bleak. Recent studies by the Statistical Research Agency has established that the rates of both employment and unemployment have now reached a state of parity between Protestants and Catholics. In other words, there is now a genuine basis for economic and social equality between those two communities. All political parties also recognise that any form of future devolved government must involve both major communities at executive level.

It is also acknowledged that the political reunification of the island can only be achieved through peaceful and democratic means. There is an awareness that relations between the two parts of Ireland need to be developed on the basis of genuine cooperation and mutual respect. All of these developments mark significant changes in the conditions that prevailed in the decades that led up to the outbreak of the Troubles and give reason to hope for the future.

35.
Collateral Damage

Ingeborg Niedermayer remained in Northern Ireland for seven years after her husband's abduction. She told one journalist that she had decided to stay because she had lived in Northern Ireland for so long that she now regarded it as her home. She said she had also been moved by the support she had received from members of the public. In 1978, she pursued a case against the Northern Ireland Office (NIO) for Criminal Injuries. In order to assess her claim for compensation, the NIO requested an examination by a consultant psychiatrist. The report that he wrote provides valuable insight into Ingeborg's psychological condition at that time.

She told the psychiatrist that she had received treatment for depression in the years leading up to her husband's kidnapping. She attributed this, in part, to the incessant demands that his work made on him, which resulted in his frequent absences from their home. She also believed that the 'very full social life' they led, following his appointment as the Honorary German Consul, had caused some tension to arise between them. She said that, in the immediate aftermath of the abduction, she had lost several stone in weight and the psychiatrist noted that she was still markedly underweight. Ingeborg also told him that she had felt under enormous personal stress in the months after Thomas's disappearance and had contemplated suicide on more than one occasion.

Ingeborg was declared a widow by a German court in 1976, but she told the psychiatrist that she continued to pray that Thomas was still alive and had done so every day since the night of his abduction. She believed that if she 'knew for certain what had become of [her] husband' she might feel better. It was 'the not-knowing,' she said, 'that continually nags at my mind and brings on periods of depression and anxiety'. Since the kidnapping, she confided, she had only managed to survive 'from day to day'. The psychiatrist observed that she had become extremely isolated and lived without much social contact: 'I get lonelier and lonelier,' she told him. 'People don't want to know me anymore.'

In the aftermath of the kidnapping, Ingeborg had stopped attending the Lutheran Church that was frequented by many German expats in Northern Ireland. It seems that some of those attending the church had become nervous that she might draw down unwelcome attention on other members of their community from the IRA or other paramilitary groups. Instead, Ingeborg began to attend a Presbyterian church at Harmony Hill in County Antrim where she maintained a deliberately low profile. In the years that she waited for news of her husband's fate, she engaged with other aspects of life in Northern Ireland; volunteering to work as a children's nursing assistant and answering phone calls for the Samaritans from people struggling with various mental health challenges, including suicidal thoughts.

Kidnapping derives its malignant power from the ways in which it can manipulate human emotions by denying the victims and their families any real control over both their ordinary lives and the extraordinary situation in which they find themselves. This severe loss of personal control can lead to intense and profound feelings of helplessness and distress. Judith Herman had observed that, when such feelings are present, they can also connect and regenerate prior traumas and psychological disruptions. If there is a degree of social isolation and a lack of therapeutic support, this can become evident in physical, cognitive and affective ways. In this sense, the real targets of most kidnappers are not the unfortunate people they have abducted, but their families.

In the case of Thomas Niedermayer's family, they were kept for years in a state of fearful suspense with critical information withheld from them by both the British government and – principally – by the IRA. In other words, the trauma they experienced was made even worse by the powerlessness that had been ruthlessly imposed on them by Thomas's killers. According to Rogelio Alonso, a leading historian of terrorism in Europe, 'when bodies are disappeared, (the terrorists) are going the extra mile in their cruelty. They are denying the relatives any proper closure or mourning for their loved ones.' Denis Lehane described the impact of this deliberate withholding of critical information in powerful and telling words: 'The silence of the dead says, Goodbye. The silence of the missing says, Find me.'

The subsequent fallout of Thomas Niedermayer's disappearance was extreme but not exceptional. Psychologists have recorded the feelings of shame, anger, self-blame and depression among other families who have gone through similar experiences. The levels of extreme and conflicting emotions that these families undergo can produce great internal stress, which can impair their everyday functioning, even within previously close families. In that context, conflicts can remain unresolved for years and family members can become estranged and isolated from each other.

Sadly, the impact of Thomas Niedermayer's abduction appeared to have fractured the unity of his immediate family. Ingeborg complained to the psychiatrist who examined her for the NIO that her elder daughter, Gabriele, never came to visit her and he described her relationship with Renate, the younger daughter, as 'strained': it appeared that they lived 'separate lives' in the same house and seldom spoke to each other. It was also clear that Ingeborg's mental stability had been profoundly affected by what had occurred five years previously. 'I'll never be the same,' she told the psychiatrist, 'my whole life is completely messed up.'

There seems to have been a tendency for Ingeborg and her children to blame themselves and each other quite unfairly for what has happened on that cold December night and to feel a crippling mixture of guilt, anger and resentment. If Ingeborg had not been in the hospital, she might, perhaps, have been able to prevent the abduction; if Renate had not opened the door to the kidnappers, her father might possibly still be alive; if Gabriele had been at home, things might, conceivably, have been different. Those are the sort of agonising thoughts that are groundless but can easily distort perceptions and produce intense feelings of liability and shame. Sometimes such feelings can lead to further tragedies.

Ingeborg returned to Germany soon after the burial of her husband in 1980. It is difficult to imagine what comfort she found there. The world of East Prussia in which she had grown up was gone for good. It had been dismembered and absorbed by Russia, Poland and Lithuania. In the aftermath of the world war, Stalin had insisted that the USSR should be given access to the Baltic Sea, and Ingeborg's home village was now part of the Oblast of Kaliningrad – a small Russian enclave located hundreds of miles from the rest of the Soviet Union. All ethnic Germans had been expelled and the region had been re-populated with settlers from across the USSR. Land, houses and personal property had been distributed to those settlers. Even the names of the towns and villages that Ingeborg had known when growing up in had been erased and replaced. The German language was no longer spoken in the region, and most of the evidence of its previous history had been totally eradicated. Indeed, while researching this book, I could only locate Ingeborg's birthplace by consulting Lutheran church records: its name had literally been wiped off the map.

By 1980, Ingeborg had not lived in West Germany for almost two decades and may have felt almost as much of an outsider there as she had once been in Northern Ireland, She had once been officially classified as a 'displaced person' and perhaps that label always impacted her sense of identity, even though she did her best to remain optimistic. Writing to a friend in Northern Ireland in November 1983, she observed that 'the weather is cold here, I just shrivel up in it, but soon the soft sunshine will come. I look forward to it. We all do.' In the same letter, she confessed that she had felt 'so down mentally and physically all the time (since) my husband was taken away'. But she was determined to be positive: 'I do know I will come out of [this]', she continued, 'Only time and my faith in God have brought me through. I know in my heart that God will not leave me alone even in Germany. In time, I hope I will find some friends who will like and maybe love me for myself.' However, 'at the moment', she confessed, 'I am home-sick for Ireland and I miss my friends.'

From time to time, she would visit her daughters and their families. Her granddaughter, Tanya, can remember Ingeborg's visits. She recalls her as 'a very small, timid lady who just seemed incredibly sad. She may have been there is person but it didn't feel that she was there in spirit.' There were also times when it seemed to Tanya that Ingeborg couldn't cope: 'She went down into what appeared to be pits of depression.' Tanya attributes some of this to the trauma Ingeborg experienced during her flight from East Prussia: 'She was put on a refugee train to escape the Russian armies (and she) lived among the dead and dying for more than six months. As Jürgen Müller-Hohagen observed, that traumatic history had left wounds that could never fully heal.

Ingeborg came back to Ulster from time to time over the next few years to see Renate and also to visit the home in which they had all once lived together as a family. According to its new residents, she would ask if she could visit the living room and would sit there in silence for an hour or so before quietly leaving the house. In January of 1990, she wrote to her friend that her daughter, Gabriele, 'had invited me to spend Christmas and New Year with her and her family [in England]. It was wonderful to see my daughter after three long years and be together for a while.' Her granddaughter, Rachel, remembers that 'it was like having a ghost in the house'. Ingeborg had been tempted to use the opportunity of that visit to go back to Ireland: 'I was thinking to take a plane to Belfast and see my friends again, but the weather was cold and very windy.' 'One fine day,' she concluded, 'I will come back.'

A few months later, Ingeborg did return to Ireland. In June of that year, she travelled south of the Irish border and booked into O'Shea's Hotel in Bray, a seaside resort south of Dublin in County Wicklow. She asked for a room with a sea view and a double bed, telling hotel staff that she found the sight of two single beds upsetting since the death of her husband, which they found a puzzling comment. Her choice of hotel had its own significance: Ingeborg and Thomas had once spent a romantic weekend there not long after he had taken up his new job at the Grundig factory. It was a time when a new and exciting chapter in their lives was about to open. They were both, after all, starting off in a country that was unfamiliar to either of them – and which was quite unlike the societies in which either of them had grown up.

Three days after Ingeborg booked into the hotel in Bray, the staff noticed that she had not occupied her room during the previous night.. Three days after that, a jogger came across her body, which had been washed up on the north beach of Greystones, a residential town further down the coast. Ingeborg was fully dressed in a beige coat, blue skirt and black shoes. There are sometimes said to be three principal motives for suicide: relief, revenge and reunion. Judith Herman believes that the last of these – the desire for reunion – can sometimes explain clusters of related suicides, and 'the belief that one might join the people one has lost – a fantasy that you will meet them on the other side and then you'll be together again'. Perhaps such an idea was in Ingeborg's mind when she let the Irish Sea carry her away – or perhaps she simply sought relief from another day of suffering.

Her suicide took place during the Italia '90 soccer World Cup. That event generated great public excitement in both Germany and Ireland and may partially explain why her death received little press coverage in either country. It was a week before her body could be identified. Her brother-in-law, Alfred Niedermayer, travelled from Germany to make the final arrangements: Ingeborg was cremated at Glasnevin Cemetery and, in accordance with her wishes, her ashes were scattered in the garden of her former home in Belfast. It seems ironic yet somehow fitting that the remains of Thomas and Ingeborg should rest in the country where they had arrived with such high hopes, but which had eventually claimed both their lives. As one of Ingeborg's granddaughters has observed, the fact that Ingeborg returned to Ireland to kill herself was itself a 'very big statement'. Others have felt that, in effect, Ingeborg did not commit suicide, but was murdered by the IRA 'as surely as if they had put a gun to her head and shot her at point-blank range'.

At the time of her mother's death, Renate Niedermayer – the younger of Thomas's daughters – lived in South

Africa. It was Renate who had opened the door to her father's killers and had gone to rouse Thomas from his sleep. She had worked for a time as a journalist for a local newspaper in Lisburn, County Antrim, where she never mentioned the circumstances of her father's death to any of her co-workers. They remember her love of animals – as well as her mother's constant anxiety that Renate was not eating properly. In fact, in the years that followed her father's abduction, Renate developed a serious eating disorder. She never married and by the early 1990s was living in South Africa on her own while volunteering in an animal sanctuary: she received only a very small stipend for her work there, but, as she pointed out to a friend, she had 'free accommodation, electricity and TV'.

Writing to her friend in Ireland, Renate admitted that life in South Africa was very difficult for her. This was, she wrote, in part because her mother's suicide had 'hit me very hard'. She was also dealing with a number of serious health issues directly related to her eating disorders, but was unable to afford any hospital treatment. She described her living conditions as 'very spartan' and conceded that it had been difficult to 'get a life together here'. She asked, 'What is Ulster like now? What is Belfast like?' but she could not see herself ever going back to her former home, and wonders 'what on earth would I do in Ireland?'

Within a year of her mother's death, Renate was also dead. The eating disorder that she developed in the aftermath of her father's abduction continued in the following decades. One of those who knew her when she lived in South Africa noticed her frequent recourse to powerful laxatives and her consistently underfed appearance. It seems somehow appropriate that her last home was attached to a refuge for wounded and abandoned creatures.

By the time of her death, Renate had made little contact with her sister for some time. On the night of her father's abduction, Gabriele – the elder of his two children – was staying overnight with a friend. Like her sister, she subsequently moved away from Northern Ireland. Unlike her sister, she married – almost exactly a year after her father's abduction. The wedding was in England, but the location of the venue was kept secret from the press for security reasons and so that '[no] move could be made against the family': further evidence of the fear that the abduction had produced. Subsequently, Gabriele had two daughters, Tanya and Rachel.

Gabriele attempted suicide in the years that followed her sister's death and, in 1994, she died of carbon monoxide poisoning from a car she had rented for the purpose of taking her own life. But this awful sequence was not yet complete for the girls: a few years after their mother's death, their father, Robin, also killed himself.

Gabriele left letters for both her daughters in which she expressed her undying love for both of them. According to Tanya and Rachel, Gabriele had never described the circumstances of their grandfather's death and perhaps her deep distress at his murder had been compounded by the long years of silence. It was only after their parents' suicides that the children discovered their family's troubled history: 'We were never told about any history or about our family at all,' Rachel said, 'my mum never spoke about it. So it wasn't until my father died and Tanya and I went back to the house to sort out the possessions and found all the old newspapers that related to Thomas's death [that] we realised that there was a whole background.' Through the collection of Irish newspaper cuttings, the granddaughters became aware for the first time of the background to the grim succession of deaths in their family.

Tanya believes her father's later suicide was a further effect of the kidnapping: 'If it hadn't been for that, Mum wouldn't have killed herself. And that loss affected Robin horrendously. In the years that followed, he finally succumbed to depression. He was a victim as well. [...] In that sense, he is also a genuine victim of this abduction.'

In the course of making our film about this case, we were able to meet one of the men who killed Thomas Niedermayer. He expressed regret for what had happened to the German businessman and claimed that he often thought with remorse about what he had done. 'I am not an animal,' he said, 'I never meant to kill that man.' He left the IRA soon after the killing, and it was obvious that the murder had continued to haunt him in the decades that had passed since Thomas's death. There is clearly no moral equivalence between an innocent victim and the men who beat him to death, but it must be acknowledged that some of the families of those involved in terrorist crimes had sometimes to pay a high price for that connection. Their ordeals may not have been as dreadful, as prolonged or as tortured as those of Ingeborg, Gabriele and Renate, but their families often had their loved ones absent from their homes for many years.

After the trial of McManus and Bradley had concluded and sentences had been passed on both men, Ingeborg performed an act of extraordinary kindness. She cycled all the way from her home to Bradley's house – a round trip of about 13 miles. His family lived in the middle of Turf Lodge and Ingeborg risked entering this IRA stronghold in order to tell his wife of her sorrow that she was also now a single parent and having to raise a young family on her own. That was just what Ingeborg had been compelled to do and she told Bradley's wife that she recognised they had both, in their different ways, lost husbands to the Troubles. She hoped no one else would endure the same loss and suffering.

We know that Ingeborg found strength and solace in her religious faith. No doubt, she believed that this visit to the wife of her husband's killer was her Christian duty. But it remains a remarkable and rare instance of common humanity displayed in what was often a cruel, callous and brutal conflict.

36.
It Ends Here

Even by the brutal standards of Northern Ireland's Troubles, the long-term impact of Thomas Niedermayer's abduction and killing is exceptional. Its aftermath reveals the long-term and corrosive effects that acts of political terrorism can have on succeeding generations – and even on ones that are yet to be born. In this case, a German family stumbled into a long-running domestic dispute in Ireland – whose intensity they couldn't begin to understand – and all of them ended up dead.

While the dreadful effects of the Troubles on the Niedermayer family may be exceptional, they are, sadly, not entirely unique. Recent research has indicated that thousands of adults in Northern Ireland suffer from some sort of mental health issues that are directly related to the Troubles. Further research suggests that many of these victims have passed their trauma on to the next generation. A study by the Commission for Victims and Survivors in 2015 found that the legacy of the Troubles was also connected to Northern Ireland's dramatic rise in suicides.

There are now increasing concerns about the ways in which post-traumatic stress disorder can cascade down from parents to their children. There is even some evidence that a parent's trauma can be passed on to a child's biological stress response. This biological transmission was first identified in the children of Holocaust survivors, and it may help to explain why the suicide rate in Northern Ireland is now substantially higher than in any other region of the UK. Indeed, the unpalatable truth is that more people have killed themselves in Northern Ireland in the twenty years that followed the Good Friday Agreement than were killed in the previous thirty years of political violence.

Both Tanya and Rachel feel that the process of making this book, and our film, has helped them to learn more about their family's history in Ireland and perhaps to come to terms with that troubled legacy. They both recognise just how much Ingeborg had suffered during the Second World War: losing her home and almost all of her family in that terrible conflict. But, in the aftermath of the world war, she and Thomas had tried to create new and fulfilling lives for themselves in a new country. In many ways they had succeeded in that goal. Rachel reminded us that Ingeborg had become 'a wife to a successful husband and a mother to two beautiful, intelligent girls. But then she was hit again'.

Ingeborg had spent many years nurturing her family, but then Rachel believes that 'the strain and uncertainty of not knowing whether Thomas was alive or dead meant that her family disintegrated'. Despite the anguish that she had endured, Ingeborg remained mindful and compassionate. She visited the family of a man who had helped to kill her husband and she expressed her human sympathy for his family's predicament. She worked as a children's nurse, and volunteered with the Samaritans and to help those who were also struggling with psychological or emotional crises.

Tanya and Rachel are aware that the trauma of their family was prolonged for almost seven years after their grandfather's abduction. Tanya believes that the refusal of those who had taken and killed Thomas to accept responsibility for their actions was an act of monstrous and deliberate inhumanity. She and Rachel know that the impact of what happened to Thomas not only affected those who were directly involved, but also impacted on further generations of their family. They are also aware that Ingeborg and her children were left to deal with their pain and confusion largely on their own and without adequate advice and support. As Jürgen Müller-Hohagen of the Dachau Institute has commented, 'It was a crime to leave a family in such uncertainty for so long – a crime of extraordinary recklessness and cruelty.'

Now the focus of both sisters is on the future. Tanya wants her family 'to be remembered for the people that they were, and not simply as victims of a tragedy'. She does not absolve the people who murdered her grandfather from their moral responsibilities: 'I'm not saying that I am full of forgiveness and light, because I'm not. It is their fault that this happened to our family. But I've got two wonderful children. They light up my life. I have been adamant that they will not suffer in the same way that Rachel and I did.'

Rachel moved to Australia very soon after she graduated from university. She wanted 'to start a new life without a constant reminder of the pain we'd gone through'. Since then, she has established a very successful career there as an environmentalist, researching animal behaviour, which includes 'everything from sharks to lions'. Her goal is to understand why animals do what they do, and she has established an impressive reputation in her chosen field. 'But I don't think,' she admits, 'that I'll ever understand human behaviour, or how one tragic event could have had such a massive impact on my whole family for generations.'

Both Tanya and Rachel are determined that the damage inflicted on their family by an act of terror should end with them. 'The damage that's happened to our family has to stop with myself and Tanya,' says Rachel. 'I don't want to see it trickle down to the next generation. I don't want to see any of our children's lives impacted any further by that event.'

While making our film, we accompanied Tanya and Rachel on a visit to Bamberg – the picturesque Bavarian town where Thomas and Ingeborg first met, fell in love and married. They were able to meet their German blood relatives who still reside there, and to renew contact with one side of their family after a silence of many years. Ingeborg's sister-in-law Marianne Niedermayer movingly remarked that, when she looked at Tanya, she felt she was looking at Ingeborg once again.

Together, they listened to voices that had not been heard for over sixty decades: the audio letter that Thomas and Ingeborg had recorded back in 1962 – soon after they arrived in Northern Ireland – had never been sent, and due to the out-of-date format that it had been recorded on, until that moment had been unlistenable. This was the tape in which they spoke of the beauty of their new country, and their hopes for the future in Ireland.

How precisely the legacy of political violence – and events such as the kidnapping and killing of Thomas Niedermayer – can be processed and understood remains problematic in Northern Ireland. Michael Longley explored the emotional sacrifices that can be involved in making peace in his poem 'Ceasefire'. He drew some suggestive parallels between the Troubles in Northern Ireland and the Trojan War. In Longley's eloquent poem, Priam, the last king of Troy, understands and accepts 'what must be done' to recover the body of his son, Hector, from the Greeks so that he can be given a respectful burial by his family. He kneels to kiss the hand of Achilles, the man who killed his son. The implication here is that demanding and painful acts of conciliation are sometimes necessary if the most bitter of wars are ever to end.

At the beginning of this book, I cited David Rieff's argument that a 'measure of communal forgetting is actually the *sine qua non* of a peaceful and decent society'. He has also questioned if, on some occasions, 'the human and social cost of the moral demand to remember is too high a price to be worth paying'. In other words, Rieff has suggested that sometimes we must at least pretend to forget and forgive and he has argued that 'whereas forgetting does an injustice to the past, remembering does an injustice to the present'.

His words might seem particularly apposite in the case of Northern Ireland where the memories of wrongs inflicted by one side of the conflict are invariably countered by the recital of wrongs committed by the other. Perhaps Rieff is right: perhaps, deliberate forgetfulness is the price that sometimes has to be paid for an end to political violence. Perhaps, like King Priam in Longley's poem, we should sometimes be prepared to 'kiss Achilles' hand'.

But, perhaps, there are also times when the price paid for peace needs to be re-negotiated. There are times when it is important to contest some historical narratives before they take firm root in the popular imagination. And there are indications that some of those narratives have already taken hold both in Ireland and elsewhere. A *Sunday Times* poll, conducted in 2023 to mark the 25th anniversary of the Good Friday Agreement, revealed startling levels of ignorance among young Irish people about the nature of the Northern Troubles. The poll found that, for example, those under the age of 35 were much more likely to attribute the majority of killings during the conflict to the British army, and not to the IRA. In reality, the British army was responsible for 10 per cent of all deaths while the IRA and other republican terrorist groups accounted for more than 60 per cent of those fatalities. One headline in the *Sunday Times* seemed to sum up the poll's findings: 'The Country Is Losing its Memory'.

Over 80 per cent of those under 35 who were polled also admitted that they had never heard of any of those who, like Thomas Niedermayer, were 'disappeared' by the IRA. I hope this book will serve to challenge that selective amnesia by reminding people of his and others' existence. I believe that it remains imperative to contest any narratives that present the history of the Troubles as if political violence were both inevitable and fully justified. It can prove too easy to erase the lives of those human beings who were victims of terrorism from our collective memory. I think we owe them more than that.

Bibliography

As I hope this book has made clear, the lives of both Thomas and Ingeborg Niedermayer cannot be wholly defined by the years they spent in Northern Ireland. They were both, in different ways, the products of the world war that raged throughout much of their teenage years. Some of the horrors that Ingeborg Niedermayer is likely to have experienced in her desperate flight from East Prussia are described in two short books. One is *Ahead of the Bear* by Annette Reddy, which records her mother's harrowing journey from the Russian Front in 1945 – as well as her mother's poignant visit, fifty years later, to the farm where she grew up. *Last Minute* by Rosemarie Miles Apsel provides a chilling account of its author's flight from East Prussia. She was just nine years old in 1945 but, in a postscript to her book that was written almost seventy years later, she states that with the passage of the years she had come to realise that Germany was 'not defeated at the end of World War Two, but liberated' from the tyranny of Nazism.

The psychological impact of the defeat of Nazi Germany on its citizens is illustrated by the waves of mass suicide that washed over the country in the closing months and the aftermath of the world war. Christian Goeschel's *Suicides in Nazi Germany* examines the connection between the self-immolation of leading Nazis, such as Hitler, Goebbels, Himmler and Goring – who exalted 'death before dishonour' – and the wider pattern of suicide in Germany that emerged during the collapse of the Nazi regime. He argues that there is a clear difference between those who killed themselves because they wished to escape justice, and those who killed themselves for other reasons – including their fear of the Red Army, or their inability to conceive a world in which National Socialism had been defeated and ceased to exist.

A comprehensive account of the brutal warfare and indiscriminate violence that took place during the Soviet invasion of East Prussia is provided by Prit Buttar in *Battleground Prussia: The Assault on Germany's Eastern Front 1944–45*. Given the confused nature of much of the military action, Buttar's account of this theatre of war is both detailed and coherent. His critical analysis of the bloody engagements between the Wehrmacht and the Red Army is supported by many first-hand testimonies drawn not only from Soviet and German military sources, but also from some of the civilians caught up in that dreadful conflict.

A sense of the difficulties that immigrants from East Prussia and elsewhere encountered is also conveyed by Harald Jähner in *Aftermath: Life in the Fallout of the Third Reich, 1945–1955*. This is an unflinching account of the extraordinary ways in which German society as a whole began to re-build itself after a war that had reduced many of its cities to rubble and left many of its citizens deeply traumatised – to say nothing of the loathsome legacy that the Nazi regime had bequeathed to their country.

A detailed and deeply disturbing account of the mass suicides that took place in the small German town of Demmin is given by Florian Huber in *Promise Me You'll Shoot Yourself: The Downfall of Ordinary Germans in 1945*. Hundreds of Demmin's citizens chose to kill themselves and their families rather than endure the depredations of the Red Army. Huber notes that 'of all the different ways of committing suicide, drowning was the most common in Demmin'. Demmin was situated close to the village where Ingeborg grew up and lived, and it is hard not to connect that observation with her subsequent suicide.

Two writers, in particular, helped me to understand the psychological impact of the war on Thomas and Ingeborg as well as the profound effects of the kidnapping of Thomas and the protracted anguish and uncertainty that was forced upon the entire Niedermayer family. In *Trauma and Recovery*, Judith Lewis Herman explores the ways in which prolonged periods of trauma can have devastating consequences for those who are caught up and feel trapped by circumstances beyond their control. Jürgen Müller-Hohagen, in *Dialog Statt Trauma* (written with Ingeborg Müller-Hohagen), argues that our understanding of traumatic experiences, such as those endured by the Niedermayers, is much greater today than it was when Thomas was abducted. It is now widely recognised that dialogue and discussion are preferable to the silences that often followed such traumas in the past.

Many books have been written about political violence in general, and, in particular, about the Troubles in Northern Ireland. Rather than provide an exhaustive (and exhausting) catalogue of them all, I've listed some of those that have been most useful to me in writing this book.

In his provocative work *In Praise of Forgetting: Historical Memory and its Ironies*, David Rieff questions whether remembrance can ever 'inoculate' the present against repeating the errors of the past. He argues that a focus on historical wrongs can inhibit conciliation. One need not accept all or any part of his argument to recognise the value of such questioning. Rieff has also suggested that Irish society has been particularly prone to the mythologising of historical events.

In *History and Memory in Modern Ireland*, Ian McBride has edited a stimulating collection of essays that explores this relationship between the past and present. The collection includes an analysis of how certain groups have appropriated and ritualised incidents in the recent Troubles in order to support their own political narratives. Edna Longley's essay 'Northern Ireland: Commemoration, elegy, forgetting' stands out for me due to the originality and subtlety of her analysis.

Rosemary Harris's *Prejudice and Tolerance in Ulster* is based on her research as a social anthropologist in the 1950s. This pioneering fieldwork was conducted in and around a small town close to the Irish border and explored the sectarian divisions in Northern Ireland with an unprecedented degree of analytical rigour. The picture that Harris drew of Protestant and Catholic communities was one in which their apparent tolerance of everyday social contact was accompanied by underlying feelings of suspicion and fear. Her work gave some indication of the inter-communal violence that was yet to come. However, in the 1950s, Harris's research encountered opposition from those academics who believed that her approach was better suited to Africa than Western Europe, and the book was not published until the 1970s.

Lost Lives: The Stories of the Men, Women and Children Who Died as a Result of the Northern Ireland Troubles by David

McKittrick, Chris Thornton, Seamus Kelters and Brian
Feeney is an indispensable reference work which provides
comprehensive details of all those who died in the Northern
Ireland Troubles – both civilians and combatants (for want
of a better word). The book makes for sobering reading,
but, if it were to include all of those injured or damaged in
other ways, it would be many times longer.

Watching the Door: A Memoir 1971–1978 by Kevin Myers can
almost be read as a companion book to *Lost Lives.* While
the latter is rigorously objective in the way it records the
thousands of deaths that took place during the Troubles,
Myers' book conveys a vivid, insightful and passionate
sense of what it was actually like to live through events
and to report on them. Myers subjects his own conduct
as a reporter to as much critical scrutiny as he does to his
fellow journalists, and he is candid about the mistakes
that he made at that time.

Paul Bew's and Gordon Gillespie's *Northern Ireland: A
Chronology of the Troubles* provides, as its name indicates,
an excellent source of information about the history of
politics and political violence across the decades. The book
includes a number of illuminating short essays that focus
on some of the major events and incidents of those years.

J. Bowyer Bell wrote a number of books about the
Troubles in Northern Ireland. He was one of the first

to interview and document several generations of IRA members, although his writing might now be considered to be excessively romantic and impressionistic. His best-known work, *The Secret Army*, alleges that a small West Belfast (IRA) unit, 'frustrated at the organisation's lack of progress at getting the Price sisters home from prison in England', acted 'almost on the spur of the moment and without authorisation' when it kidnapped Thomas. What we now know makes that claim unsustainable.

Patrick Bishop and Eamon Mallie's *The Provisional IRA* is a well-informed and compelling history, particularly in its incisive and comprehensive account of that organisation's formative period.

Henry Patterson's *Ireland since 1939: The Persistence of Conflict* not only offers a rigorous and balanced analysis of the Troubles, but also makes an important contribution to an understanding of the development of both Irish states during the past half-century, their shared histories, and the complex ways in which they have diverged from and mirrored each other. In particular, Patterson challenges many of the conventional narratives, easy assumptions and clichéd stereotypes that have seldom been contested in the past. Patterson is also the co-author, with Paul Bew and Peter Gibbon, of *Northern Ireland 1921–2001: Political Forces and Social Classes*, which covers the period between the partition of Ireland and the cessation of the IRA's most recent armed campaign. This critical work, which has gone through several editions, has served to undermine the widespread perception of Ulster's Protestants as a social and political monolith and has drawn attention to the underlying economic and social factors that contributed to the downfall of the unionist regime.

Marianne Elliott's *The Catholics of Ulster* is a complex and important work of scholarship. Elliott argues that Ulster's Catholics can be distinguished from their co-religionists elsewhere in Ireland. They are also clearly distinct from Ulster's Protestants, but Elliott suggests that the two northern communities actually depend to a great extent on each other for a sense of their respective identities. Elliott is also the author of *Wolfe Tone*, an outstanding biography of the United Irishmen leader. In this study, she situates Tone's revolutionary beliefs firmly in the context of the European Enlightenment. That raises questions, in turn, about the way in which the subsequent adulation of Tone by Irish nationalists, such as Patrick Pearse, has served to obscure Tone's actual opinions and allowed his memory to be appropriated for what have sometimes been sectarian purposes.

In *A Broad Church: The Provisional IRA in the Republic of Ireland 1969–1980,* Gearóid Ó Faoleán examines the ways in which the Irish Republic was used by the IRA as an essential base for its campaign in Northern Ireland. Ó Faoleán argues persuasively that the amount of tacit and explicit support that republican violence received south of the Irish border was central to the maintenance of IRA lines of supply and finance and helps to explain the longevity of the Troubles.

Shane Ross's *Mary Lou McDonald: A Republican Riddle* is an account of the Sinn Féin politician's life and actions, written in a lively journalistic style. According to Ross, McDonald's political agility has allowed her to follow perceived shifts in public opinion on a range of issues – such as the EU – and may help to explain her current popularity in the Irish Republic.

In *Ulster Loyalism and the British Media*, Alan F. Parkinson has written an original and challenging analysis of how Ulster's unionists were represented by the British press and broadcast media. He argues that some British journalists still find it hard to overcome their cultural aversion to the various manifestations of Ulster loyalism – particularly when it is articulated by working-class loyalists. However, Parkinson also suggests that the negative treatment that the Protestant community tended to receive in the early years of the Troubles has been gradually modified as the complexity of the history and politics of Northern Ireland have become more apparent.

There are relatively few sympathetic accounts of Orangeism, but one of them is provided by Ruth Dudley

Edwards in *The Faithful Tribe: An Intimate Portrait of the Loyal Institutions*. While her book is not uncritical, she treats the Orange Order as a more complex and diverse institution than its common representation in the media.

In *A Political History of the Two Irelands: From Partition to Peace*, Brian Walker focuses on the ways in which conflicting ideas of identity have contributed to political violence in Northern Ireland. He argues that the island of Ireland has now entered a new era of political accommodation, although he is, perhaps, overly optimistic about the extent and strength of pluralism on either side of the Irish border.

In *The Provisional IRA in England: The Bombing Campaign 1973–97*, Gary McGladdery examines the impact of the IRA's English campaign on British government policy towards Northern Ireland. The book analyses the internal politics of the republican movement, exploring the reasoning and assumptions behind the use of particular tactics and raises fundamental questions about the effectiveness of the IRA's bombing campaign in England.

Ruan O'Donnell provides an account of IRA prisoners in the United Kingdom in *Special Category: the IRA in English Prisons, Vol. II: 1978–1985*. As I have mentioned in the preceding text, he gives some credence to the IRA's claim that Thomas Niedermayer died of 'natural causes', but gives no explanation of why he favours that flawed account of his death. In a sense, I suppose, everyone dies of natural causes – but that explanation seems somewhat evasive when heavy blows to the head have immediately preceded death.

Martin Dillon has written a number of well-informed and insightful books about both republican and loyalist paramilitaries. In *The Enemy Within*, he provides a thorough description of the London bombings of March 1973.

Patrick Radden Keefe's book *Say Nothing* provides a detailed and dramatic account of the abduction and murder of Jean McConville and its long-term effects on her children and on some of those involved in her 'disappearance'. Based upon a redacted transcript of an interview by Ed Moloney with Dolours Price and details from other sources, Keefe has suggested that it was Marian Price who fired the shot that killed McConville. However, Ed Moloney has denied that the redacted sections of his interview named Marian Price as the killer. Through her solicitor, Price has also 'vehemently denied' that she shot Jean McConville.

In 2018, a feature-length documentary about Dolours Price, called *I, Dolours,* was produced by Ed Moloney and Nuala Cunningham. This is a very well made and powerful film that was funded by RTÉ, Ireland's national broadcaster and by Fís Éireann/Screen Ireland (formerly the Irish Film Board). The documentary draws primarily upon Price's own version of certain critical events, both in a lengthy interview with Ed Moloney and in dramatised sequences using actors, and so some of the assertions expressed and enacted in the film cannot be regarded as entirely reliable.

Paul Wilkinson's *Terrorism and the Liberal State* was an early attempt to address this issue on a global basis, but much of his book is focused on Northern Ireland. Although elements of his analysis may now seem dated, or have been overtaken by events, some of his arguments have proven to be all too prescient.

In *The British State and the Northern Ireland Crisis, 1969–73: From Violence to Power-Sharing*, William Beattie Smith has examined the early years of the Troubles and has analysed in cogent detail how they developed into political turmoil and violence. He has also examined the policies followed by successive British administrations in their efforts to restore peace and civil order.

Graham Walker's *History of the Ulster Unionist Party: Protest, Pragmatism and Pessimism* provides a thorough examination of the development of the party across the decades. In particular, the book provides valuable insights to the conflicts and tensions between the various different groupings within the unionist political alliance.

The Autobiography of Terence O'Neill reveals a good deal about the character of the fourth Prime Minister of Northern Ireland – though, perhaps, not always to his advantage. While his political and social skills may have been limited, the role O'Neill played in the history of Northern Ireland remains of critical and historic importance.

Brian Faulkner's autobiography, *Memoirs of a Statesman*, was published posthumously – which may explain its somewhat portentous title. Although the book seeks to explain and justify Faulkner's political decisions – including his failures – it also conveys some of its author's pragmatic character and reveals his intuitive understanding of the political culture of Northern Ireland.

Gerry Adams has written an autobiography, *Before the Dawn*, but, since he denies ever having been a member of the IRA, the insights it offers to that organisation are necessarily limited. Not surprisingly, Adams devotes considerable space to incidents of violence from the British army and loyalist paramilitaries. The killings for which republicans have admitted responsibility – and which amount to more than 60 per cent of all the deaths in the Troubles – receive much less attention. One of Adams' recent publications consists of an anthology of his tweets. They are apparently intended to showcase the 'lighter side' of his character and feature his whimsical musings on teddy bears, chocolate creme eggs and strawberry pavlova.

In *Gerry Adams: An Unauthorised Life*, Malachi O'Doherty has attempted to chart and analyse the life of the long-term Sinn Féin president. His book is both informative and illuminating and, if Adams' character remains somewhat elusive, that may not be the fault of the author.

In *James Chichester-Clark: Prime Minister of Northern Ireland*, the penultimate premier is portrayed as a decent and honourable man. The author, Clive William Scoular, attempts to refute the widespread perception that Chichester-Clark was unsuited or unfit for the job of Prime Minister. If he fails to achieve that objective, the fault may, once again, lie more with the subject of this biography than with its author.

Dean Godson's *Himself Alone: David Trimble and the Ordeal of Unionism* is an extremely detailed and penetrating political biography of the man who led the Unionist Party into the Good Friday Agreement. Although Godson is clearly sceptical about the benefits that the Agreement brought to Northern Ireland, he shows considerable respect for Trimble's ability

to overcome opposition within his own party and negotiate a historic compromise with Ulster's nationalists. Godson
also reveals Trimble to be a more complex, capable and sympathetic figure than his public image might suggest.

In their well-researched and highly readable book, *The
UVF: The Endgame*, Henry McDonald and Jim Cusack
recount the development of this loyalist paramilitary
organisation from its origins through to its involvement
in the Good Friday Agreement.

In *Gunsmoke and Mirrors* Henry McDonald challenges
the narrative of the Troubles that had been promoted by
Sinn Féin and its apologists and which has been accepted,
tacitly or otherwise, by many mainstream journalists. He
also questions the memorialist culture, which supports
that narrative and has been used retrospectively to justify
the political violence of previous decades.

Kidnapped by A. J. Davidson provides valuable information
about some of the circumstances in which Thomas
Niedermayer was abducted, along with accounts of a
number of other cases of kidnappings in Ireland.

In *Hostage*, Paul Howard provides detailed accounts of
five abductions (excluding that of Thomas Niedermayer)
committed by the IRA. With one possible exception,
none of these proved effective from the kidnappers'

point of view. In one case, a group of IRA gunmen were apprehended by armed Gardaí while attempting to abduct an Irish-Canadian businessman. The leader of the IRA unit on that occasion was subsequently employed by Sinn Féin as a 'political manager'.

In *A Secret History of the IRA*, Ed Moloney provides a thorough, well-informed and credible account of the history of that organisation. Much of his focus falls on the role played by Gerry Adams in the run-up to the Good Friday and St Andrew's Agreements. He suggests that Adams exerted a great deal of personal control over Sinn Féin and the IRA and that he led (and misled) his colleagues down a path that eventually resulted in the end of their military campaign. In that process, Moloney suggests that Adams was also able to outmanoeuvre Tony Blair and leading members of his administration. It remains to be seen if the current leadership of Sinn Féin can prove as adroit and manipulative – or as effective.

In *Voices from the Grave: Two Men's War in Ireland*, Moloney presents the testimony of two former paramilitary leaders, one loyalist, one republican. Both men provide insight into the actions and motives of their respective groups, the UVF and the IRA. Brendan Hughes, a former high-ranking IRA member, had become an opponent of Adams' political strategy and offers convincing testimony regarding Adams' direct involvement in some notorious incidents of violence.

In the past, Moloney has collaborated with Anthony McIntyre, a former IRA prisoner in the Maze who was jailed for murder. In his *Good Friday: The Death of Irish Republicanism*, McIntyre argues that Gerry Adams and the Sinn Féin leadership have surrendered some of the essential principles of Irish republicanism – such as its previous rejection of the so-called unionist veto. However, McIntyre does not agree with those republican dissidents who believe that a campaign of political violence should be continued.

Since the end of the Troubles, a number of former IRA members have written accounts of their work as agents of the RUC Special Branch. In the past, the word 'informer' has been considered a term of abuse in Ireland, but these writers have not expressed any regret for their actions in passing information to the security forces. In fact, they remain proud of their work as police agents and have claimed that the information they passed on to their RUC or MI5 handlers was able to save many innocent lives. In several respects, *The Informer* by Sean O'Callaghan is one of the most important of these accounts to emerge. O'Callaghan was elected as a Sinn Féin councillor and held a key position in the IRA's Southern Command. While working as an agent for the Gardaí's Special Branch, he was familiar with many other senior republicans and he used that access to provide information of critical importance to the Irish security forces. He eventually turned himself in to the police in England. The police offered him witness protection, but he refused and pleaded guilty to two murders committed on behalf of the IRA. While in prison, he began to write *The Informer*. On his release, he continued to write and was also prepared to give evidence in open court against his former comrades.

In *The Volunteer: A Former IRA Man's True Story,* Shane Paul O'Doherty provides an authentic and compelling first-hand account of his path from volunteering to join the IRA in Derry when he was still a young teenager to the one-man bombing campaign that he conducted in London in the early 1970s. Unlike Brian Keenan, he refused to recognise the British court at his eventual trial for terrorist offences and was sentenced to life imprisonment. O'Doherty spent several years in solitary confinement and 'on the blanket' when he refused to wear a prison uniform. Eventually, he came to renounce the IRA and all forms of political terrorism. In his book, he is as unsparing in his critique of himself and his IRA activities as he is of his former comrades. He has chosen to live outside Ireland.

In *Fifty Dead Men Walking*, author Martin McGartland names a number of leading IRA figures who were active in Belfast, including Davy Adams, the Sinn Féin leader's nephew. McGartland was finally exposed as an SB agent and only escaped execution by jumping out of a window on the third floor of a block of flats. He was subsequently re-located by British Intelligence in England but was shot and seriously wounded in 1999, when the IRA was supposedly on a ceasefire. In his second book, *Dead Man Running*, McGartland argues that he was abandoned by British Intelligence in the following years and, in late 2017, told one journalist that he believed he was still living 'on borrowed time'.

Raymond Gilmour was a member of both the Irish National Liberation Army (INLA) and the IRA in the late 1970s and early 80s. He also worked as an agent of the RUC Special Branch and his book *Dead Ground: Infiltrating the IRA* is one of the early accounts of that role given by a Special Branch agent. Gilmour also became one of the first 'super-grasses' and gave evidence in court against many of his former colleagues. However, his evidence was regarded by the presiding judge as not credible and their trial collapsed. Gilmour died in 2016. On the day of his death, his estranged son, also called Raymond, posted: 'Today is a very good day. There is a God.'

Unlike Gilmour, Eamon Collins did not work as an RUC agent and he did not give evidence in court against the IRA. However, he did become disillusioned and sickened while working as an IRA intelligence officer and broke away from that organisation. His memoir *Killing Rage* provides powerful and disturbing evidence of the intimate nature of much of the IRA's campaign during the Troubles. While working as a customs official, Collins set up one of his own colleagues for assassination by the IRA. Subsequently, he found himself sitting opposite the dead man's daughter on a train journey; an incident that affected him deeply and led to his eventual repudiation of political terrorism. Following the publication of his book, Collins was beaten and stabbed to death. His body was buried in Newry's Monkshill Cemetery close to the grave of a Catholic RUC officer whose assassination he had helped to organise. Several members of the IRA were arrested and questioned by the RUC but no one has ever been charged with his murder.

In *Children of the Revolution: The Lives of Sons and Daughters of Activists in Northern Ireland*, Bill Rolston interviewed the children of both republican and loyalist paramilitaries. In this revealing book, they try to assess as adults the impact of their parents' activities on the course of their lives. Some of them recount their experiences with a degree of ambivalence and a mixture of pride and shame. One of the contributors is Jeannette Keenan, the daughter of Brian Keenan. In her at-times moving piece, she suggests that the long-term effects on activists and their children have often left both unable 'to talk about how they feel or cope with their feelings'.

Richard English's *Armed Struggle: The History of the IRA* offers a detailed, comprehensive and, in some respects, sympathetic account of the various republican campaigns since 1916.

Rogelio Alonso's *The IRA and Armed Struggle* represents a sustained critique of the campaign waged by the IRA across four decades. What is unusual about Alonso's analysis is that it rests upon a large number of candid interviews with ordinary members of the IRA. Most of them appear to have joined the organisation when they were very young – in many cases, when they were still teenagers – and most of those featured in the book seem to have become thoroughly disillusioned with the IRA's violence.

Chris Ryder's *The RUC: A Force Under Fire* provides a comprehensive and insightful history of Northern Ireland's police force from its roots in the old Royal Irish Constabulary to the ways in which it was radically transformed during the Troubles.

There have also been a number of accounts of the Troubles written from the perspectives of former members of the RUC. Alan Simpson was the RUC officer who interrogated and 'turned' the IRA member known as 'Disciple' into working as a police informant. He also directed the search for the body of Thomas Niedermayer. In his book, *Deceit and Deception*, Simpson describes in considerable detail the background to his investigation as well as providing a valuable and original insight into other operations conducted by the RUC during the Troubles.

Colin Breen also served in the RUC and in *A Force Like No Other* he allows a number of former officers to describe their experiences during the Troubles. These range from the mundane to the terrifying and Breen's book makes a valuable contribution to the documenting of such experiences.

Johnston Brown's *Into the Dark: 30 Years in the RUC* is, as its title may suggest, an intense and vivid account of his service in the CID division of the RUC and what he terms the 'continual friction with the SB'. His book expresses a level of frustration experienced by CID officers when they had to turn agents they had recruited over to SB handlers who were prepared, according to Brown, to allow them to participate in the commission of serious crimes. Brown also relates the remarkable case of one former IRA volunteer who went on to join the loyalist UVF and who eventually became a CID informant.

Dr William Matchett is one of the few former officers in the RUC Special Branch to have written about the Troubles. In *Secret Victory: The Intelligence War that Beat the IRA*, he examines the contentious role played by the SB in successive decades. Although he is clearly writing from a particular viewpoint, Matchett's book is an important and credible corrective to a widely accepted narrative that often presents the SB in wholly negative terms.

Alastair Campbell was the chief spin-doctor to Tony Blair, the British prime minister, during the negotiations that led to the Good Friday Agreement. He has published multiple volumes of dairies and memoirs from that period, including *The Irish Diaries: 1994–2003*. These provide a unique – though often self-regarding – perspective on British policies in relation to Northern Ireland.

Jonathan Powell was Tony Blair's Chief of Staff and chief negotiator in the run-up to the Good Friday Agreement. (Curiously, his elder brother, Charles, played a comparable role in Margaret Thatcher's administration.) Powell's *Great Hatred, Little Room: Making Peace in Northern Ireland* provides a detailed account of the convoluted political background to the Agreement. His account is, in some respects, both more sophisticated and more naive than that of Alistair Campbell, although a similar frisson of excitement can be detected in the writing of both men when they come face to face with real-life IRA commanders. Perhaps, as Jenny McCartney has suggested, it is a feature of a particular type of Englishman that he is 'rightly repelled by manifestations of extreme English nationalism, yet bizarrely soppy over its Irish equivalent'.

Robert Ramsay served as the Principal Private Secretary to Brian Faulkner when he was Prime Minister of Northern Ireland. *Ringside Seats: An Insider's View of the Crisis in Northern Ireland* provides, as its title suggests, a credible, penetrating and well-written description of the civil rights campaign and the rise of the Provisional IRA as they were viewed from Stormont's government buildings.

Sir Kenneth Bloomfield was the highest-ranking civil servant in Northern Ireland during the worst years of the Troubles. *A Tragedy of Errors: The Government and Misgovernment of Northern Ireland* gives a valuable account of his experiences in dealing with a range of British, Irish and Northern Irish officials. Bloomfield is particularly critical of both the political and the personal commitments of successive ministers and governments of the UK.

Noel Dorr served as Secretary General in the Irish Department of Foreign Affairs. In *Sunningdale: The Search for Peace in Northern Ireland*, he suggests that the Irish government acted, during this critical period, as the effective interlocutor for the SDLP and for John Hume in particular.

I was also able to consult the *Family Report* issued by the Historical Enquiries Team (HET) in response to a request from Thomas Niedermayer's two granddaughters, Tanya and Rachel. This report largely consists of synopses of contemporary RUC files and post-mortem findings. Unfortunately, the report also contains a number of factual errors and omissions, and some of these are of the most basic kind.

Acknowledgements

Many people contributed to the making of both this book and the documentary whom I would like to acknowledge.

The documentary film that we made about this story received critical and invaluable support from Fís Éireann/ Screen Ireland, and, in particular, from Greg Martin, Céline Haddad and Désirée Finnegan. Greg's advice was extremely helpful in the production of the feature-length film.

I would also like to thank the commissioning editors with the three broadcasters who each contributed to the production of our documentary film. Colm O'Callaghan at RTÉ was the first to commit to the production and he continued to provide invaluable support and insightful advice throughout the production process. I would like to thank Eddie Doyle and Mary McKeagney in BBC Northern Ireland for their support of this project and for the critical perspective that they brought. I would like to thank Thorge Thomsen and Alexander von Harling from ARTE for the valuable support and advice that they gave during the lengthy gestation and production period of our film. I would also like to thank Peter Crawford-McCann for his advice, insights and practical help over the years – and for the (unexpected) time we spent together in Dubai. I would like to thank Haydn Keenan of Smart Street Films for his advice and assistance both in Australia and in more general terms. I would also like to thank Kenny Donaldson of the South East Fermanagh Foundation, who has proved a powerful and effective advocate for the victims/survivors of terrorism in Northern Ireland.

I must also thank Gerry Gregg, the director of our documentary film, not only for his creative input, but also for his analytical skills, his good humour and his dogged persistence in helping to ensure that our film was produced in what were often very demanding and difficult circumstances. Catherine O'Flaherty, our Executive Producer, also played a central role in the film's production.

I must also pay tribute to the many ways in which we were helped in making our film by Tanya Williams-Powell and Rachel Williams-Powell, Thomas and Ingeborg Niedermayer's only grandchildren. They were open to our approach and most generous in the time, trouble and assistance that they gave to us over many months.

I must also acknowledge the contribution made and the hospitality shown by Jürgen Müller-Hohagen, when we interviewed him in Dachau. Jürgen is the author, along with his partner, Ingeborg, of the important text *Dialog statt Trauma*.

I would like to thank Professor Judith Herman, Professor of Psychiatry at the Harvard School of Medicine for her hospitality when I met and interviewed her in Boston.

I am also grateful to Alan Simpson for the time he gave us and the courtesy and hospitality that he extended to us when we interviewed him for our documentary film, and also to the number of former RUC Special Branch and CID officers and former members of the IRA who agreed to speak with me, but who in some cases – and for obvious reasons – preferred to remain anonymous.

The newspapers that I have consulted in writing this book include the *Belfast News Letter*, the *Belfast Telegraph*, the *Irish News*, the *Irish Press*, the *Irish Times*, the *Sunday Independent* and the *Sunday Times*. I am grateful to the staff at the Public Records Office of Northern Ireland in Belfast, Cartlann Náisiúnta na hÉireann (the National Archives of Ireland) in Dublin and the National Archives (United Kingdom) at Kew in England for access to their files and to the Archive Library in RTÉ and the RTÉ Player.

Vinnie Beirne, an editor and director with whom I have collaborated on many film projects, was involved from the start – in fact, even before the start, since he urged me to make a film about this case over a period of almost ten years. He brought not only his technical skills but his editorial judgment to bear when the film was being cut – and I am grateful for both.

I would like to acknowledge again the importance of the radio documentary made by Joe Duffy and Ciaran Cassidy. I would also like to thank Ann Marie Hourihane for bringing that programme to my attention, and for the subsequent research that we conducted together. In particular, I would like to acknowledge the critical importance of the documents that she obtained in the German Foreign Office's Political Archive in 2013. Professor Tom Inglis read an early draft of the text and gave some very pertinent advice. Maurice Earls, the co-founder of *The Dublin Review of Books*, was also good enough to read and comment on some of the chapters.

My friend Brian Kinkead also read and commented on the early drafts. I am grateful to Dr Barry O'Halloran for his informed and helpful comments on the first complete draft of this book. My son Dr Jamie Blake Knox brought a professional historian's perspective to bear and was also of great assistance. The other members of my family also gave their usual unstinting – if not uncritical – support.

I would like to thank Dan Bolger, my former editor at New Island, for the enthusiasm he showed for this story: it was Dan who convinced me to write this book. I would also like to thank Aoife K. Walsh of New Island for her help and support during the various stages of making this book. Finally, I must thank my editors, Ruth Hallinan and Kerri Ward – whose close and perceptive reading of my text proved especially valuable – and also my copy-editor Djinn von Noorden, whose fluency in German far exceeds my own.

Once again, I should stress that, whatever faults this book contains, they are entirely my own responsibility.

INDEX